Secondary Education in Ethiopia

A WORLD BANK STUDY

Secondary Education in Ethiopia
Supporting Growth and Transformation

Rajendra Dhoj Joshi and Adriaan Verspoor

THE WORLD BANK
Washington, D.C.

© 2013 International Bank for Reconstruction and Development / The World Bank
1818 H Street NW, Washington DC 20433
Telephone: 202-473-1000; Internet: www.worldbank.org

Some rights reserved

1 2 3 4   16 15 14 13

World Bank Studies are published to communicate the results of the Bank's work to the development community with the least possible delay. The manuscript of this paper therefore has not been prepared in accordance with the procedures appropriate to formally edited texts.

This work is a product of the staff of The World Bank with external contributions. Note that The World Bank does not necessarily own each component of the content included in the work. The World Bank therefore does not warrant that the use of the content contained in the work will not infringe on the rights of third parties. The risk of claims resulting from such infringement rests solely with you.

The findings, interpretations, and conclusions expressed in this work do not necessarily reflect the views of The World Bank, its Board of Executive Directors, or the governments they represent. The World Bank does not guarantee the accuracy of the data included in this work. The boundaries, colors, denominations, and other information shown on any map in this work do not imply any judgment on the part of The World Bank concerning the legal status of any territory or the endorsement or acceptance of such boundaries.

Nothing herein shall constitute or be considered to be a limitation upon or waiver of the privileges and immunities of The World Bank, all of which are specifically reserved.

Rights and Permissions

This work is available under the Creative Commons Attribution 3.0 Unported license (CC BY 3.0) http://creativecommons.org/licenses/by/3.0. Under the Creative Commons Attribution license, you are free to copy, distribute, transmit, and adapt this work, including for commercial purposes, under the following conditions:

Attribution—Please cite the work as follows: Joshi, Rajendra Dhoj, and Adriaan Verspoor. 2013. *Secondary Education in Ethiopia: Supporting Growth and Transformation*. Washington, DC: World Bank. doi: 10.1596/978-0-8213-9727-5 License: Creative Commons Attribution CC BY 3.0

Translations—If you create a translation of this work, please add the following disclaimer along with the attribution: *This translation was not created by The World Bank and should not be considered an official World Bank translation. The World Bank shall not be liable for any content or error in this translation.*

All queries on rights and licenses should be addressed to the Office of the Publisher, The World Bank, 1818 H Street NW, Washington, DC 20433, USA; fax: 202-522-2625; e-mail: pubrights@worldbank.org.

ISBN (paper): 978-0-8213-9727-5
ISBN (electronic): 978-0-8213-9730-5
DOI: 10.1596/978-0-8213-9727-5

Library of Congress Cataloging-in-Publication Data

Joshi, R. D. (Rajendra Dhoj)
  Secondary education in Ethiopia : supporting growth and transformation / by Rajendra Dhoj Joshi and Adriaan Verspoor.
    p. cm.
  ISBN 978-0-8213-9727-5—ISBN 978-0-8213-9730-5
  1. Education, Secondary—Ethiopia. I. Title.
  LA1517.J67 2012
  373.63—dc23
                                                                                                    2012035451

Contents

Foreword   xi
Acknowledgments   xiii
About the Authors   xv
Abbreviations and Acronyms   xvii
Executive Summary   xxi

Chapter 1	**Macroeconomic Context and Human Capital Challenges**	**1**
	Recent Economic Performance	1
	The New Growth and Transformation Plan	3
	Human Capital Implications	6
	Contribution of Education to Economic Growth	16
	Conclusion	18
	Notes	18
	References	19
Chapter 2	**Education in Ethiopia: Achievements and Challenges**	**23**
	Modern Education in the Twentieth Century	23
	Education Development Since 1991	25
	Implementing the 1994 Education and Training Policy	26
	Trends in Education Expenditure	28
	Challenges: Access	29
	Challenges: Quality and Learning Achievement	34
	Conclusion	37
	Notes	38
	References	39
Chapter 3	**The Place of Secondary Education in an Economic Transformation Strategy**	**41**
	Evolving Skill Profile	42
	Enrollment Profile of Middle-Income Countries	44
	The Importance of Mathematics and the Sciences	46
	Vocational Training: Middle-Income Country Profile	48
	Education for Growth and Transformation	49
	Priorities for Educational Development in Ethiopia	51

	Conclusion	54
	Notes	55
	References	56
Chapter 4	**Curriculum: Quality and Relevance**	**59**
	Current Curriculum	60
	International Trends in Curriculum Reform	68
	Priorities of Ethiopian Curriculum Reform	72
	Conclusion	85
	Notes	88
	References	89
Chapter 5	**Teacher Preparation and Development**	**91**
	The Teacher Training System	91
	Teacher Demand and Supply	93
	Improving Teacher Effectiveness	97
	Teacher Management	104
	Conclusion	111
	Notes	113
	References	114
Chapter 6	**Strengthening Governance and Management**	**117**
	School-Based Management: International Experience and Approaches	119
	Decentralization in Ethiopia	123
	Strengthening School-Based Management	130
	Capacity Building for School-Based Management	134
	Implications of School-Based Management for the Secondary Education System	138
	Conclusion	140
	Notes	141
	References	142
Chapter 7	**Diversifying the Provision of Secondary Education**	**145**
	Nongovernmental Schooling in Ethiopia	146
	Expanding Nongovernmental Provision of Secondary Education	149
	Toward Public-Private Partnerships	154
	Conclusion	158
	Notes	158
	References	158
Chapter 8	**Financing the Development of Secondary Education**	**161**
	Cost Per Student: Benchmarks	162

Contents | vii

	Fiscal Envelope for the Education Sector	164
	Updated ESDP IV Simulation Model	166
	Reducing the Financing Gap	171
	Alternative Scenarios for Secondary Education Financing	173
	Implementing Reforms	177
	Conclusion	180
	Note	182
	References	182
Chapter 9	**Conclusion: Priorities for Policy Reform and Action**	**183**
	Implement Curriculum Reform	184
	Ensure Sustainable Financing	185
	Strengthen Governance and Management	186
	Expand Access	188
	Promote Equity	189
	Improve Quality	192
	Implementation and Phasing of Reforms	195
	Note	197
	References	197

Appendixes

	A Curriculum Documentation	199
	B Facilities and Equipment for Science Teaching	201
	C Adding Value to Achievement Tests	211
	D Teacher Recruitment and Screening	215
	E Pedagogical Content Knowledge	219
	F Quality Assurance in Teacher Education	221

Boxes

Box 1.1: Labor Skills and Productivity in Ethiopia	9
Box 1.2: Economic Reform in Vietnam	14
Box 1.3: Recent Estimates of Returns to Secondary Education and Training	17
Box 4.1: Types of Chemical Reaction Taught in Grade 9	63
Box 4.2: New Science Curriculum in Qatar, 2004	65
Box 4.3: The Disappointment of the Plasma TV Learning Program	67
Box 4.4: Counseling Support Groups in Namibian Schools	72
Box 4.5: Responses to the Changing TVET Environment	77
Box 4.6: Curriculum Elements that Develop Metacognitive Skills	78
Box 4.7: Local Content in Secondary Education Curricula	82
Box 5.1: Calculating the Number of Required Secondary Teachers	94
Box 5.2: Induction Programs for Beginning Teachers	101
Box 5.3: Goals of CPD in Ethiopia	102
Box 5.4: South African Science Centers	104
Box 5.5: Teaching Standards in the United States	106

Box 5.6: Australia: National Program Standards for Accreditation
of Initial Teacher Education Programs 109
Box 6.1: Types of Control in School-Based Management 120
Box 6.2: Guiding Principles for Implementing School-Based
Management 122
Box 6.3: Ethiopian Policy on Educational Organization and Management .. 124
Box 6.4: Options for Capacity Development Training for Principals 135
Box 6.5: Networking Options for In-Service Support to Secondary
School Management Teams 138
Box 6.6: Preparing for School-Based Management Reform in Ethiopia .. 140
Box 7.1: Private Schools in Mauritius and Korea 149
Box 7.2: Examples of Public Support for Private Provision
of Secondary Education 150
Box 7.3: IFC Private Sector Support Program in Africa 156
Box 9.1: Expanding Secondary Education in Thailand 190

Figures
Figure 1.1: GDP Growth Rate Comparison 2
Figure 1.2: Change in Employment by Sector, East Asia, 1999–2010 6
Figure 1.3: Average Number of Years of Schooling Completed
by Individuals Aged 15+ Years, 1980–2010 7
Figure 1.4: Economywide Measures of Routine and Nonroutine Task
Input, United States, 1969–98 10
Figure 1.5: Share of Firms Rating Skills of Managers, Professionals,
and Skilled Workers as Important, Indonesia, 2008 11
Figure 2.1: Enrollments in Primary and Secondary Education, 1967–2009 .. 27
Figure 2.2: Trends in Secondary Education GER, 1994–2011 27
Figure 2.3: Enrollment Pyramid for Students in Poorest Quintile,
by Age, 2005 31
Figure 2.4: Rural and Urban Enrollment Compared, by Age, 2005 31
Figure 2.5: Secondary Education Gross Enrollment Rate,
by Region, 2009/10 32
Figure 2.6: Primary and Secondary Enrollment Rates, by Age
and Wealth, 2005 33
Figure 3.1: Comparison of Educational Attainment of Population Aged
15+ over Time, Korea, Rep., and Vietnam 42
Figure 3.2: Educational Attainment of Workforce Aged 15+, Selected
Middle-Income Countries, 1990 and 2010 43
Figure 3.3: Educational Attainment of Ethiopian Labor Force,
Various Years 43
Figure 3.4: Gross Enrollment Rates by GNI per Capita, Ethiopia and
Selected Middle-Income Countries, 2010 or Latest Available Year ... 45
Figure 3.5: Graduates of Tertiary Scientific and Engineering Programs,
Selected Middle-Income Countries, 2009 or Latest Available Year ... 47

Figure 3.6: TVET as Percentage of Enrollments in Upper Secondary Education, Selected Countries, Latest Available Year	49
Figure 3.7: Percent Labor Force in Manufacturing and Secondary School Enrollment in Asia	50
Figure 6.1: Increasing Accountability: The Short Route	118
Figure 6.2: Classification of SBM Reforms Implemented in Various Countries	120
Figure 7.1: Enrollments in Nongovernmental Secondary Schools, Selected Years	147
Figure 8.1: Education as a Share of GDP, Selected Countries, Groups, and Regions	166
Figure 8.2: Base Case Scenario	170
Figure 8.3: Base Case Scenario: Allocation of Education Budget by Subsector, 2009/10–2024/25	171
Figure 8.4: Deep Reform with Education Budget of 4.6 Percent of GDP	175
Figure 8.5: Moderate Reform with Education Budget of 5.2 Percent of GDP	176
Figure B.1: Diagram of Multipurpose, Science, and General Teaching Rooms	206

Tables

Table E.1: Possible Phasing of Secondary Education Reforms	xxxi
Table 1.1: Ethiopia: Basic Indicators, 2009	1
Table 1.2: Evolution of the Structure of the Ethiopian Economy	3
Table 1.3: Projected Growth and Structure of GDP, by Economic Sector, 2010–25	4
Table 1.4: Composition of GDP of Selected Middle-Income Countries, 1994 and 2009	5
Table 1.5: Ethiopian Firms that Find Worker Skills a Severe or Very Severe Constraint on Business	9
Table 1.6: Links between Education and Economic Development in Korea, Rep., 1960s–present	14
Table 1.7: Private Returns to Education in Ethiopia, Selected Studies	16
Table 2.1: Participation Rates in Education by Grade Level, 2010/11	28
Table 2.2: Education Expenditures as Percentage of Government Spending and GDP, by Fiscal Year	29
Table 2.3: Progress toward ESDP IV Enrollment Targets	30
Table 2.4: Comparison of Target and Actual Efficiency Indicators for Secondary Education	34
Table 2.5: Percentage of Students Scoring below 50 percent on NLA Tests, 2010	35
Table 3.1: Projected Education Enrollment Targets Compared to LMIC Average	52

Table 3.2: Composition of Educational Spending and Per Student Cost in 17 Countries in Sub-Saharan Africa	53
Table 3.3: Per Student Cost of Education in Ethiopia, 2009/10	54
Table 4.1: Comparison of Educational Systems, Various Countries	61
Table 4.2: Comparison of Mathematics Curricula in Five Countries	64
Table B4.1: Elements of Science Curriculum in Qatar	65
Table 4.3: Some Characteristics of Curriculum Reform, 1960s–2010s	68
Table 4.4: Comparison of Five Syllabi: "Physics—The Study of Movement"	70
Table 4.5: Guidelines for Three Grade 12 Examinations by Topic, South Africa, 2005	71
Table 5.1: Actual and Projected Enrollment and Teacher Requirements, 2009/10–2024/25	93
Table 5.2: Teacher Requirements by Subject in Grade 9–12 School of 1,440 Students	95
Table 5.3: Projected Third-Year University Enrollments by Field of Study, Selected Years	96
Table 5.4: Estimated Teacher Demand and Supply by Subject, 2019	96
Table 5.5: Content of MOE Teacher Education Modules	99
Table 6.1: Assessment of Progress toward Decentralization to Subnational Governments	126
Table 6.2: Assessment of Progress toward School-Based Management	128
Table 6.3: Possible Phased Implementation of School-Based Management in Ethiopia	132
Table 6.4: Composition of School Management Committee in the Community-Control SBM Model	133
Table 7.1: Regulatory Framework for Nongovernmental Schools in Ethiopia	153
Table 8.1: Comparison of Total Public Per-Student Spending	163
Table 8.2: Typical Per-Student Spending Patterns in Relation to Rates of Economic and Secondary Enrollment Growth	164
Table 8.3: Trends in Public Education Expenditures in Ethiopia	165
Table 8.4: ESDP IV Education Budget Parameters, 2009/10	167
Table 8.5: Key Parameter Values of Base Case Scenario	168
Table 8.6: Potential of Policy Options to Reduce Financing Gap in Base Case Scenario	172
Table 8.7: Share of Financing Gap Assigned to Various Education Subsectors	173
Table 8.8: Policy Reform Packages for Reducing Cost of Public Service Delivery	174
Table 8.9: Alternative Scenarios for Expanding Secondary Education	174
Table 8.10: Ability of Alternative Scenarios to Cover the Education Sector Financing Gap	176
Table 9.1: Possible Phasing of Secondary Education Reforms	196
Table B.1: Comparison of Science Kit Equipment Costs	208

Foreword

Traditionally the main purpose of secondary education has been to prepare students for higher education. Two recent trends in low-income countries in Africa—progress toward achieving universal primary education and a strong drive to achieve middle-income status—make a compelling case to revisit this traditional approach. In today's Africa, secondary education should prepare students for *both* higher education and the job market. However, many developing countries have yet to transform their secondary education systems in accordance with this dual objective.

The economic transition from low- to middle-income status requires changes in the skills that meet the demands of the labor market, and thereby sustain economic transformation. As the demand for higher levels of cognitive, behavioral, and technical skills increases, education systems will need to evolve. At the same time, a larger proportion of young people will enter secondary education, making the range of students' aspirations and abilities more diverse. Instead of predominantly aiming to enter higher education, an increasing number of lower secondary students will seek to enter the job market and/or prepare for technical and vocational education and training. A secondary education system that mainly seeks to prepare students for higher education will therefore fail to meet the aspirations of the majority of its students. This is a situation that African countries can ill afford.

Developing a policy response to these challenges is particularly important in Ethiopia. With one of the fastest-growing economies in Sub-Saharan Africa, Ethiopia has set its sights on becoming a middle-income economy by 2020–23. The secondary education reforms required to sustain this economic objective need to be carefully prepared, based on broad consultations with all stakeholders. This report has been prepared with the intention of contributing to this process. It focuses on the agenda for secondary education reform, particularly in the areas of curriculum, governance and management, and financing.

I hope that the study will stimulate discussion of the secondary education reform agenda not only in Ethiopia but also in other countries in the Africa region.

Ritva S. Reinikka
Director
Human Development Sector
Africa Region, The World Bank

Acknowledgments

This publication was prepared by Rajendra Dhoj Joshi (Task Team Leader) and Adriaan Verspoor (consultant, Education Development). The following people prepared background papers for the publication: Andrew S. Clegg (curriculum), Richard Kraft (teacher preparation and development), Harvey N. J. Smith (governance and management), Michael Latham (private provision of secondary education), and Derebssa Dufera Serbessa (education sector development and governance and management in Ethiopia). Girma Woldetasadik made a significant contribution by helping collect materials and providing comments and logistical support. Jemal Mohammed Omer provided inputs for macroeconomic projections. Shimeles Worku conducted case studies of secondary schools and collected materials in Ethiopia. Ravi Somani provided clarifications on the simulation model used for projections in Ethiopia's Education Sector Development Plan IV.

The team gratefully acknowledges Peter Nicolas Materu, Sector Manager, and Michel Welmond, Cluster Leader, for their guidance and encouragement. And they express special appreciation to H. E. Ato Fuad Ibrahim, State Minister for General Education of Ethiopia. They also thank Directors Solomon Shiferaw and Girma Alemayehu of the Ministry of Education of Ethiopia for their guidance and comments. Acknowledgments are also due the following peer reviewers: Keiko Inoue, Kin Bing Wu, Peter Darvas, and Toby Linden. The team also acknowledges the valuable comments of Tawhid Nawaz.

Peggy McInerny provided excellent editing of the content. The team gratefully acknowledges the financing for the study provided by the Norwegian Post-Primary Education Fund, Africa Region.

About the Authors

Rajendra Dhoj Joshi, a Nepalese national, is a senior education specialist at the World Bank. He has worked for the Bank in Nepal, Ethiopia, the Russian Federation, Kazakhstan, Afghanistan, Bangladesh, Bhutan, and India. Before joining the Bank he was a professor of electrical engineering at Tribhuvan University in Nepal. While at the university he worked in various managerial positions, including the Dean of Faculty of Engineering. He left the university as an established reformer. He has experience working at all levels of education. His key focus has been increasing the efficiency and effectiveness of service delivery through reforms. He is associated with the following reforms in the education sector: increasing cost sharing in higher education, including the introduction of full cost-recovery programs; decentralization of university administration; performance-based financing of schools and higher education institutions (public and community); opening the textbook supply to the private sector; the transfer of schools to community management; and the introduction of per capita financing for schools. He has authored a publication on higher education reforms in Nepal entitled "Reforms at the Institute of Engineering, Tribhuvan University, Nepal" (2002), published by the World Bank.

Adriaan Verspoor is an education consultant specializing in policy analysis and the design and management of education development programs. He has worked on issues of education in developing countries for more than 40 years. Among the various positions that he has held at the World Bank are lead education adviser for the Africa region, manager of Bank education programs in India, and manager of the Bank's education policy and research programs. He has field experience in 25 countries in Africa and Asia and has authored and coauthored numerous refereed books and journal articles on education issues in developing countries. He led a taskforce on quality improvement in basic education in Africa launched by the Association for the Development of Education in Africa and was the lead author of the World Bank 2007 report, *At the Crossroads: Choices for Secondary Education in Sub-Saharan Africa*.

Abbreviations and Acronyms

ABE	Alternative Basic Education
AC	Alternating current (electricity)
ADB	Asian Development Bank
AfDB	African Development Bank
AIDS	Acquired immune deficiency syndrome
BA	Bachelor of Arts
Br	birr (Ethiopian currency)
BS	Bachelor of Science
CIE	Cambridge International Education
CPD	Continuous professional development
CRT	Criterion-referenced test
CSA	Central Statistical Agency
CTE	College of Teacher Education
DHS	Demographic and Health Survey
EC	Ethiopian calendar
ECBP	Engineering Capacity Building Program
ECE	Early childhood education
ELQIP	English-Language Quality Improvement Program
EMI	Ethiopian Management Institute
ESDP	Education Sector Development Program
ESSA	Education Statistics Annual Abstract
ETS	Educational Testing Service
FAS	Foundation-Assisted Schools, Pakistan
FAWE	Forum for African Women Educationalists
FEMISE	Forum Euroméditerranéen des Instituts de Sciences Économiques (Euro-Mediterranean Forum of Economic Sciences Institutes)
FET	Further education and training
GC	Gregorian calendar

GCE	General Certificate of Education
GCE-A	General Certificate of Education-Advanced Level
GCE-N	General Certificate of Education-Normal Level
GCE-O	General Certificate of Education-Ordinary Level
GDP	Gross domestic product
GEQIP	General Education Quality Improvement Program
GER	Gross enrollment rate
GET	General education and training
GNI	Gross national income
GNP	Gross national product
GPI	Gender parity index
(G)SE	(General) Certificate of Secondary Education
GTP	Growth and Transformation Plan (2010/11–2014/15)
HERQA	Higher Education Relevance and Quality Agency
HDP	Higher Diploma Program
HIV	Human immunodeficiency virus
IB	International Baccalaureate
ICT	Information and communication technology
IGCSE	International General Certificate of Secondary Education
IMF	International Monetary Fund
INSET	In-service education and training
IT	Information technology
JSE	Junior Secondary Examination
KHURUSAPHA	Teachers' Council of Thailand
LAMP	Leadership and Management Program
LMIC	Lower-middle-income country
MLC	Minimum learning competency
MOE	Ministry of Education
MOFED	Ministry of Finance and Economic Development
NBTS	National Board for Professional Teacher Standards, USA
NCATE	National Council for Accreditation of Teacher Education, USA
NEAEA	National Educational Assessment and Examinations Agency
NER	Net enrollment rate
NGO	Nongovernmental organization
NLA	National Learning Assessment
NRT	Norm-referenced test
OCT	Ontario College of Teachers, Canada

OLPC	One laptop per child
PASEC	Programme d'Analyse des Systèmes Educatifs (Program on the Analysis of Education Systems)
PCK	Pedagogical content knowledge
PGDT	Post-Graduate Diploma in Teaching
PIRLS	Progress in International Reading Literacy Study
PISA	Programme for International Student Assessment
PLSE	Primary School-Leaving Exam
PPP	Public-private partnership
PSSA	Private Secondary Schools Authority, Mauritius
PSSP	Private Sector Support Program, IFC
PTA	Parent-teacher association
PTC	Parent-teacher congress
PTSC	Parent-teacher-student committee
R&D	Research and development
REB	Regional Education Bureau
SACMEQ	Southern and Eastern Africa Consortium for Monitoring Educational Quality
SBM	School-based management
SEIA	Secondary Education in Africa, World Bank
SET	Science, engineering, and technology
SIP	School Improvement Plan
SMC	School Management Committee
SNNPR	Southern Nations Nationalities and Peoples Region
SOE	State-owned enterprise, Vietnam
STA	Scientific Teaching Aids, South Africa
TEAC	Teacher Education Accreditation Council, USA
TEI	Teacher Education Institution
TIMMS	Trends in International Mathematics and Science Study
TV	Television
TVET	Technical and vocational education and training
UIS	UNESCO Institute of Statistics
UK	United Kingdom
UNESCO	United Nations Educational, Scientific, and Cultural Organization
UNEVOC	UNESCO International Centre for Technical and Vocational Education and Training, Bonn
UNICEF	United Nations Children's Fund

URL	Uniform resource locator
USA	United States of America
VIT	Victorian Institute of Teaching, Australia
WDI	World Development Indicators database
WEF	World Economic Forum
WEO	Woreda Education Office; also World Economic Outlook (database), IMF

All dollar amounts are U.S. dollars unless otherwise noted.

Executive Summary

This report on secondary education was prepared by the World Bank as a contribution to the Government of Ethiopia's longer-term education strategy development. The report analyzes the challenges of secondary education in the context of the government's Growth and Transformation Plan (GTP, 2010/11–2014/15) and its stated goal of becoming a middle-income country by 2020–23. It does not aim to provide a definitive set of recommendations for expanding secondary education to meet the demands of a middle-income economy. Rather, the report informs policy makers about the options available in the context of Ethiopia. It aims to equip them to chart a path for sustainable expansion of the subsector, enabling secondary education to play an important role in transforming the country from a low- to middle-income economy.

The report begins with an investigation of the participation rate in secondary education that would support a middle-income economy. It then examines whether the current secondary curriculum can ensure a supply of secondary graduates compatible with the needs of this economy. The report also analyzes how teacher preparation, development, and management, together with school-based management, can contribute to ensuring quality secondary graduates. Based on the quantity and quality of secondary graduates required, the report then assesses the options for ensuring sustainable financing for the subsector. It concludes with a summary of policy options for the expansion of secondary education. The most critical reform areas identified in the study relate to the curriculum, financing, and governance and management of secondary education, particularly school-based management.

Macroeconomic Context and Human Capital Challenges

The Ethiopian economy has been one of the fastest-growing economies in Africa in recent years, with real gross domestic product (GDP) growth at or near double-digit levels since 2003. The country's progress toward becoming a lower-middle-income country (LMIC) will involve the transformation of an economy that—notwithstanding its recent growth performance—has a large subsistence agriculture sector and is dominated by low-productivity activities. This economy must grow into one in which labor is more productive and modern agriculture, manufacturing, and services are increasingly important. Reaching the annual 11.2 percent growth rate in GDP projected by the GTP will require significant improvements in labor productivity (chapter 1). Building a workforce that has the level of education and training required to support the economy on its path to middle-income status is therefore a central development challenge.

Education in Ethiopia: Achievements and Challenges

Throughout much of the twentieth century Ethiopia was one of the most educationally disadvantaged countries in the world, where most people had little access to schooling. This legacy continues to affect its human resources (chapter 2). Only 36 percent of the country's adult population is literate. But great strides have been made in education since 1994, and much of this progress has been realized in the context of recurring regional conflicts, fragile natural resources, and a high level of human immunodeficiency virus/acquired immune deficiency syndrome (HIV/AIDS) prevalence. Access to education has surged, especially at the primary level, where more than 85 percent of the relevant age group is now in school. At the secondary level, the gross enrollment rate (GER) for grades 9–10 has more than doubled since 2000. Yet key challenges remain in secondary education: (1) a low primary education completion rate constrains the growth of secondary enrollments; (2) access to secondary education remains inequitable; and (3) levels of student learning are disappointing.

Secondary Education and Economic Transformation

Addressing these issues is critically important, given that the experience of middle-income countries suggests that sustained economic progress is associated with a rapidly evolving skill profile of the labor force. Vietnam in 1960 had a labor force education attainment profile that was roughly similar to that of Ethiopia today. Between 1960 and 2010 the proportion of the Vietnamese population with no schooling declined from 41.9 percent to 4.2 percent, and the proportion with secondary education increased from 17.3 percent to more than 30 percent. In other words, its education attainment pyramid inverted during the period (chapter 3). At the primary level Ethiopia has almost reached middle-income country enrollment rates, with a GER of 96 percent and a net enrollment rate of 85 percent, compared to the LMIC averages of 107 percent and 83 percent, respectively. However, it lags substantially behind the LMIC average for all other levels of education. The lower and upper secondary (preparatory) GERs for Ethiopia are 38 percent and 8 percent, respectively, compared to the respective LMIC averages of 72 percent and 45 percent.

Policy development ultimately is determined by national conditions and priorities, but international experience can be helpful when planning a long-term strategy. The experience of LMICs suggests that a number of observations be taken into account. First, although universal general secondary education (grades 9–10) is an important policy objective, a lower secondary GER of roughly 80 percent should be adequate to support the needs of a lower-middle-income economy. Second, a number of students will want to enter the labor market and get a job upon completion of general secondary education (grade 10). These students will seek, whenever possible, to benefit from in-house training offered by employers, but will not enter full-time technical and vocational education and training (TVET) programs. Third, the current target for upper secondary (preparatory) education admissions (20 percent of grade 10 graduates) is much lower than the average LMIC target. And finally, the well-justified goal of natural science enrollments of 70 percent at both the preparatory and tertiary level may be difficult to achieve with an acceptable level of graduate quality, although it provides a clear indication of policy direction.

Emerging Education Policy Priorities

The education system in Ethiopia as currently organized, together with existing education policies, has served the country well as it has transitioned from a country with some of the lowest enrollment ratios in the world to one where universal primary education is within reach. Opportunities for further education and training are now expanding rapidly. But the development context has changed with the progress that has been realized in both the economy and the education sector. Education policy over the next 15 years will be driven by the need to expand access to a broad range of education and training opportunities. The policy framework for secondary education must ensure that (chapter 3):

- All primary education graduates who are academically able and interested have access to general secondary education and can complete 10 years of schooling.
- General secondary education curricula are designed to prepare students for a range of future education, training, and career options.
- Preparatory education evolves into a program that has a broader purpose than preparation for university entrance.
- The proportion of students admitted into grade 11 gradually increases to reach middle-income levels.
- Policies that promote learning achievement, especially in mathematics and science, are an integral part of the country's secondary education development strategy.
- A diverse range of TVET and "second-chance" general education programs are available to graduates of primary, secondary, and preparatory education who do not wish to continue formal general education programs, but may seek further education or training either upon leaving academic programs or later in life.

Curriculum

The current secondary curriculum is not designed to meet the demands of universal general secondary education; it is too difficult and academic for that purpose (chapter 4). The level of the science and mathematics curricula are, moreover, higher than what is common in middle- and high-income countries. These issues are an important reason for the low student learning performance already observable at current participation rates. Meanwhile, the 80 percent of students who do not enter grade 11 are not adequately prepared for further education and training or for the world of work.

By about 2024/25 the number of students enrolled in general secondary education is expected to represent close to 80 percent of the relevant age cohort. In this kind of system the curriculum will have to cater to the educational needs of a student body with a much wider range of backgrounds, abilities, and aspirations than has previously been the case. Such a curriculum must be learner centered rather than subject centered and incorporate strategies that address differences in learners' abilities and needs. This secondary system should not brand slower learners as failures and must not put a brake on the progress of the most able. These requirements mean redefining the purpose of the curriculum to ensure that its conceptual demands match the conceptual abilities of a wide range of learners. As a result, secondary education will be sufficiently flexible to allow all students to realize their potential and complete at least 10 years of education.

Equally important is a reconsideration of the purpose of the preparatory level of secondary education, with a related redefinition of the curriculum toward more flexibility and differentiation. As has happened in most LMICs, the number of students entering this level should be growing faster than the numbers entering higher education, especially as current enrollments are far below the LMIC average at the preparatory level. An increasing proportion of graduates will leave grade 12 looking for opportunities other than university entrance, including work and TVET programs. The curriculum should be adjusted accordingly through further differentiation, especially curriculum changes that respond to the increasing "academic foundation" demands of TVET programs.

It is also crucial to consider revisions that change the purpose of assessments from selection of students for higher education to certification of a broad array of competencies. At the same time, changes are needed to provide enhanced local content and create a positive learning environment for girls and ethnic minorities. Perhaps most important, secondary schooling must be designed to develop higher-order skills, including metacognitive skills, in line with the demands of a rapidly growing economy and the need for lifelong learning.

The single most important policy choice to be made in Ethiopia is to measure the success of students in general secondary education in terms of their ability to pursue higher education or their capacity to learn according to their abilities and aspirations and, ultimately, be of use to society. Although this choice concerns secondary education, it will have a significant impact on the development of human resources in the country as a whole and hence, its success in becoming a middle-income-country. As such this issue deserves to be discussed in a broad forum of stakeholders, including politicians, teachers, development practitioners, academicians, and civil society representatives, among others. This discussion would also benefit from the experience of middle-income and developed countries.

Teacher Preparation and Development

Ethiopian classrooms remain primarily teacher centered, where didactic instruction is the norm. There is little evidence of active student learning, inquiry processes, metacognitive skill development, or opportunities for creativity. Improving the quality of instruction involves not only ensuring that necessary equipment and infrastructure are in place, but also improving the quality of teaching. The latter goal requires a two-pronged strategy (chapter 5). The first prong is to develop teachers' instructional competence through pre- and in-service programs. The second prong is to implement a policy framework for teacher management that establishes clear standards of teacher performance and provides incentives for teachers to reach these standards.

Developing teachers' instructional competence is a career-long process that starts with quality pre-service education and induction support for new teachers, and proceeds through continuous professional development (CPD) programs. Priorities in this process include:

- Improving the effectiveness of university programs for teachers
- Providing induction support to Post-Graduate Diploma in Teaching (PGDT) graduates
- Providing systematic and continuous school-based support and supervision to longer-serving teachers through principals and lead teachers
- Developing a CPD system with capacity at the regional and *woreda* (district) levels that can provide support to schools and lead teachers
- Strengthening the capacity of principals to act as instructional leaders and effective school managers via short courses and decentralized support systems.

The priority of teacher management should be to create, through gradual enhancement of incentives, an environment in which these incentives become the main driver of teachers' professional development, as opposed to a professional development system that mainly focuses on the supply side. There is considerable evidence that teacher motivation may be the most critical element of effective teacher performance. This is partly a function of salary and working conditions, but also of selection procedures and criteria that emphasize the longer-term interests of teacher candidates and those in the teaching profession.

The starting point for improving the country's teacher management framework must be the definition of standards and indicators for expected teacher performance. These standards and indicators can then be used as the foundation for a fair and forward-looking teacher evaluation system, including performance improvement plans. Standards will also provide the basis for the accreditation of university teacher education programs, the licensing and relicensing of teachers, and a future merit-based career progression system. For example, pre-service (that is, PGDT) and in-service training programs should be explicitly linked to this new career ladder. Ultimately a standards-based teacher management system requires the creation of a professional administrative body responsible for establishing standards and accrediting teacher education institutions. This agency would be independent of both the Ministry of Education and the universities, but governed by a board with broad representation of all major stakeholders.

Strengthening Governance and Management
In the last two decades decentralization has been one of the key reforms implemented in Ethiopian schools, with important responsibilities transferred to the regions and woredas. Nonearmarked and nonsector-specific block grants are now transferred from the federal to the regional governments, which in turn transfer these grants to woreda governments. Woredas have full authority to allocate the grants, together with their own income, among as well as within the various sectors. Regions and woredas also have the authority to create teacher and other staff positions, fill those positions, and take disciplinary action. In addition, community engagement in the management and financing of school education has increased due to the institutionalization of parent-teacher associations (PTAs) elected by parents.

Ethiopia aspires to further deepen its decentralization policies, specifically by expanding the scope of school-based management (SBM). SBM can make a significant contribution to achieving national secondary education goals because it substantially enhances the effectiveness and efficiency of schools. This type of management involves transferring the authority for academic administration, financial and human resources management, and procurement to the school level. The specific features of the SBM model and the phasing of implementation require considerable further analysis and broad stakeholder consultation. But ideally, a School Management Committee (SMC) or School Board, formed by parents and under their leadership, would have overall responsibility for school performance, including major management decisions. While an SMC would primarily focus on resource generation, external linkages, and the monitoring of school activities and performance, the school principal would focus on school administration and academic management (chapter 6).

SBM is a major reform that radically changes the power structure within an education system. Adoption of a clear legal framework that establishes a solid foundation for SBM, together with sustained political commitment, are prerequisites for its successful implementation. One critical challenge associated with SBM is the need for capacity building at all levels of the education system.

This suggests a phased approach, with careful monitoring of implementation experience and continuous capacity building.

Diversifying the Provision of Secondary Education

The 1994 Education and Training Policy (ETP) commits the government to creating the conditions needed to encourage and support private investors to open schools and establish other education and training institutions. Nevertheless the government currently remains the almost exclusive provider of general education, enrolling some 95 percent of primary and secondary students. Enrollments in nongovernmental (private) secondary schools have been increasing steadily since 2000; nevertheless, they represented only about 5.2 percent of total secondary enrollment by 2010. This share is much lower than that in countries such as Mauritius (59 percent), Indonesia (49 percent), Chile (55 percent), Vietnam (21 percent), Jordan (18 percent), or Ghana (15 percent).

Mobilizing the nongovernmental sector to support the development of secondary education will require streamlining the regulatory framework and allowing the nongovernmental sector to respond to unsubsidized market demand on the order of roughly 10–20 percent of the school-age population (chapter 7). More ambitious targets for nongovernmental sector participation can be envisaged for the longer term; however, such targets would require moving beyond acceptance of the sector as a self-financing parallel system toward a public-private partnership in which the government supports the development of nongovernmental providers as an integral part of its secondary education development strategy. The savings to the government budget resulting from these strategies could be significant. Yet implementation will require substantial efforts to work out a partnership framework that is satisfactory to all parties.

Ensuring Sustainable Financing

Building an education system that effectively supports a middle-income economic development trajectory requires financing for both expansion of access and sustained quality improvement. These twin goals must largely be achieved with national resources, as it is unlikely that external support will be increased beyond existing levels.

A base case scenario, which reflects the most likely course of secondary education expansion within the framework of existing policies and practices, was formulated for the purpose of financial analysis (chapter 8). This scenario targets a secondary education GER of 80 percent by 2024/25 and assumes that the current level of public financing for education of about 4.6 percent of GDP will be maintained. The base case scenario also assumes that the share of nonsalary recurrent expenditures will be 40 percent in order to "ring fence" inputs for quality enhancement. These assumptions result in a projected financing gap for the education sector that averages 24 percent over the period 2015/16–2024/25.

Simulations conducted for this study showed that it would not be possible to fully fund the required development of secondary education solely by increasing public financing; the financing needed is estimated at 6 percent of GDP, but the maximum likely envelope for the sector is only about 5.4 percent. The scope for reducing the financing gap through policy measures aimed at enhancing the efficiency of available resources and mobilizing additional nongovernmental resources was then assessed. The policy measures that were considered were decreasing the teacher-section ratio, continued double-shift use of classrooms, decreasing classroom construction costs, and increasing both the share of enrollment in nongovernmental schools and community contributions to classroom construction. Simulations revealed, however, that even the most radical package of reforms based on these policy measures would not yield sustainable financing of secondary education.

Since sole reliance on either increased public financing or reforms was unfeasible, simulations were conducted for a mix of increased public financing and reforms. The results of these simulations showed that public education financing of 5.2 percent of GDP, complemented by policy measures designed to utilize available resources more efficiently and mobilize additional nongovernmental resources, could help achieve sustainable financing of the secondary subsector. The specific policy measures in this simulation would:

- Decrease the teacher-section ratio from 1.6 to 1.2 for general secondary education and from 1.7 to 1.4 for preparatory secondary education by 2024/25.
- Continue double-shift use of 20 percent of all classrooms through 2024/25.
- Decrease the construction costs of new classrooms from Br 425,000 to Br 340,000, starting in 2014/15.
- Increase enrollment in nongovernmental schools to 20 percent in 2024/25 from 10 percent in 2014/15.

It is important to note that this simulation also assumed that similar reforms will be carried out in other subsectors of education.

The combination of increased public education financing and policy reforms described above is one of many possible combinations that could result in sustainable expansion of secondary education. Due to the uncertainties associated with long-term economic growth forecasts, the simulation results discussed here should be treated as indicative rather than definitive. In other words, the above scenario does not constitute a recommended set of reforms and a specific level of increased public financing. Rather, the financial projections methodology used in this report is offered as a guide for policy makers when considering financing options.

Expanding Access

Progress toward universal general secondary education is predicated on the success of current efforts to improve the quality of primary education and increase primary graduation rates. It also requires that modalities be developed to make secondary education easily accessible in rural areas. Inevitably, this means adopting a "small-school" strategy, that is, a model for delivering good-quality education in a cost-effective way in secondary schools that have no more than two or three sections (chapter 9). These schools will often simply be extensions of existing primary schools in which grades 9 and 10 are integrated under a single principal, with shared common infrastructure.

In such schools, qualified subject teachers may be shared among grades 7 through 10 and multigrade and multilevel classes may be offered in low population-density areas. In addition, innovative approaches—such as traveling teachers who teach a year-long course in one semester and then move on to another school—may be required. Science and social studies subjects may need to be taught as respective integrated courses. Finally, financial incentives may be needed to encourage teachers to work in remote areas and information and communication technology used to support teachers and students (and provide learning enrichment activities not otherwise easily available in rural areas).

Notwithstanding progress to date in education in Ethiopia (chapter 2), gender inequities in access persist. In 2009/10, the gender parity index in general secondary education (grades 9–10) was 0.80 and in preparatory education (grades 11–12), 0.57. The first step in reducing this gap is to continue and, where necessary, intensify efforts to establish gender equity at the primary level. The second step includes making general secondary schools accessible closer to home, building awareness among parents, offering gender-sensitive role models, strengthening gender-sensitive instructional strategies, and offering separate sanitary facilities to ensure consistent progress in girls' enrollment and learning achievement.

Poverty remains the dominant factor explaining low educational achievement in the country (see chapter 2). There is a stark difference in access to secondary education between the secondary age groups belonging to the richest and poorest quintiles. It will be impossible to reduce this gap in any meaningful way without policy measures to assist students from poor households, such as fee waivers in government schools; scholarships to nongovernmental preparatory schools; and scholarships to governmental and nongovernmental boarding schools for students from areas that lack an accessible public school.

To be financially sustainable, this kind of financial support needs to be carefully targeted. Over time, its scope will diminish as the network of secondary schools expands geographically. The challenge is to ensure that limited public resources actually reach the neediest students.

Enabling Conditions

Ethiopia has made considerable progress in improving enabling conditions for effective learning. Yet, challenges remain, especially in the most disadvantaged areas, with 35 percent of secondary schools not having a sufficient number of classrooms and only 20 percent having Internet access. Many laboratories lack basic equipment and supplies and it is unclear how well libraries are stocked. Finally, average class sizes in general secondary education have recently grown to 64 students (2009) and PTAs are often constrained in their ability to contribute to a school's educational performance.

It will therefore be important to agree on minimum enabling conditions for effective education service delivery. On the basis of such conditions, investments should be targeted to schools where remaining resource gaps are so large that they, in effect, preclude effective instruction.

School Leader Effectiveness

School improvement is critically dependent on the management skills of stakeholders. The starting point here must be a sustained effort to enhance the effectiveness of school leaders. Skills of these leaders include instructional leadership (chapter 5), financial and human resources management (chapter 6), forging effective working relationships with the line staff of educational agencies, and winning the confidence of parents and School Management Committees. The pay-off in terms of improved student learning performance is likely to be substantial. Reaching this goal will require, among other things, competency-based selection criteria for school leaders; well-designed training programs prior to appointment; decentralized arrangements for the continuous professional support and supervision of school leaders; and effective professional networks for peer support and learning.

Implementation and Phasing of Reforms

The challenges of secondary education development in Ethiopia are multiple and daunting. Successful implementation of needed reforms requires evidence-based strategies, broad communication of challenges and achievements, sequencing, local support, and adapting reform packages to local conditions. These elements all underscore the importance of closely monitoring the impact of reforms, making adjustments that reflect the lessons of implementation experience, and involving all stakeholders in the process, from design through implementation.

It will be important to initiate further analysis of the issues raised in this report as soon as possible, with stakeholder consultations on options for the long-term development of secondary education. What is clear is that the absence of action is unlikely to result in a secondary education system that can effectively support Ethiopia's progress toward a middle-income economy. The policy framework for the Education Sector Development Plan IV period is clearly set. But the time has come to assess progress to date, consider needed adjustments, and set the stage for the design and implementation of reforms that will be required in the medium (2015/16–2019/20) and long (2020/21–2024/25) term. Table E.1 provides a possible phasing scenario for the implementation of reforms.

Table E.1 Possible Phasing of Secondary Education Reforms

Phase I: 2012/13–2014/15	Phase II: 2015/16–2019/20	Phase III: 2019/20–2024/25
Equitable access. Intensify GEQIP efforts to improve quality and student retention rates in primary education. Update specification for minimum enabling conditions (MECs) for quality instruction at the primary and secondary levels.	Pilot approaches for increasing access to secondary education for girls and students from sparsely populated rural and pastoralist areas, as well as students from poor families.	Scale up nationwide program for equitable access to secondary education. Continue funding schools to meet MECs.
Prepare strategy and programs for equitable access to secondary education for girls and students from pastoralist and sparsely populated rural areas, as well as students from poor families.	Fund schools to meet MECs.	
Curriculum reform. Review international experience with curriculum differentiation, including examination systems. Initiate consultations and decide on options appropriate for the Ethiopian context. Revise curriculum framework with a view to developing curriculum differentiation and an examination framework.	Revise curriculum for differentiated content; prepare new learning materials. Implement revised curriculum and examination system.	Continue implementation of revised curriculum and examination system.
Teacher preparation and development. Review the PGDT curriculum with a view to preparing teachers to teach more than one subject; prepare curricula for certification of grade 9 and 10 teachers who want to qualify to teach additional subjects. Adapt policies related to accreditation of teacher education faculties of universities.	Revise PGDT to enable teachers to teach more than one subject. Establish an accreditation system for PGDT.	Monitor, evaluate, and adjust accreditation, CPD, and licensing system.
Prepare a plan to strengthen the teacher induction and CPD system. Adopt a career progression system for teachers that is linked to a licensing (and relicensing system) and a robust performance evaluation system.	Put in place a strengthened system of teacher induction and CPD. Implement licensing and relicensing system, together with a revised system for career progression of teachers.	
School-based management. Adopt a regulatory framework for SBM and launch a communication campaign. Build the capacity of schools to implement SBM, and of the woredas, regions, and MOE to support SBM.	Implement the first phase (that is, resource generation and utilization, strengthening accountability, simple disciplinary actions, selection of teachers and staff for further training, and recognition of good staff work) and initiate the second phase (that is, management of salary and capital budget; hiring principals; moderate disciplinary actions with respect to staff).	Complete implementation of the second phase and implement the third phase (that is, hiring and promotion of all staff; serious disciplinary actions with respect to staff, teachers, and principals).

(table continues on next page)

Table E.1 Possible Phasing of Secondary Education Reforms *(continued)*

Phase I: 2012/13–2014/15	*Phase II: 2015/16–2019/20*	*Phase III: 2019/20–2024/25*
Nongovernmental provision. Streamline regulatory framework for nongovernmental provision of education. Prepare a plan to develop public-private partnerships (PPPs).	Implement revised regulatory framework for nongovernmental provision. Pilot PPPs.	Take PPPs to national scale, making them an integral part of the financing strategy for secondary education.
Financing. Update the ESDP IV financial projection model. Chose a set a policy reforms that will ensure sustainable financing of secondary education by enhancing the efficiency of public resource use and mobilizing additional nongovernmental resources and public financing. Draw up a plan to implement these reforms.	Implement reforms.	Implement reforms.

Note: CPD = Continuous professional development, ESDP = Education Sector Development Program, GEQIP = General Education Quality Improvement Program, MECs = Minimum enabling conditions, MOE = Ministry of Education, PGDT = Post-Graduate Diploma in Teaching, PPP = Public-private partnership, SBM = School-based management.

CHAPTER 1

Macroeconomic Context and Human Capital Challenges

Ethiopia's economy has been one of the fastest growing economies in Africa in recent years. The country aims to sustain an annual rate of economic growth of more than 10 percent and become a middle-income country by the period 2020–23. This goal will require significant improvements in labor productivity. As the economy develops and the industrial and service sectors adopt more complex production techniques, a workforce with more advanced levels of education and technical skills will be necessary. International experience suggests that investments in secondary education are especially important in order to both avoid shortages of middle-level manpower and provide a strong foundation for high-quality tertiary education.

Recent Economic Performance

Ethiopia remains one of Africa's poorest countries (table 1.1), yet its economy has been one of the continent's fastest growing in recent years.[1] With real annual gross domestic product (GDP) growth at or near double-digit levels since 2003/04, the country has outperformed most other countries in Africa. In fact, it has expanded at a rate much faster than the continentwide average (figure 1.1).[2]

Table 1.1 Ethiopia: Basic Indicators, 2009

Population (millions)	82.8
Population growth (annual %)	2.6
GDP (current $, billions)	28.5
GDP per capita (current $)	344.0
GDP growth (annual %)	8.7
Life expectancy at birth (years)	55.7
Infant mortality rate (per 1,000 live births)	67.1
Female youth literacy rate (% of females aged 15–24)	33.3

Source: World Development Indicators (WDI).
Note: GDP = Gross domestic product.

Figure 1.1 GDP Growth Rate Comparison
percentage

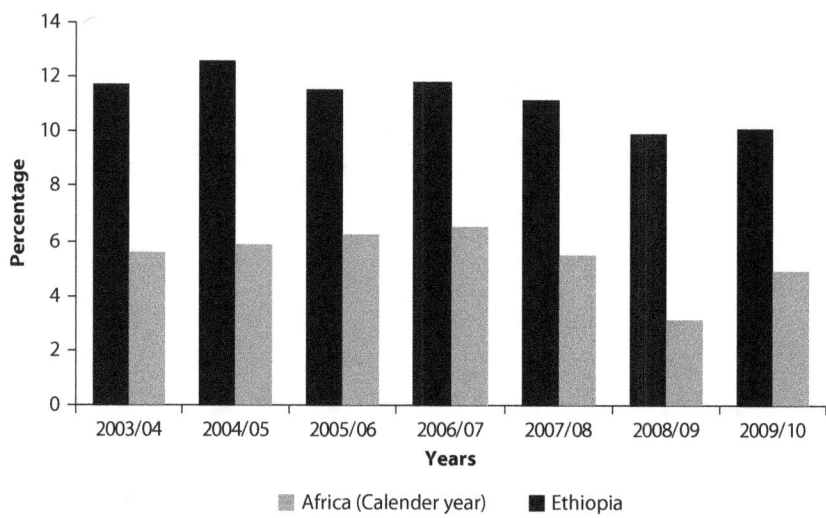

Sources: For 2003/04–2007/08, AfDB 2010; for 2008/09 and 2009/10, WDI.

This accelerated growth has been a key factor in reducing poverty in Ethiopia. According to the country's 2004/05 Household Income and Expenditure Survey, the proportion of people below the poverty line (that is, the share of the population that cannot afford to buy a basic basket of goods) declined from 44.2 percent in 1999/2000 to 38.7 percent in 2004/05 (Ethiopia 2007).[3] Based on International Monetary Fund (IMF) data, *The Economist* projects continued strong growth performance for the country during the period 2011–15, with average annual GDP growth of 8.1 percent (*The Economist* 2011).

This prospect reflects the success of the government's growth and poverty reduction strategy, which focuses on infrastructure development, the commercialization of agriculture, improving access to basic services, and private sector development (including the creation of appropriate regulatory and institutional frameworks to support private business). Requirements and procedures for business registration and licensing have been streamlined, leading to a reduction in transaction costs. Improvements in policies, plus major public investments in infrastructure, have led to a rise in output and services, as well as an expansion and diversification of exports. Incentives provided for new economic activities have started to yield results. For example, flower exports have expanded from less than $10 million in 2004/05 to close to $170 million in 2009/10. And the Ease of Doing Business Index of 2010 (World Bank and IMF 2010) ranked Ethiopia 104 out of 183 countries, higher than Greece (109), Indonesia (121), the Russian Federation (123), Brazil (127), and India (131).

Although agriculture remains the largest sector of the economy, the base of economic growth is broadening, with industry making increasing contributions

Table 1.2 Evolution of the Structure of the Ethiopian Economy
percentage of GDP

	1989	1999	2008	2009	2010
Agriculture	53	50	44	51	48
Industry	12	13	13	11	14
of which Manufacturing	5	6	5	4	5
Services	34	38	43	38	38

Source: WDI.
Note: GDP = Gross domestic product.

to GDP (table 1.2). The share of GDP generated by agriculture declined only slightly from 1989 to 2010, from 53 percent to 48 percent, and the sector remains an important source of growth. However, given mounting pressure on the land, sustaining higher rates of growth in agriculture over the medium term will require substantial improvements in factor productivity. Transforming the structure of agriculture (which is mostly subsistence based at present) to more commercially oriented small-scale production, including for export, will be crucial to sustaining growth in the sector.

Services—dominated by financial intermediation, public administration, and retail business activities—are the second largest sector of the economy, with a share that has remained fairly stable over the past decade. The share of GDP generated by industry remains small, but is gradually increasing in importance, particularly since 2009. Accelerating growth in this sector will be critical to sustaining high overall economic growth over the long run. This will require more private investment in both export-oriented and import-substituting industries, supported by further public investment in infrastructure.

The Ethiopian economy has navigated the global economic crisis much better than most developing countries. Strong growth—estimated by a recent IMF mission at 7.5 percent (IMF 2011)—has continued in 2010/11. Yet, the robust growth performance and considerable development gains of the 2003–07 period came under threat in 2008 and 2009 with the emergence of the twin macroeconomic challenges of high inflation and a difficult balance of payments situation. Yet exports, remittances, and foreign investment, after falling modestly in 2007 and 2008, have recovered to exceed their precrisis levels, with overall economic growth reaching 10.1 percent in 2010. The government has taken a number of measures in the last two years, among them, tightening fiscal policy, reducing domestic borrowing, importing cereals to mitigate the impact of high food prices, tightening the money supply, depreciating the local currency, and introducing price caps on selected goods.

The New Growth and Transformation Plan

Two economic development plans—the Sustainable Development and Poverty Reduction Program (2002/03–2004/05) and the Plan for Accelerated and Sustained Development to End Poverty (2005/06–2009/10)—guided economic development through 2010. Based on lessons learned and its national development vision, the government launched a new five-year plan for 2010/11–2014/15 called the "Growth and Transformation Plan" (GTP) (Ethiopia 2010). The new plan aims to continue rapid broad-based development in a sustainable manner, achieve the Millennium Development Goals (MDGs) and make Ethiopia a middle-income country by the 2020–2023 time frame. The GTP envisions a major leap, not only in terms of economic structure and income level but also in terms of social indicators. The long-term vision of the country enunciated in the plan (Ethiopia 2010, 21) is:

> . . . building an economy which has a modern and productive agricultural sector with enhanced technology and an industrial sector that plays a leading role in the economy; sustaining economic development and securing social justice; and, increasing per capita income of citizens so as to reach the level of those in middle-income countries.

Clearly, the overriding development agenda of the GTP is to sustain the growth witnessed over the past several years and eventually end poverty in Ethiopia. To this end, the plan seeks to maintain annual GDP growth between 11.2 percent and 14.9 percent (table 1.3). Agricultural production is expected to double by the end of 2014/15 through the commercialization of the sector and development of agrobusiness; ambitious targets have been set for flower, coffee, and meat production. The GTP also has a strong focus on industrialization, especially in the sugar, textile, garment, and leather industries.

In terms of infrastructure, the plan includes important investments in transportation, energy, and telecommunications. Accordingly, it seeks to increase access to electricity from 41 percent to 100 percent of the population and total access to safe water from 68.5 percent to 98.5 percent. Social sector objectives include a reduction in the infant mortality rate from the current 101 per 1,000 births to 67 per 1,000, cutting the maternal mortality rate by more than half (from 590 to 267 per 100,000 births), reaching a primary net enrollment ratio

Table 1.3 Projected Growth and Structure of GDP, by Economic Sector, 2010–25

percentage

Sector	GDP growth, 2010/11–2014/15		GDP structure by industrial origin, 2014/15		GDP structure by industrial origin, 2024/25	
	Base case	Higher case	Base case	Higher case	Base case	Higher case
Agriculture and related activities	8.6	14.9	36.9	41.0	33	32
Industry	20.0	21.3	18.8	16.9	23	21
Services	10.6	12.8	44.3	42.1	44	47
Real GDP	11.2	14.9	n.a.	n.a	n.a.	n.a

Source: MOFED 2010; World Bank staff estimates for 2024/25.
Note: GTP = Growth and Transformation Plan (2010/11–2014/15), GDP = Gross domestic product, n.a. = Not applicable. Base case and higher case refer to base case and higher case scenarios of GTP.

of 100 percent, and more than doubling the number of students enrolled in undergraduate programs in government universities.

While ambitious, the general directions of the GTP respond to the needs of the country. The analysis in this and subsequent chapters analyzes the implications of this projected economic growth scenario for secondary education.

Toward a Middle-Level-Income Country

In order to reach the GDP of a lower-middle-income country—one that exceeds $1,000 per capita (in 2010 dollars)—from its current per capita level of $330 (WDI), Ethiopia will need to grow at a projected base case scenario average annual rate of 11.2 percent for 14 years, with annual population growth of 2.6 percent. In the higher case scenario in which the country grows at a 14.9 percent average annual rate, it would take about 10 years to reach this goal. In both cases, growth will entail the transformation of a largely agricultural economy dominated by low productivity to an economy in which labor is more productive and manufacturing and services play an increasingly important role, as has been the case in several countries in East Asia over the past decade.

The GTP foresees a transformation in this direction, with agriculture and related services expected to grow, at a minimum, at an average annual rate of 8.6 percent and industry and services, at 20.0 percent and 10.6 percent, respectively. The industrial sector is clearly expected to be the driving force of projected growth; its share of GDP is projected to increase from 12.9 percent in 2010/11 to 18.8 percent in 2014/15, while the share of agriculture is projected to decrease from 41.6 percent to 36.9 percent and the service sector, from 45.6 percent to 44.3 percent, over the five-year period. According to the GTP, these trends are expected to continue through 2025. The decline in the share of GDP represented by agriculture is consistent with the experience of countries that have reached middle-income levels. In some of these countries the shift has been toward the services sector, while in others, such as Vietnam and Indonesia, the industrial sector has been the engine of growth (table 1.4).

Table 1.4 Composition of GDP of Selected Middle-Income Countries, 1994 and 2009

percentage

Country	Agriculture		Industry		Services	
	1994	2009	1994	2009	1994	2008
Ethiopia	58	51	10	11	32	39
Ghana	42	32	28	19	31	49
Kenya	33	23	17	15	49	62
China	20	10	47	46	34	43
India	29	18	27	27	46	55
Indonesia	17	16	41	49	41	35
Vietnam	27	21	29	40	44	39

Source: WDI.
Note: Totals may not add up to 100 percent due to rounding.

Human Capital Implications

Projected growth targets for the Ethiopian economy will also affect the composition of employment by sector. The trend has been very clear in East Asia, where the movement of workers out of agriculture provided the labor to support rapid growth in the industrial and service sectors (figure 1.2).

This sectoral shift is generally accompanied by major efforts to upgrade the skills of the labor force, regardless of the region. In China, for example, the average years of educational attainment increased from 4.7 to 8.2 years between 1980 and 2010. In Ghana over the same period, educational attainment rose from 5.0 to 7.7 years (figure 1.3).

Ethiopia is still in the early phase of similar changes in the supply of human capital. There, the large-scale movement of people out of agriculture has not yet begun. In 2005, 80 percent of the labor force was employed in agriculture, 13 percent in services, and only 7 percent in industry (Ethiopia 2005).

Similarly, recent efforts to expand access to education in the country have not yet impacted average educational attainment. Ethiopia is also starting from a low educational base. In 2008, for example, the literacy rate in the country was estimated to be 36 percent and the average educational attainment of the population of 15 years and older, 1.5 years. By contrast, when the economic take-off began in China in 1990, the literacy rate in the country was estimated at 78 percent; when Vietnam began a similarly rapid growth trajectory in 2000, its literacy rate was estimated at 90 percent (EdStats).

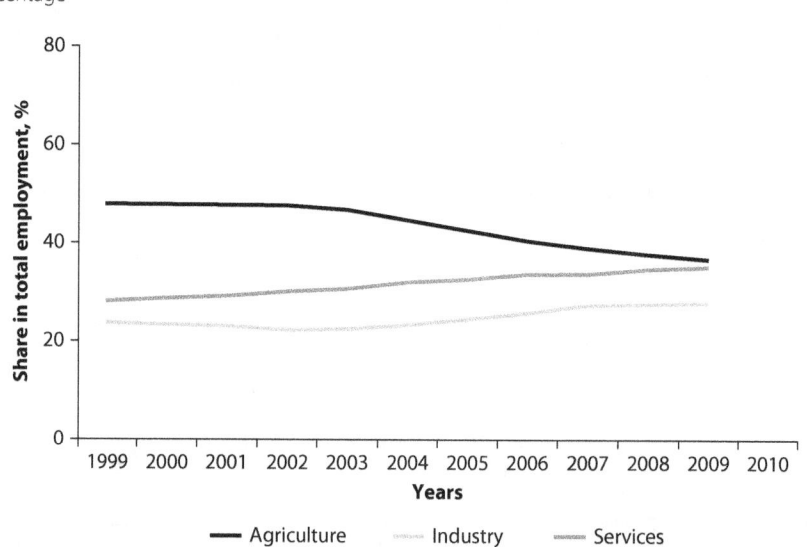

Figure 1.2 Change in Employment by Sector, East Asia, 1999–2010
percentage

Source: Reproduced from ILO 2011, *Global Employment Trends 2011* (Geneva: ILO), 83, figure R5 (bottom panel). Copyright © International Labour Organization 2011.

Figure 1.3 Average Number of Years of Schooling Completed by Individuals Aged 15+ Years, 1980–2010

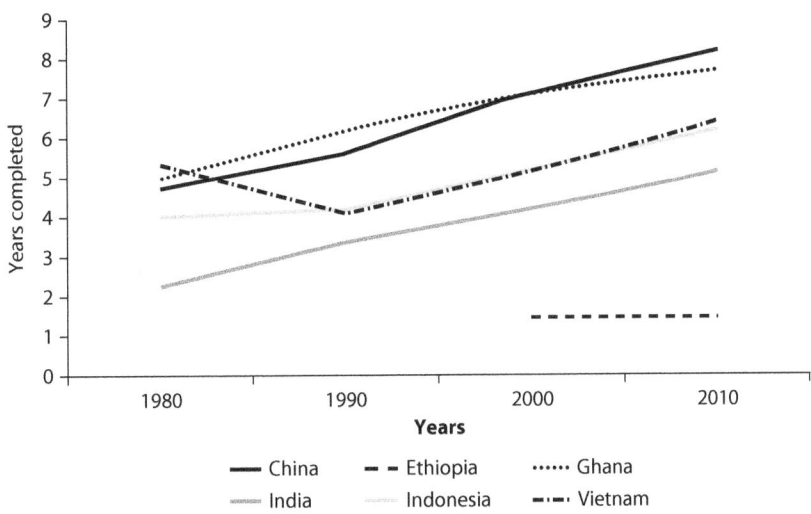

Sources: Barro-Lee Dataset; UNDP 2011.

As noted earlier, reaching the rates of growth projected in the GTP, including a GDP per capita of $1,000 by 2024/25, will require significant improvements in labor productivity. Compared with almost all its peers, labor productivity remains very low in Ethiopia. Moreover, the country's domestic wages are one-third of the average wage in Sub-Saharan Africa. Given substantial investments in infrastructure over the past decade, the economy should be able to compete in a range of export commodities, but this competitiveness has been slow to develop. A recent investment climate assessment of Ethiopia (World Bank 2009c) suggests that productivity is held back by structural and economic factors, which combine to make the economy less flexible and less responsive to incentives. The financial sector, land policies, patterns of inter-firm contracting, and the state of market institutions are all contributing factors that distort or limit competition, resulting in a situation where the most productive enterprises do not systematically increase their market share at the expense of less productive competitors.

Tackling these constraints is necessary, but may not be sufficient to ensure industrial growth in a low-income Sub-Saharan country such as Ethiopia, where the vast majority of workers and firms are trapped in low-productivity, low-skilled informal activities and have little access to markets, skills, technology, or finance. Poor labor skills can severely limit economic growth. When workers are unable to read instructions or operate machines properly, product rejection rates rise. While differences in skill levels are difficult to capture precisely in numerical terms, they are manifested in lower-quality finished products that sell at lower prices, as well as in related wage differentials.

The wage differential between skilled and unskilled workers is only 14 percent in China, but 81 percent in Ethiopia. Although the marginal difference in wage rates in China may indicate a shortage of unskilled workers, it suggests that even unskilled workers in China possess some technical skills that warrant a wage closer to that received by skilled workers. Unskilled workers in China also require less supervision than those in Ethiopia. The ratio of skilled to unskilled labor in China is estimated to be 1 to 10, while in Ethiopia it is 1 to 4 (Dinh et al. 2012).

Yet low-skilled workers in the best-managed firms in Africa achieve Chinese levels of productivity in leather shoe manufacturing (seven pieces per worker per day) and close to Chinese levels in garment manufacturing (80 percent in Lesotho and 60 percent in Ethiopia). This underscores the importance of the quality of management: while workers' may have poor skills in poorly managed firms, in well-managed firms low-skilled workers can acquire good skills through on-the-job training and reach high levels of productivity, especially when they have completed basic education (Dinh et al. 2012). Box 1.1 shows that the comparative advantage of Ethiopia associated with lower wages may be offset by a lack of skills among workers or a labor force that could benefit from on-the-job training. A good supply of primary and general secondary graduates who have acquired minimum competencies prescribed for the corresponding educational level will therefore be critical to Ethiopia's competitiveness in the long run.

Skills for Growth and Transformation

A 2009 investment climate assessment for Ethiopia highlighted the constraints posed by skilled worker shortages (World Bank 2009c). A large proportion of large-scale firms, especially in the services sector (100 percent), but also in manufacturing, reported that a shortage of educated and skilled manpower was a severe or very severe constraint on their operations (table 1.5). To sustain economic progress, then, it is essential that Ethiopia's basic education system produce a literate workforce—one that may have limited technical skills, but can be easily trained to operate simple but modern machines.

Literacy alone, however, will not suffice. Even in simple light manufacturing industries, the quality of managers' skills and their motivation are important—even more important than those of workers. Good managers working under competitive pressure can train and motivate low-skilled workers to reach high levels of productivity in three months or less (Dinh et al. 2012). In addition, as the economy develops more complex manufacturing and service sectors, the need for workers with education beyond the basic level will rapidly increase. To effectively prepare students for further education, basic education will need to emphasize generic, academic, and technical skills—especially in science and technology—so that students, whether they pursue further education and training or join the labor market, are well prepared for their future paths.

Box 1.1

Labor Skills and Productivity in Ethiopia

Labor efficiency. On average, labor efficiency in medium-size and large firms in Ethiopia is about 50 percent of that in similarly sized firms in China and Vietnam, in large part because of less training, smaller-scale operations, poorer organization of functions and tasks, and less reliance on productivity bonuses. (Even in the best-managed firms in the country, labor efficiency is only slightly more than 70 percent of the Chinese level). The lower wages of low-skilled workers, however, more than compensate for Ethiopia's lower efficiency. In small and micro (often informal) firms in the country, labor efficiency is less than 20 percent of the Chinese level, largely due to the lack of both task specialization and scale, as well as inferior equipment.

Input efficiency. While well-managed firms in Ethiopia achieve high input efficiency, average waste and product rejection rates often reach 15 percent each—compared with roughly 5 percent in both China and Vietnam—largely due to poor labor training. These inefficiencies represent a significant penalty, since inputs account for more than 60 percent of total product costs.

Source: Dinh et al. 2012.

Table 1.5 Ethiopian Firms That Find Worker Skills a Severe or Very Severe Constraint on Business

percentage

	Services	Manufacturing
Ethiopia as a whole	15	26
Type of firm		
Small	10	19
Medium	40	33
Large	100	43
Domestic	16	26
With foreign investment	0	24
Nonexporting	15	25
Exporting	25	32

Source: World Bank 2009c.

Recent studies reiterate the importance of combining skills and technology development in order to achieve higher productivity. A recent World Bank study (2009a, xxi), for example, observes that "... micro studies are identifying links between skills and higher productivity at the level of the firm, while research using macro data is showing that R&D [research and development] raises productivity, as does the quality of education." All of these data make it clear that improving worker productivity requires both unskilled workers with a solid basic education and a strong and diverse supply of personnel with middle- and higher-level technical and professional skills.

Higher-Order Skills

As Ethiopia progresses toward becoming a lower-middle-income country, it will need to intensify its efforts to produce ever greater numbers of workers with the knowledge and skills demanded by an increasingly complex, knowledge-based economy. These demands will be driven by changes in production technology and the challenges of moving up the economic value chain, a progression that requires being able to manufacture more complex products and/or deliver advanced services. Employer surveys show that employers in Ethiopia anticipate these changes and are already looking for workers who can solve problems, communicate well, and work in groups—creative, higher-order reasoning, scientific, and metacognitive skills that are at a premium in knowledge economies.

Figure 1.4 presents a visual perspective on changes in the demand for skills in the United States over time. With 1969 set as the baseline year, the importance of different types of skills in the economy is graphed for subsequent years as a percentile change along the y axis. Obviously, the current Ethiopian economy cannot be compared to the economies of developed countries. However, trends in the organization of work and the demand for different types of skills also affect developing countries—including Ethiopia—as these countries aim to establish their own competitive advantages in the global market of the twenty-first century.

In recognition of changes in the global economy, school systems in developing countries need to bring about reforms in teacher training, curricula, and educational structures so that they can prepare students with the needed

Figure 1.4 Economywide Measures of Routine and Nonroutine Task Input, United States, 1969–98

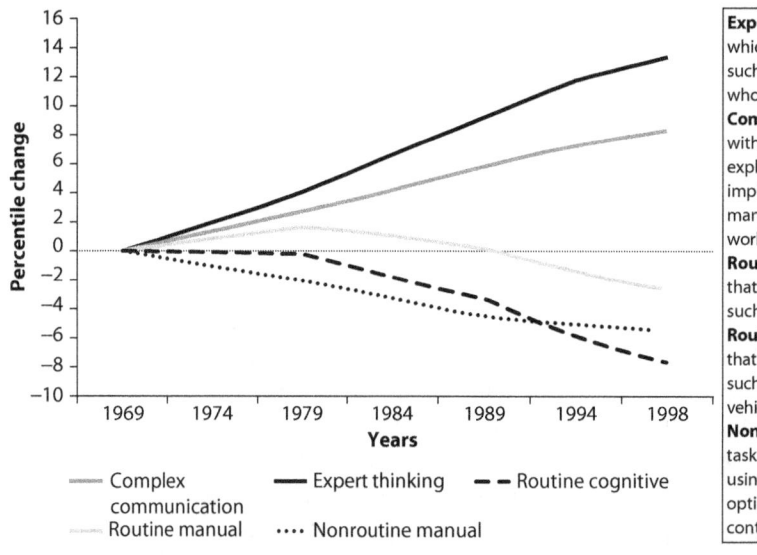

Sources: Left panel—reproduced from Levy and Murnane 2004, 50, figure 3.5; right panel—World Bank 2005b, 81.

skills. A strong case can be made that in order to meet new global realities, general academic secondary schools and technical and vocational education and training (TVET) in Ethiopia, current and future, must prepare for continual change in curriculum organization and content. Without teachers who have mastered new curricula, are experts in both pedagogy and content, and able to impart more than nonroutine manual or routine cognitive skills, Ethiopia will be unable to achieve the progress demanded by its economic development vision.

The graph shown in figure 1.4 makes clear that in most developed and developing countries many of the skills taught in the traditional curricula of primary and secondary schools—and in vocational training programs—may no longer be sufficient to prepare the workforce for the labor market by 2025. Mastery of basic skills remains, of course, essential. It is the major focus of basic education in all educational systems throughout the world. These skills fall under the category of routine cognitive tasks and unless they are mastered, students' success at the secondary education level (lower and upper) becomes highly problematic. These challenges should guide education development in Ethiopia. There is little doubt that an increasing number of Ethiopian graduates of not just TVET programs, but also of preparatory school (grade 12) and general secondary education (grade 10), already need higher-level expert and communication skills in order to effectively participate in the labor force.

Figure 1.5 shows the skills that Indonesian employers perceive as being most important for managers, professionals, and skilled workers. Not surprisingly,

Figure 1.5 Share of Firms Rating Skills of Managers, Professionals, and Skilled Workers as Important, Indonesia, 2008

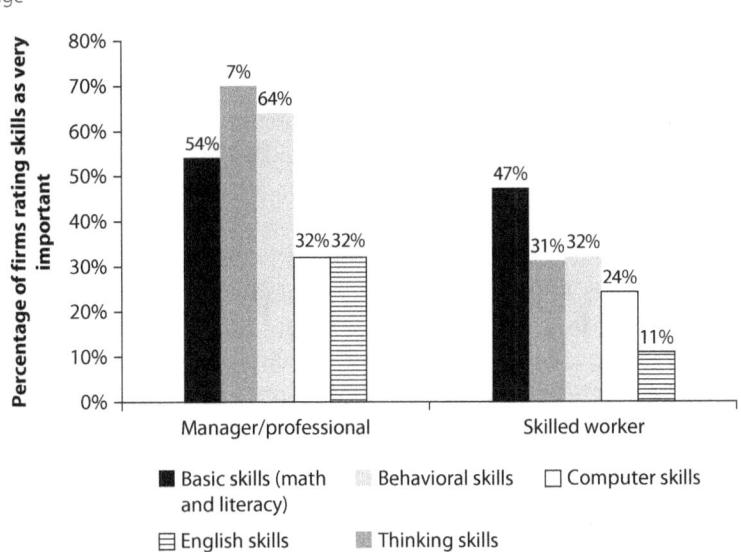

Source: Reproduced from di Gropello 2011, 80, figure 2.20.

thinking and behavioral skills are more highly valued for managers and professionals, while basic skills in mathematics and literacy are seen as most important for skilled workers. The graph underscores the importance of ensuring that education systems provide good-quality basic education, as well as advanced education and training that imparts the cognitive and behavioral skills expected of managers and professionals.

Middle-Level Skills

An often neglected, but critical, challenge for countries aspiring to progress toward a middle-income economy is the preparation of middle-level skilled personnel. In many middle-income countries skills shortages are especially severe at this level after an initial economic take-off, as illustrated by the recent experience of India, Indonesia, Vietnam, and Ghana.

In India most employment growth over the past 10 years has taken place in skilled services (for example, information technology, financial services, telecommunications, tourism, and retail) and skill-intensive manufacturing, all of which require, at a minimum, secondary education. Meanwhile, employment has declined in low-skilled occupations and stagnated in agriculture, with agricultural value-added growth decelerating sharply in the second half of the 1990s. Even in rural areas, job prospects are better for the more qualified. In fact, the shortage of skilled and semi-skilled workers is adversely impacting the competitiveness of Indian industry. Skills shortages appear when employers try to expand production (that is, fill new vacancies), upgrade existing employees to more technology-intensive production processes, or replace employees lost to higher-paying employers. Shortages exist across many segments of industry in India today, including the oil and gas, biotechnology, food processing, information technology, aviation, health care, construction, automotive, mining, textiles, plastics, finance, insurance, chemicals, and pharmaceuticals industries (World Bank 2009b).

While unskilled positions in Indonesia are almost by definition easy to staff, a recent survey found that employers in the country consider it difficult to staff director- and professional-level jobs (as reported by 80 percent and 60 percent of employer respondents, respectively). The manufacturing and export sectors in Indonesia tend to report greater problems in finding employees with the required skills, but services also face serious difficulties. The widest gaps across professional profiles are for English-language and computer skills, followed by thinking and behavioral skills. Gaps in the latter are particularly critical, given their overall importance to employers; those in computer and English skills are likely to be more important in export- and technology-oriented sectors and subsectors. Within the category of behavioral skills, leadership, team orientation, and the ability to work independently are considered particularly weak among Indonesian workers. The survey confirmed that the strongest gaps in job-specific skills were in theoretical and practical knowledge of a given job, in accordance with the most important job-specific skills (di Gropello 2011).

A similar skills shortage prevails in Vietnam, where the economy grew rapidly during the period 2002–07, with GDP increasing at an annual average rate of 7.9 percent. This growth was propelled largely by the industrial and services sectors, which grew at annual average rates of 10.3 percent and 7.6 percent, respectively. Agriculture also grew, but at the slower average annual rate of 3.9 percent. In terms of the structure of the economy, agriculture in 2007 accounted for only 20.3 percent of GDP, while industry accounted for 41.6 percent and services, 35.1 percent. However, with the latter two sectors expanding rapidly, Vietnam is now confronted with a shortage of technical personnel, skilled workers, and middle managers. Indeed, lack of skills has been reported as a constraint by a high proportion of firms in several surveys. Moreover, projections indicate a growing demand for skilled labor; for example, skilled workers were expected to account for 24 percent of the total workforce by 2010. At present, however, only 13 percent of the employable workforce in the country has vocational education qualifications (ACCC 2010).

The shortage of highly skilled workers in Vietnam has now reached an alarming level, particularly in enterprises that have received foreign investment. Within the manufacturing sector, continued growth is projected for the electro-mechanical, shipbuilding, textiles, food processing, and petrochemical industries. As in the past, tourism also continues to be a growth sector. Information and communications, professional, scientific, and technical services remain small, but are growing rapidly. Their growth reflects the priority that the Vietnamese government has given to high technology, including new-materials technology, biotechnology, automation technology, and nanotechnology. Policies to raise the skills of workers who are entering or already working in the labor force are consequently essential to achieve needed productivity gains and economic growth (ACCC 2010).

Employers in Ghana also identify a shortage of skilled workers as a problem at the firm level, with 50 percent of respondents in a recent Employers Association survey reporting hard-to-fill vacancies in their firms. Some 80 percent of this group noted that the vacancies had been unfilled for the past 12 months. The top three causes cited for such vacancies were lack of technical or practical skills, an insufficient number of suitably qualified people, and lack of practical work experience (World Bank 2011).

In East Asian countries that have achieved high growth rates, such as Singapore, the Republic of Korea, and more recently, Vietnam, the vision for national economic development has been closely linked to policies to develop the education system. Educational priorities have evolved over time in response to the increasing complexity of the economy as each country moved from manufacturing simple products to developing heavy industry and, today, to knowledge-based production and service industries (table 1.6). The national vision of these countries is built on the interaction between education and the economy, with a clear understanding that these two priorities are mutually dependent and reinforcing.

Table 1.6 Links between Education and Economic Development in Korea, Rep., 1960s–present

Educational investments	Targeted skills education
Elementary and secondary education (1960s)	• Labor-intensive light manufacturing
Vocational-technical high schools (1970s–1980s)	• Capital-intensive heavy and chemical industry
Higher education (1980s–present)	• Electronics, high-tech knowledge industry

Source: Lee 2006, slide 11.

Emphasis on the development role of education, however, goes well beyond economic issues. Education has been assigned a key role in nation building, including building the moral values and national cohesion required to make a multiethnic society work. For example, many African countries today—some 40–50 years after independence—still consider the content of their curricula too reflective of their colonial heritage and not sufficiently adapted to their national realities. Singapore, Korea, and Vietnam, by contrast, "renovated" their educational curricula almost immediately following independence so that schools could serve overarching national economic and nation-building goals (Verspoor 2008).

It is, of course, much too simplistic to posit a direct link between investment in education and economic development. The experiences of the "Asian Tigers" (Hong Kong, Singapore, Korea, and Taiwan; see World Bank 1993) in the 1980 and 1990s and more recently, Vietnam (box 1.2), suggest that it may be possible to sustain rapid growth in the short term through simple factor accumulation. In the longer term, however, it becomes essential to pursue a broad package of policy reforms that enhance factor productivity, including making investments in human capital (especially secondary education).

Box 1.2

Economic Reform in Vietnam

Launched in 1986, the *Doi Moi* economic reforms emerged from the recognition that Vietnam needed comprehensive reform of the agricultural, services, and manufacturing sectors. The country also needed a gradual implementation approach that would allow state-led enterprises to coexist with new private initiatives as the reforms created property rights and markets. Key elements of the *Doi Moi* reforms were:

- *Property rights over land*. Reversing the collectivization of farmland was a critical first step, with agricultural land given to rural households on an egalitarian basis. The 1993 Land Law then created tradable land-use certificates that could be mortgaged. Constraints that hindered the import of fertilizers were also reduced. By 2000, 11 million land titles had

(box continues on next page)

Box 1.2 Economic Reform in Vietnam *(continued)*

been issued. Land reform coincided with a boom in coffee prices and rice yields, which raised rural productivity and incomes.
- *Human capital investments.* Vietnam invested heavily in education as part of these reforms, increasing upper secondary enrollment from 7.2 percent in 1993 to 41.8 percent in 2002, with enrollment of the poorest segments of the population in lower secondary rising from 12 percent to 54 percent.
- *Competition and privatization.* In the 1990s Vietnam removed price controls on many products, lowered barriers to market entry, and allowed an increasing number of firms to export and import. It also gradually liberalized tariffs while maintaining protections for key industries. Competition among state-owned enterprises (SOEs) was permitted as the government began to restructure them either by gradual equitization (large enterprises) or selling them to directors and workers (small enterprises).
- *Creation of a new private sector.* Economic and institutional reforms at first permitted the creation of 5,000 private firms each year. The emergence of an informal, and then formal, private sector allowed for off-farm income and the movement of labor from agriculture to industry and services. In early 2002, a special Communist Party Central Committee meeting endorsed private sector development and deepened market reforms. Formal annual firm creation had already jumped from 5,000 to over 15,000 by 2000; special economic zones supported the reforms by attracting foreign direct investment.
- *Creation of a new financial sector.* Credit as a percentage of GDP increased from 13 percent in 1990 to 44 percent in 2000. This increase was based on: (1) a liberalization of interest rates that began in 1996; (2) removal of social mandates from the missions of state commercial banks and efforts to deal with nonperforming SOE debt; (3) permission first for private (joint stock) banks and then foreign banks to operate in the country alongside state banks. In addition, substantial progress has also made in building market institutions, such as security pledge registries, a credit bureau, and an enabling legal framework, while regulatory capacity continues to be developed.
- *Economic openness.* Twenty years after the *Doi Moi* was launched, Vietnam was invited to join the World Trade Organization, capping its remarkable commitment to removing barriers to trade. The country also leveraged foreign direct investment early in the reform process, with $12 billion in such investments approved through 1994.
- *Credibility and macroeconomic stability.* Periodic decisions by Communist Party Congresses signaled major reform milestones, removed contradictory policies, and guaranteed the irreversibility of the reforms at key junctures in the process. Over time, Vietnam's record of macroeconomic stability contributed to investor confidence. Throughout the 1990s, with the exception of the years of the Asian financial crisis of 1997–98, Vietnam's macroeconomic indicators were ranked among the top quintile worldwide.

Sources: World Bank 2009c; based on World Bank 2002; Klump 2007.

Contribution of Education to Economic Growth

The economic benefits of education in terms of increased individual earnings are well documented. A review of the literature by Psacharopolous and Patrinos (2002) found that an additional year of schooling has a large effect on workers' earnings, with a 10 percent average rate of return to an additional year of schooling, based on a sample of 100 countries. The relative scarcity of human capital in low-income countries is the main factor for the high returns to education (Jimenez 2008). In low-income countries with poor primary education participation rates, the private and social returns to primary education have typically been higher than those to other levels of education. But as an increasing proportion of young people complete primary education, the value of secondary education increases. Recent analyses accordingly show higher returns to secondary than to primary education (box 1.3), especially in countries experiencing rapid economic growth.

No recent estimates of the returns to education are available for Ethiopia. Table 1.7 summarizes private rates of return documented in studies conducted in the country the 1990s (see World Bank 2005a), which are mostly moderate to high. These rates can be seen as a partial explanation for rising enrollment rates in recent years. The simultaneous rapid growth of GDP is likely to have increased the wage differentials between skilled and unskilled labor and increased the returns to both secondary and higher education.

Education Quality and Economic Growth

Although moderate to high rates of return to education provide a justification for prioritizing public investment in the sector, rates of return are based on enrollment or school attainment data at the microlevel; in other words, they do not account for educational quality, as measured by learning outcomes. A recent impact evaluation of World Bank support to basic education in Ghana, for example, found "that gains in educational outputs are directly linked to better school quality" (World Bank 2004a, i).

Table 1.7 Private Returns to Education in Ethiopia, Selected Studies

annual percentage

	Urban areas			Rural areas	All areas
		Private sector			
	Public sector	Formal	Formal and informal	Public and private sectors	Public and private sectors
Rate of return by level					
Primary	10.6	—	..	—	32.5
Secondary	15.0	—	8.2	—	19.2
Higher education	15.1	—	21.5	—	22.4
Year of survey	(1997)		(1997)		(2000)

Source: World Bank 2005a.
Note: .. = Negligible (estimate not statistically different from 0), — = Not available.

Box 1.3

Recent Estimates of Returns to Secondary Education and Training

Tanzania: A wage earner who completed primary education earned 75 percent more than an uneducated wage earner; an employee who completed lower secondary education made 163 percent more; and one who completed upper secondary education earned 181 percent more (World Bank 2006a).

Burkina Faso: The returns to education in Burkina Faso were estimated at 16 percent for secondary education, compared to 9 percent for primary education (World Bank 2006c).

Mali: The rate of return on education is about 10 percent for initial years of schooling and increases substantially with the number of years of education: 15 percent for a complete primary education and about 25 percent for a complete secondary education (World Bank 2006d).

Mauritania: An analysis that covered different segments of the economy, including the informal sector, found low overall average rates of return for an additional year of education (3.4 percent). Earnings were, however, found to rise with more education, with especially high increases associated with a complete secondary education. Earnings of workers in the informal and formal sectors were rather similar and exceeded earnings in government jobs by as much as 30 percent (World Bank 2006e).

Mozambique: For male workers outside of agriculture, returns to primary education range from 14 percent to 24 percent; returns to lower secondary education range from 23 percent to 40 percent; and those to upper secondary, from 60 percent to 74 percent. For female workers and workers in agriculture, returns to education are substantially lower, but follow a similar pattern, with a 7 percent return for agricultural workers with five years of education or less (World Bank 2006b).

Rwanda: The returns to general secondary education are estimated at 21.5 percent, compared to 13.2 percent for primary education and 18.4 percent for secondary vocational education (World Bank 2004b).

Sénégal: At 18 percent, the return to lower secondary education in the modern economic sector exceeds the returns to primary education (11 percent), upper secondary (14 percent), and tertiary education (0.1 percent). Returns to all three levels of education are higher in the informal economic sector (29 percent, 27 percent, and 29 percent, respectively) than in the modern sector (UNESCO BREDA 2005).

Sources: UNESCO BREDA 2005; World Bank 2004b, 2006a, 2006b, 2006c, 2006d, 2006e.

More recently, Hanushek and Wößmann (2007) reviewed the relationship between educational quality—measured by student performance in mathematics and the sciences—and economic growth. They found strong evidence that educational quality—rather than years of school attainment alone—was powerfully and causally related to an individual's earnings, the distribution of income, and economic growth. The authors concluded that concentrating on years of school attainment or enrollment rates leads to misleading analysis, arguing that educational quality is the key issue for assessing the education policies of developing countries.

Conclusion

Ethiopia's recent economic performance has been impressive. Sustaining this performance over the coming 15 years will require significant improvements in productivity, which must be achieved through improved management, the application of technology, and the upgrading of human capital.

As the country follows a path toward becoming a lower-middle-income country, subsistence agriculture will become less important and commercial agriculture, industry (including agroprocessing), and services will grow more rapidly. An increasing proportion of the workforce will be employed outside of the agricultural sector. In the immediate future industrial growth may be driven by investments in light manufacturing; it is sufficient that this sector have a workforce with good basic education (enabling them to easily learn to operate simple machines). But in the medium and longer term, a workforce with more advanced levels of education and technical skills will be needed if Ethiopia is to increase economic productivity and sustain growth.

Shortages of skilled labor are likely to increase the wage premium to education and training in the country, as well as fuel social demand for education beyond the basic level. The experience of other lower-middle-income countries suggests that ensuring an adequate supply of personnel with middle-level skills is critical. The need for these types of workers underscores the urgency of expanding secondary education and providing young Ethiopians with the analytical, problem-solving, and communication skills that are demanded by employers.

There is little doubt that investments in education in Ethiopia can yield high returns to both individuals and society. To capture these benefits, however, it will not be enough simply to increase the number of students who attend school for more years. Improved student learning achievement is the key to reaping these high returns. Ensuring that its education system both imparts students with middle-level skills and facilitates improved learning achievement is probably the most critical challenge that Ethiopia faces.

Notes

1. This section draws heavily on AfDB 2010.
2. All years cited in this publication refer to the Gregorian calendar (GC) unless the Ethiopian calendar (EC) is specifically indicated. The Ethiopian fiscal year begins on July 7 in the Gregorian calendar.
3. Citations of Ethiopian government documents prior to 1995 are indicated by "Ethiopia" in this publication; citations of such documents after 1995 are indicated by

the acronym of the government ministry or agency. For practical purposes, a fiscal year in Ethiopia corresponds to an academic year, hence both are indicated as fiscal years (for example, 1985/86).

References

ACCC (Association of Canadian Community Colleges). 2010. "Viet Nam: Skills Enhancement Project." In association with SRI (Socioeconomic Research Incorporated) and Strategic Consultancy Company Limited. Technical Assistance Consultant's Report, Project No. 41339-01. Submitted to Asian Development Bank, Manila, Philippines. http://www2.adb.org/documents/reports/consultant/41339-VIE/41339-01-vie-tacr.pdf.

African Development Bank (2010) Ethiopia's Economic Growth Performance: Current Situation and Challenges Economic Brief Vol 1, Issue 5.17 September 2010.

Barro-Lee Educational Attainment Dataset. Economics Department, Korea University, Seoul. http://www.barrolee.com.

di Gropello, Emanuela. 2011. *Skills for the Labor Market in Indonesia: Trends in Demand, Gaps, and Supply.* With Aurelien Kruse and Prateek Tandon. Directions in Development Series. Report 60812, World Bank, Washington, DC.

Dinh, Hinh T., Vincent Palmade, Vandana Chandra, and Frances Cossar. 2012. *Light Manufacturing in Africa: Targeted Policies to Enhance Private Investment and Create Jobs.* Washington, DC: World Bank.

The Economist Online. 2011. "Africa's Impressive Growth." January 6. http://www.economist.com/blogs/dailychart/2011/01/daily_chart.

EdStats (database). World Bank, Washington, DC. http://go.worldbank.org/85XM5TBQA0.

Ethiopia, Federal Democratic Republic of CSA (Central Statistical Agency). 2005. "Report on the 2005 National Labour Force Survey." *Statistical Bulletin* 365. CSA, Addis Ababa.

———. 2007. "2004/05 Household Income, Consumption, and Expenditure Survey: Volume II, Statistical Report." *Statistical Bulletin* 394. CSA, Addis Ababa.

Ethiopia, Federal Democratic Republic of MOFED (Ministry of Finance and Economic Development). 2010. "Growth and Transformation Plan, 2010/11–2014/15." MOFED, Addis Ababa.

Hanushek, Eric A., and Ludger W. Wößmann. 2007. "The Role of Education Quality in Economic Growth." Policy Research Working Paper 4122, World Bank, Washington, DC.

ILO (International Labour Organization). 2011. *Global Employment Trends 2011.* Geneva: ILO.

IMF (International Monetary Fund). 2011. "Statement by an IMF Staff Mission on the 2011 Article IV Consultation with Ethiopia." Press Release 11/207, IMF, Washington, DC.

Jimenez, Emmanuel, and Harry Anthony Patrinos. 2008. "Can Cost-Benefit Analysis Guide Education Policy in Developing Countries?" Policy Research Paper 4568, Education Team, Human Development Network, World Bank, Washington, DC.

Klump, Rainer. 2007. "Pro-Poor Growth in Vietnam: Miracle or Model?" In *Delivering on the Promise of Pro-Poor Growth: Insights and Lessons from Country Experiences*, ed. Timothy Besley and Louise J. Cord, 119–46. Washington, DC: World Bank.

Lee, Chong-Jae. 2006. "The Development of Education in Korea: Past Achievement and Current Challenges." PowerPoint presentation of background paper for Seminar Organized by the World Bank for Senior African Policy Makers, Singapore, June 23–26.

Levy, Frank, and Richard J. Murnane. 2004. *The New Division of Labor: How Computers Are Creating the Next Job Market*. Princeton, NJ: Princeton University Press and Russell Sage Foundation. Quoted in World Bank 2005b.

Psacharopolous, George, and Harry Anthony Patrinos. 2002. "Returns to Investment in Education: A Further Update." Policy Research Working Paper 2881, Education Sector Unit, Latin American and Caribbean Region, World Bank, Washington, DC.

UNDP. 2011. "Ethiopia: HDI Values and Rank Changes in the 2011 Human Development Report." Explanatory Note on HDR Composite Indexes (Human Development Report 2011; Sustainability and Equity: A Better Future for All). UNDP, New York. http://hdrstats.undp.org/images/explanations/ETH.pdf.

UNESCO BREDA (United Nations Educational, Scientific, and Cultural Organization/ Bureau Régional pour L'Éducation en Afrique [Regional Office for Education in Africa]). 2005. *Education for All in Africa: Paving the Way for Action*. Dakar, Sénégal: UNESCO BREDA.

Verspoor, Adriaan M. 2008. *At the Crossroads: Choices for Secondary Education in Sub-Saharan Africa*. With the SEIA Team. Africa Human Development Series. Washington, DC: World Bank.

World Bank. 1993. "East Asian Miracle: Economic Growth and Public Policy." Policy Research Report, Oxford University Press, New York.

———. 2002. "Vietnam: Delivering on Its Promise." Report 25050-VN, Poverty Reduction and Economic Management Unit, East Asia and Pacific Region, World Bank, Washington, DC.

———. 2004a. "Books, Buildings, and Learning Outcomes: An Impact Evaluation of World Bank Support to Basic Education in Ghana." Report 28779, Operations Evaluation Department, World Bank, Washington, DC.

———. 2004b. *Education in Rwanda: Rebalancing Resources to Accelerate Post-Conflict Development and Poverty Reduction*. World Bank Country Study. Washington, DC: World Bank.

———. 2005a. *Education in Ethiopia: Strengthening the Foundation for Sustainable Progress*. World Bank Country Study. Washington, DC: World Bank.

———. 2005b. *Expanding Opportunities and Building Competencies for Young People: A New Agenda for Secondary Education*. Directions in Development Series. Washington, DC: World Bank.

———. 2006a. "Program Document for a Proposed Adjustment Credit to the United Republic of Tanzania for a Secondary Education Development Program." Report 27631, World Bank, Washington, DC.

———. 2006b. "Project Appraisal Document on Proposed Credit to the Government of Mozambique for a Technical and Vocational Education and Training Project." World Bank, Washington, DC.

———. 2006c. "Project Appraisal Document on Proposed Credit to the Republic of Burkina Faso for a Post-Primary Education Project." World Bank, Washington, DC.

———. 2006d. "Project Appraisal Document on Proposed Credit to the Republic of Mali for a Second Education Sector Investment Program." World Bank, Washington, DC.

———. 2006e. "Rapport d'Etat sur le Système Educatif National (RESEN): Eléments de diagnostic pour l'atteinte des objectifs du millénaires et la réduction de la pauvreté" (Status Report on the National Educational System: Diagnostic Elements for Achieving the Millennium Development Goals and Reducing Poverty). Africa Education Country Status Report (Mauritania) 59239, World Bank, Washington, DC.

———. 2009a. *Accelerating Catch-Up: Tertiary Education for Growth in Sub-Saharan Africa.* Directions in Development Series. World Bank: Washington, DC.

———. 2009b. "Secondary Education in India: Universalizing Opportunity." Report 48521, v2. Human Development Unit, South Asia Region, World Bank, Washington, DC.

———. 2009c. "Toward the Competitive Frontier: Strategies for Improving Ethiopia's Investment Climate." Report No. 48472-ET, Finance and Private Sector Development Unit, Africa Region, World Bank, Washington, DC.

———. 2011. "Project Appraisal Document on a Proposed Credit in the Amount of SDR 44.9 Million (US$70 Million Equivalent) to the Republic of Ghana for a Ghana Skills and Technology Development Project." Document 59529-GH, World Bank, Washington, DC.

WDI (World Development Indicators) (database). World Bank, Washington, DC. http://data.worldbank.org/data-catalog/world-development-indicators.

World Bank and IMF (International Monetary Fund). 2010. *Doing Business 2010: Reforming Through Difficult Times.* Washington, DC: World Bank, IMF, and Palgrave McMillan.

CHAPTER 2

Education in Ethiopia: Achievements and Challenges

Throughout much of the twentieth century, Ethiopia was one of the most educationally disadvantaged countries in the world. The majority of its current population has had little access to schooling, a legacy that continues to affect the country's human resources. Only 36 percent of the adult population (aged 15 years and over) is literate. Great strides have been made in education since 1994. Access has surged, especially at the primary level, with 85 percent of children of primary-school age now in school. Enrollment growth has also been impressive at the secondary level, especially in the first cycle (grades 9–10), for which the gross enrollment rate has more than doubled since 2000. Yet key challenges remain for secondary education, including: (1) a low primary education completion rate that constrains enrollment at the secondary level; (2) inequitable access, with rural populations and girls at a particular disadvantage; and (3) student learning achievement that is disappointingly low.

Ethiopia has a long and rich educational history. Indigenous education in the country remains an important transmitter of cultural identity from one generation to the next among all ethnic and linguistic groups. Ethiopia's early Christian heritage represents a second important element of education in the country. The primary purpose of Ethiopian church education has been to prepare young men for service in the church as deacons and priests, but it has also served as the main educational preparation for civil servants. Islam is a third source of educational provision, especially in the southern and southeastern parts of the country, where a nonformal school system was established to teach the ethics and theology of Islam, with schools managed by local communities.

Modern Education in the Twentieth Century

The introduction of modern education in Ethiopia began toward the end of the nineteenth century with the establishment of a central state authority and a permanent urban seat of power, the arrival of foreign embassies, and the development of a modern economic sector.[1] Modern education officially commenced in 1908 with the opening of Menelik II School in Addis Ababa, marking a significant step in the history of education in the country.

In May 1961 Ethiopia hosted the United Nations-sponsored Conference of African States on the Development of Education in Sub-Saharan Africa. At that time, primary and secondary school participation rates in the country were among the lowest in Sub-Saharan Africa. There were shortages of both schools and teachers, as well as high dropout rates. In 1960, the primary gross enrollment ratio (GER) for boys was 11 percent and for girls, 7 percent; the respective rates for secondary education were much lower. In addition, many families were sending their children to schools operated by missionary groups and private agencies. The conference gave Ethiopia an incentive to focus on educational development. The government proceeded to expand the public school system more than fourfold between 1961 and 1971 and declared universal primary education a long-range objective. In 1971, there were 1,300 primary and secondary schools and 13,000 teachers in the country, with total enrollment of 600,000 at both levels. Yet schooling remained available only to a small urban elite, with a primary GER of only 16 percent (10 percent for girls) and a secondary GER of 4 percent (2 percent for girls) in 1971.

After the overthrow of imperial rule in 1974, the provisional military government (known as the Derg[2]) dismantled the then existing feudal socioeconomic structure through a series of reforms that also affected educational development. The National Democratic Revolution Program of the Ethiopian government of April 1976 issued an educational guideline that stated, "There will be an educational program that will provide free education, step by step, to the broad masses" (MOE 1976, 14). The new education policy emphasized the improvement of learning opportunities in rural areas as a means to increase economic productivity. As a result, primary school enrollment increased from about 957,300 in 1974/75 to nearly 2,450,000 in 1985/86, while enrollment in the country's primary, junior secondary, and senior secondary schools reached a total of 3.1 million students, up from nearly 785,000 a decade earlier. While the figure for primary enrollments represented 36 percent of the relevant age group, the combined secondary enrollment figure (grades 7 through 12) represented only 5.3 percent of the relevant age group.

Despite improved enrollment numbers, many schools did not meet minimum standards, teachers lacked basic teaching skills, and the curriculum remained deeply politicized. Further, the system was highly centralized, with instruction delivered in English and Amharic rather than in students' mother tongues. Clapham (1990) argues that "a fairly good education for a relatively small number of children had under the socialist regime been transformed into quite a poor education for a much larger number of children." The challenges of educational development in the 1980s were compounded further by a civil war and severe droughts and famines.

Education Development Since 1991

By the end of the civil war and the overthrow of the Derg in 1991, the country's infrastructure was devastated and access to education was low: gross enrollment rates were 30 percent at the primary, 13 percent at the secondary, and less than 1 percent at the tertiary level (Ethiopia 1994). The primary enrollment rate was, moreover, less than half the average GER for Sub-Saharan African countries. Girls' participation rates in primary education were much lower than those of boys, especially in rural areas. In addition, there were severe regional differences in primary GERs, ranging from 7 percent in the Afar region to 87 percent in the city of Addis Ababa (Dufera 2011). The quality of education was also poor, with inadequately trained and poorly motivated teachers and an overall lack of instructional materials. The system was both seriously underfinanced and inefficient—one-third of all students dropped out of school in their first year. Physical facilities were dilapidated due to war damage and the absence of preventive maintenance.

Education was a priority in the national development agenda of the government that took power in Ethiopia in 1991. New policy directions for the sector were set out in the 1994 Education and Training Policy, including the goals of:

- Expanded and equitable access to general education and vocational training to meet the demands of the country and the economy
- Improvement of the quality of education throughout the system
- A special focus on girls' and women's education
- Changing the curriculum to increase the relevance of education to local communities, including a shift to vernacular languages (Dufera 2011)
- Gradual decentralization of school administration, with strong community participation (Smith 2011)

In addition, the education system was restructured to better fit the context and needs of the country at that time. The "6-2-4" structure (that is, six years of primary schooling, followed by two years of junior secondary education, followed by four years of senior secondary education) that had been in place since 1962 was replaced by a new "8-2-2" structure that remains in place today. Primary education consists of an eight-year cycle divided into a basic education cycle covering grades 1–4 and a general primary cycle covering grades 5–8, followed by two years of general secondary education (grades 9–10) and two years of preparatory secondary education (grades 11–12).

General secondary education (grades 9 and 10) aims to prepare students to identify areas of interest for further education and training. The preparatory level (grades 11 and 12) prepares students for higher education or choosing a career. National examinations are now administered only at the end of grades 10 and 12; regional examinations have replaced those at the end of grade 8. Technical and vocational education and training (TVET) is institutionally separate from the regular educational system, forming a parallel track. Access to formal TVET is offered after completion of grade 10.

Students who plan to pursue higher education are required to sit for the Ethiopian Higher Education Entrance Certificate Examination at the end of the preparatory level. Those who enroll in TVET after completing grade 10 have, at present, three options to choose from, depending on their performance at the general secondary level: (1) one-year training (10+1); (2) two-year training (10+2); or (3) three-year training (10+3) (MOE 2010a).[3] Students who complete three years of training after grade 10 are considered to have completed the first year of college-level education and are eligible to join higher learning institutions to complete an undergraduate degree.

Implementing the 1994 Education and Training Policy

Within the framework of the Education and Training Policy, the government established the Education Sector Development Program (ESDP) in 1996/97, a long-range rolling plan focused on the comprehensive development of the education sector over a 20-year period. The ESDP translates the policy statement into action by providing a sectorwide implementation framework. To date the program has had four phases. ESDP I covered the first five years, 1997/98–2001/02. ESDP II and ESDP III covered the respective periods of 2002/03–2004/05 and 2005/06–2009/10. ESDP IV began in 2010/11 (see Ethiopia, 1998, 2002, 2005a, 2010b) and extends through 2014/15.

These programs have been remarkably successful in expanding access and moving primary education towards the goal of universal primary education by 2014/15, in accordance with the government's commitment to meet the Education for All targets and Millennium Development Goals. Much of this progress has been realized in the context of recurring regional conflicts, fragile natural resources, and a high level of HIV/AIDS prevalence. The ESDP I target of raising primary enrollment from 3.7 million in 1996/97 to 7 million in 2001/02 was surpassed: enrollment reached 8.1 million, representing an average enrollment growth rate of 12.8 percent. ESDP II and III continued this trend, with annual average enrollment growth rates of 11.7 percent. Subsequently primary enrollment reached 13.5 million in 2005/06 and 15.8 million 2009/10 (figure 2.1). Thus over the period 1995/96–1999/2000, the GER for primary education increased from 34.0 percent to 53.9 percent (World Bank 2005), and the net enrollment rate (NER), from 19.0 percent (Dufera 2011) to 40 percent (UIS).

Secondary school enrollment as a whole (grades 9–12) also expanded rapidly after 1994, growing roughly fivefold: from 371,000 in 1994/95 to 1.7 million in 2009/10 (figure 2.1). The GER for general secondary education (grades 9–10), rose from only 12 percent in 1998/99 to 38 percent in 2010/11; for secondary preparatory education (grades 11–12), from 3 percent in 2002/03 to 8 percent in 2010/11; and for secondary education (grades 9–12), from

Figure 2.1 Enrollments in Primary and Secondary Education, 1967–2009
millions

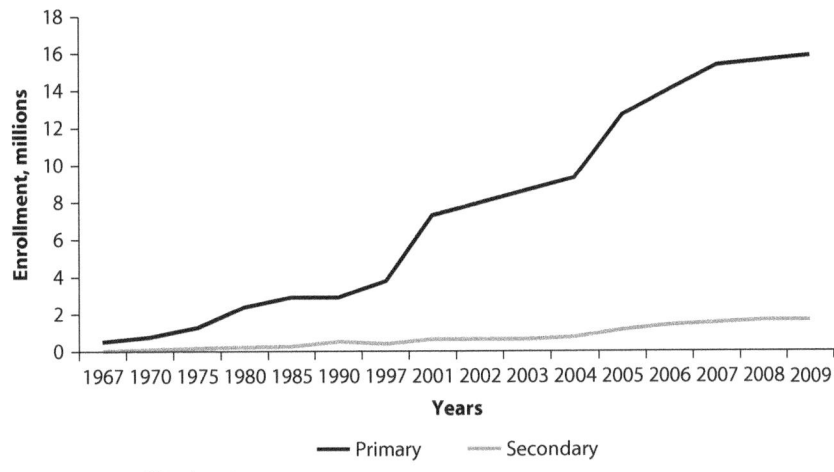

Source: MOE 2011; World Bank 2005.

Figure 2.2 Trends in Secondary Education GER, 1994–2011
percentage

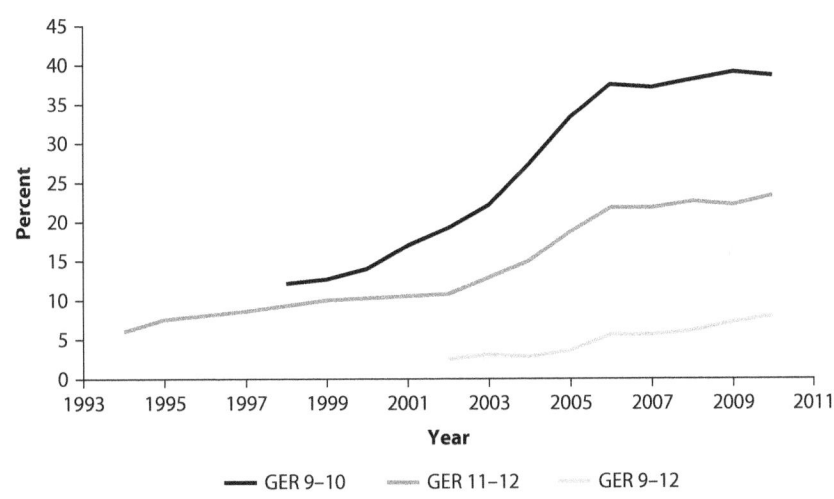

Sources: MOE 2003, 2004, 2005b, 2006, 2007, 2008a, 2009, 2010c, 2011.
Note: 1994 stands for 1994/95. Prior to 2002 data on grades 11–12 are not available; prior to 1996 data on grades 9–10 are similarly not available. GER = Gross enrollment ratio.

7 percent in 1994/95 to 24 percent in 2010/11 (figure 2.2) (MOE 2003, 2004, 2005b, 2006, 2007, 2008a, 2009, 2010c, 2011).

By 2010 good progress had been made toward universal access to the first cycle of primary education,[4] but only half of the relevant age group was enrolled in the second cycle (table 2.1). The rapid increase in enrollment was facilitated by an increase in the number of primary and secondary schools between 1996

Table 2.1 Participation Rates in Education by Grade Level, 2010/11
percentage

Grades	GER			NER		
	Male	Female	All	Male	Female	All
1–4	128.8	119.1	124.0	94.0	89.4	91.8
5–8	67.4	64.8	66.1	46.6	47.9	47.3
1–8	99.5	93.2	96.4	87.0	83.5	85.3
9–10	41.8	34.9	38.4	16.4	16.2	16.4
11–12	9.6	7.1	8.4	—	—	—
Higher education	8.4	3.6	6.3	—	—	—

Source: MOE 2010c.
Note: GER = Gross enrollment rate; NER = Net enrollment rate; — = Not available.

and 2009; the former increased from 10,394 to 26,951 (a 59 percent increase) and the latter, from 369 to 1,335 (a 262 percent increase) (MOE 2010c).

Trends in Education Expenditure

The strong commitment to educational development since 1994 is reflected in budget allocations to the sector, which increased steadily to reach more than 23 percent of total government expenditures, and 5.3 percent of GDP, in 2009 (table 2.2). Both of these percentages are high relative to per capita income by international standards. The share of recurrent education spending at the *woreda* level was estimated in excess of 40 percent during the period 2006–09 for all regions except Afar and Somali, where it was around 20 percent (MOE 2010c).[5]

The composition of government education expenditures, moreover, changed in favor of general and higher education during the years 2003–08, while the share devoted to TVET fell sharply. The share allocated to higher education is estimated to have reached 50 percent during the period 2008–10. Secondary education has been squeezed between the primary and higher education subsectors—allocated less than 10 percent of the public resources available for education in 2009/10, compared to 30 percent or more in countries such as India and Indonesia (EdStats average for 2007–09). External resources flowing through budgetary channels were estimated at Br 4.7 billion in 2009/10, representing approximately about 28 percent of total education expenditures.[6]

However, these aggregate figures mask considerable regional variation. According to Ethiopia's recent Education Public Expenditure Review (Ravishankar et al. 2010), three large regions—Amhara, Oromiya, and the Southern Nations Nationalities and Peoples Region (SNNPR)—account for over 90 percent of the roughly 200,000 additional teachers required to achieve the official norm for pupil-teacher ratios. These rates have not kept pace with enrollment increases and virtually all recurrent expenditures are spent on salaries, with few monies available for textbooks or operating costs. For example,

Table 2.2 Education Expenditures as Percentage of Government Spending and GDP, by Fiscal Year

	% of total government expenditure	% of GDP
1985/86	8.2	2.4
1990/91	10.1	2.5
1995/96	15.7	3.8
2000/01	14.2	4.1
2005/06	20.7	4.6
2009/10	23.6	4.6

Source: World Bank 2005 (1985/86–2000/01); Ravishankar et al. 2010 (2005/06); EdStats (2009/10).
Note: GDP = Gross domestic product.

education accounts for the majority of budget allocations to Gambella, but these monies are mostly consumed by salaries for teachers and education officials, with no capital or operating expenses allocated to the region. Only in 2009/10 did the government introduce school grants to increase nonsalary expenditures.

Challenges: Access

In spite of the remarkable progress in increasing educational access in Ethiopia, challenges remain in meeting government enrollment and completion targets for primary and secondary education. Progress toward ESDP IV target enrollment rates for 2014/15 is presented in table 2.3. As can be seen, extraordinary efforts will be needed to achieve NER target for grades 5–8 and the GER target for grades 9–10. In fact, phase IV of the ESDP established the goal of achieving universal general secondary education completion by 2024/25 (Dufera 2011),[7] a goal that is itself a major challenge.

In spite of the legacy of inequitable access to education for girls, rural residents, and students from poor families, increases in overall access in recent years helped narrow the gender gap, enlarged school opportunities in rural areas, and benefitted the poorest students.

Gender Gap

Traditionally, boys in Ethiopia have been more likely to attend school and less likely to drop out. In 1987, the primary GER for boys was 31.7 percent and for girls, only 20.4 percent. Promoting educational access for girls has been a central element of all phases of the ESDP. For example, the program has implemented initiatives to enhance awareness of the importance of girls' education in local communities. Efforts have also been undertaken to make schools friendlier to girls by constructing separate latrines for boys and girls and assigning female teachers and head teachers to provide girls support. Moreover, girls' clubs have been established in schools and tutorial, guidance, and counseling services provided to female students. All these endeavors have contributed to a significant increase in girls' enrollment, with the primary GER for girls rising in

Table 2.3 Progress toward ESDP IV Enrollment Targets

percentage

Grades	2008/09	2009/10	2010/11	2014/15 (targets)
NER 1–4	88.7	86.6	91.8	95.0
NER 5–8	46.0	46.4	47.3	80.0
NER 1–8	83.0	82.1	85.3	97.0
GER 9–10	38.1	39.1	38.4	62.0
GER 11–12	6.0	7.0	8.1	9.5

Source: MOE 2010b, 2011.

Note: There are some inconsistencies in the above participations rates due to revisions in population projections during the period covered in the table. NER = Net enrollment rate, GER = Gross enrollment ratio.

2010/11 to 93.8 percent, compared to 99.5 percent for boys. The gender parity index in primary education has risen from 0.66 in 1991 to 0.94 in 2010/11, and to 0.83 in general secondary education; it is also rising rapidly at the preparatory level, reaching 0.71 in 2010/11, compared to 0.46 in 2009/10 (MOE 2011).[8]

In addition, there remains a stark disparity between national gross enrollment rates and those for disadvantaged regions, such as Somali and Afar. According to regional reports, primary GER in Somali and Afar grew from 23.3 and 20.9 percent, respectively, in 2004 to 61.5 and 40.1 percent, respectively, in 2010/11. Yet the enrollment of girls continues to lag behind that of the boys: female GER in 2010/11 was 58.0 percent in Somali and 39.1 percent in Afar (MOE 2011). Moreover as data from the Ethiopia Demographic and Health Survey (DHS) 2005 (CSA and Measure DHS/ICF Macro 2006) suggest, poor girls, especially those living in rural areas, still face obstacles to accessing schools, especially secondary schools (figure 2.3).[9] The legacy of very low female enrollment is also still reflected in the very small proportion of female teachers, especially at the secondary level, where it has been stable since 2005 at 10 percent (MOE 2010b).

Rural Barriers to Access

More generally, students in rural areas—especially in Afar and Somali—still have only limited access to education beyond the primary level. The discrepancy between rural and urban rates of access is illustrated in figure 2.4, based on DHS 2005 survey data. At the primary level considerable progress has been made by reducing the distance between schools and pupils' homes, transforming existing Alternative Basic Education (ABE) centers into regular schools, establishing more ABE centers, promoting multigrade classes, and providing special support programs (including scholarships, school feeding, mobile schools, and paraboarding schools for second cycle primary students) (MOE 2010b).

The impact of these interventions has been considerable. In 2009, 80 percent of primary enrollment was in rural areas. At the postprimary level, however, the urban-rural disparity remains: only 11.2 percent of general secondary and

Education in Ethiopia: Achievements and Challenges 31

Figure 2.3 Enrollment Pyramid for Students in Poorest Quintile, by Age, 2005

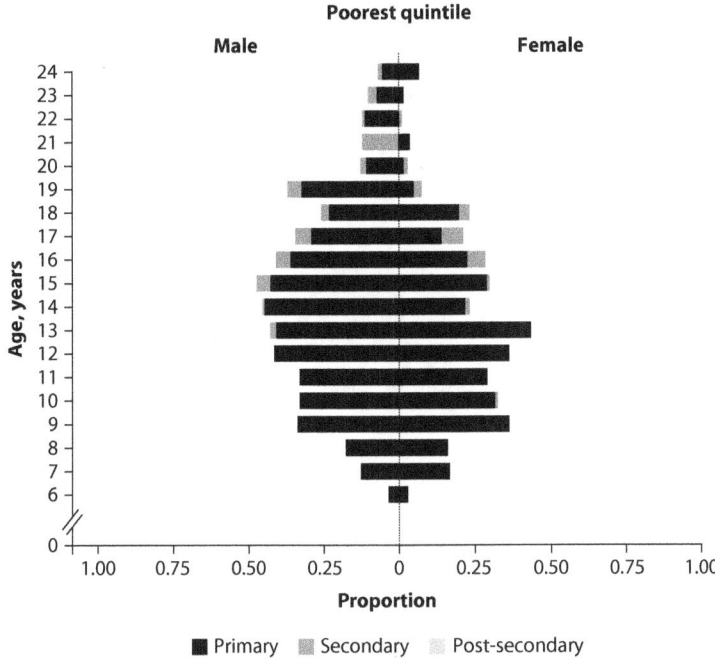

Source: Reproduced from World Bank 2009b.
Note: DHS = Demographic and Health Survey

Figure 2.4 Rural and Urban Enrollment Compared, by Age, 2005

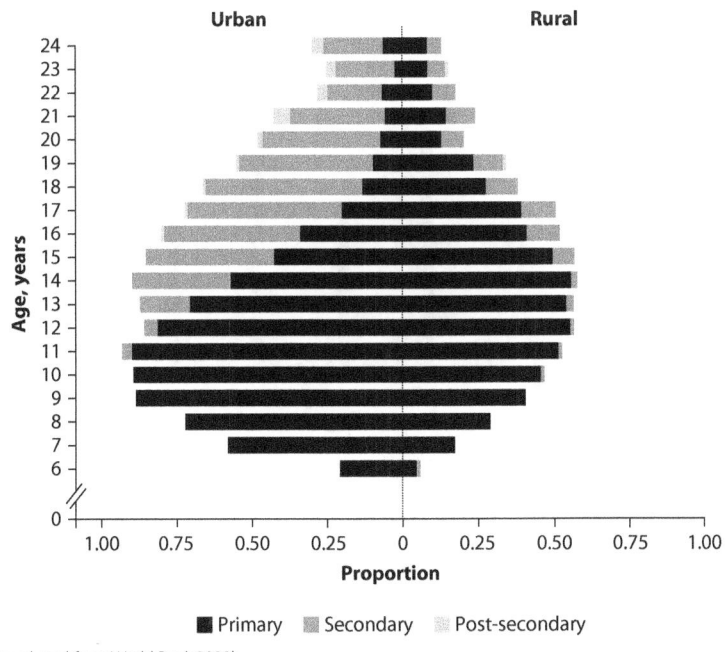

Source: Reproduced from World Bank 2009b.
Note: DHS = Demographic and Health Survey

3.6 percent of upper secondary enrollments are in rural areas (MOE 2011). The current model of secondary education provision is, moreover, dominated by large schools located in urban areas. More than 85 percent of general secondary students are enrolled in schools in urban areas; for preparatory students, the share is almost 95 percent. As of 2009/10, the average general secondary school enrolled more than 1,150 students; even schools in the emerging regions of Somali and Afar enrolled, on average, more than 500 students (MOE 2010c).

Students from Poor Families

The government is well aware of the barriers to educational equity and is committed to addressing them. At the secondary level, there are plans to establish a limited number of boarding schools, a scholarship program for vulnerable children, and a school-based accountability system for actions related to access. In addition, the survival and performance rates of girls will be improved and a commitment has been made to increase the number of teachers from emerging regions and disadvantaged groups (that is, pastoralists and indigenous groups). The differences in enrollment rates among regions are stark. At the general secondary level, Afar and Somali both have GERs far below the national level; for the second cycle at that level, Oromiya, SNNPR, and Gambela also lag behind (figure 2.5).

Figure 2.5 Secondary Education Gross Enrollment Rate, by Region, 2009/10

percentage

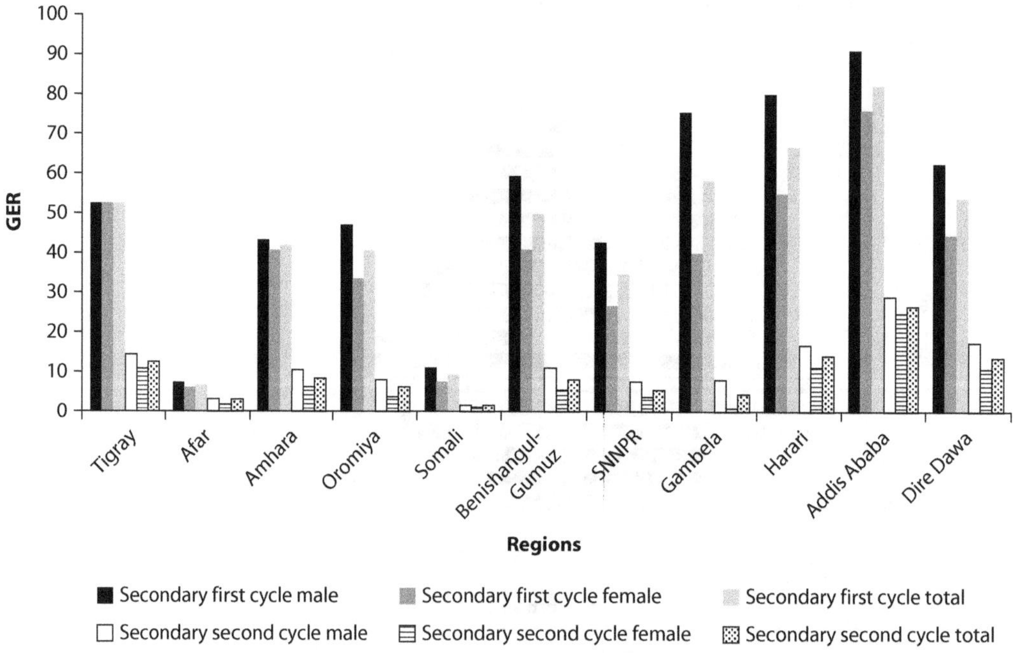

Source: MOE 2010c.
Note: GER = Gross enrollment ratio.

Poor people in particular have remained excluded from modern educational opportunities for a long time. According to 2005 DHS data, 78 percent of all 25–29-year-olds in the poorest-income quintile, and 86 percent of women in this category, have never been to school. Clearly the progress in expanding access to primary and general secondary education has changed these figures considerably, as suggested by the findings of the 2010 DHS. At the same time, even general secondary education remains largely an urban phenomenon. Students from poor families find it difficult to access this level of education (figure 2.6), especially when they live in rural areas (World Bank 2009b).

Poverty, especially among rural residents, has had a significant impact on the level of education of the labor force. Much has been achieved in past 15 years, but challenges of equity remain. Addressing these inequities is a critical priority, not only for reasons of fairness, but also to support the development objectives of the Growth and Transformation Plan for 2010/11–2014/15. Equitably sharing the benefits of growth—most importantly, the delivery of public services of acceptable quality—has been a key element in the rapid economic development of East Asian countries (Fredriksen 2008). It will therefore be important to consider strategies that could remove barriers to access for poor students and make it possible to provide secondary education of acceptable quality in sparsely populated areas in a cost-effective manner.

Figure 2.6 Primary and Secondary Enrollment Rates, by Age and Wealth, 2005

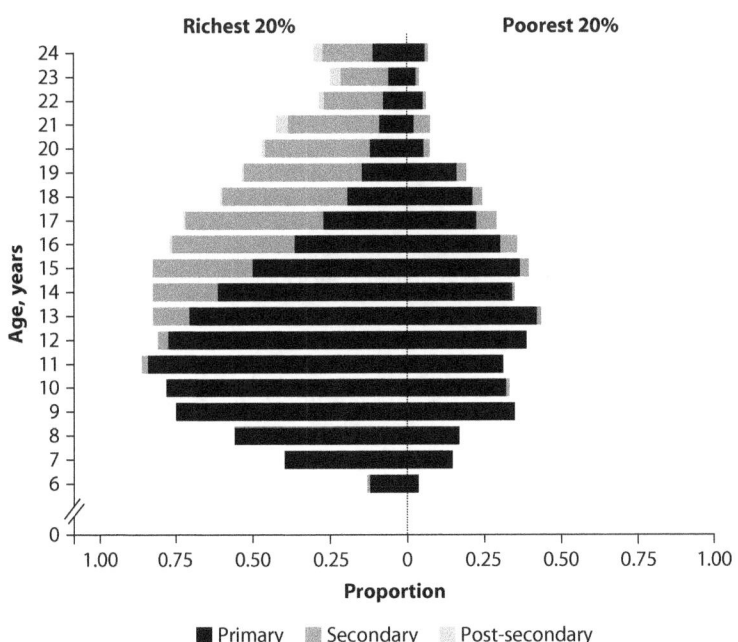

Source: Reproduced from World Bank 2009b.

Challenges: Quality and Learning Achievement

In contrast to remarkable achievements in access, progress to date in raising the quality of education in Ethiopia has been limited. Efficiency and quality input indicators, achievement tests, and classroom observations suggest that it has been difficult to maintain the quality of education during a period of very rapid enrollment expansion. Learning achievement in the education system remains unacceptably low. This has become a source of concern for government officials, educators, parents, and other stakeholders.

Lagging Efficiency and Input Indicators

Current efficiency indicators suggest issues of poor quality, including a continued high dropout rate of 28 percent in grade 1, an average national primary education repetition rate of almost 5 percent (which is nevertheless an improvement over earlier figures), a survival rate of less than 40 percent to grade 5, and a mere 49 percent primary education completion rate (MOE 2010c).

Secondary education faces similar challenges. As table 2.4 suggests, all efficiency indicators at this level are considerably below the targets formulated in ESDP IV. Yet input indicators have improved, especially the proportion of qualified teachers and student-textbook ratios; the increase in class size (that is, the number of students per section) to 64 in 2009/10 is, however, a cause of concern (MOE 2010c).

Disappointing Learning Achievement

Information on learning achievement in Ethiopia can be gleaned from national learning assessment (NLA) and national examination results.[10] For the NLA tests, a sample of grade 4, 8, 10, and 12 cohorts are tested at four-year intervals in mathematics, the sciences, and English.[11] The test instruments are based on minimum-level curriculum competencies of the relevant grade and test items are standardized by means of a pilot test. Testing also involves the collection of

Table 2.4 Comparison of Target and Actual Efficiency Indicators for Secondary Education
percent

	Repetition rate		Dropout rate	
	Target 2014/15	Actual 2009/10	Target 2014/15	Actual 2009/10
Grade 9, boys	1	14.2	1	15.2
Grade 9, girls	1	15.6	1	13.0
Grade 10, boys	1	3.8	1	4.0
Grade 10, girls	1	3.2	1	9.3
Grade 11, boys	3	5.3	2	11.9
Grade 11, girls	3	10.9	2	11.9
Grade 12, boys	3	5.4	2	10.9
Grade 12, girls	3	13.4	2	5.6

Source: MOE 2010b.

student and school background data from representative schools; results indicate that these factors contribute to the variance in scores.

Specific elements of learner achievement are also coming under scrutiny; an early-grade reading assessment in the mother tongue has been conducted and both a similar reading assessment in English and a numeracy survey are planned. With respect to national examinations, these tests are administered at the end of the year in both grades 10 and 12. The grade 10 examination is very high stakes, as only the top 20 percent of graduates are allowed to join the preparatory program (grade 11–12) that leads to higher education.

Grade 10 and 12 NLA Tests

Grades 10 and 12 were first tested in 2010. The extent of the underachievement in these tests is shown in table 2.5, which lists the proportion of students who scored below 50 percent—the minimum proficiency benchmark established by the Ministry of Education (MOE).

Given that most grade 12 learners will progress almost automatically to higher education, the 2010 NLA results have serious implications for the quality of higher education, particularly as the scores are all positively skewed and clustered at the lower end of the curve. A number of significant observations about social and educational variables emerge from test, including:

- Considerable gender differences in achievement persist in favor of boys; in addition, girls' overall scores were more highly skewed than those of boys.
- Significant differences were noted between regions and between schools. However, the proportion of the variation attributable to school differences was, perhaps surprisingly, quite small, with the most significant component being access to a textbook.
- No significant differences in scores were found between students who were and were not exposed to plasma TV-assisted instruction, with the exception of biology, where a weak positive correlation was found. Interestingly, there was a significant correlation between test results and a student's belief that plasma TV-assisted instruction helped him or her for all subjects except physics (MOE 2010).

Table 2.5 Percentage of Students Scoring below 50 Percent on NLA Tests, 2010

Subject	Grade 10 % scoring below 50 percent	Grade 12 % scoring below 50 percent
English	82.2	74.1
Mathematics	85.3	42.3
Physics	89.9	83.3
Chemistry	82.9	56.6
Biology	75.2	39.3

Source: NEAEA 2010.

Given that the NLA tests were based on minimum learning competencies for each subject and grade, the results suggest that the majority of students gain only a small part of the knowledge and skills that they are expected to learn in secondary school. The recommendations that arose from the tests, which are included in the test reports, are mainly concerned with improvements in teaching. However, the challenge probably lies deeper, particularly given that the proportion of the variance in scores attributable to school differences is quite small (16 percent and 8 percent in grades 10 and 12, respectively) (MOE 2010). The difficulty of the science and mathematics curricula (grade 10 corresponds broadly to grade 12 in South Africa, for example) may well be a significant factor. This point is analyzed in more detail in chapter 4.

National Examinations at Grades 10 and 12

Students take federally organized external examinations at the end of grades 10 and 12. These exams are conducted by the National Educational Assessment and Examinations Agency (NEAEA). The tests are all multiple choice and are marked electronically; each learner currently takes a test in about 10 subjects. Although the system is currently paper based, the vision of the agency includes some online testing in parallel with some paper-based testing.

National Grade 10 Examination Results. Results are expressed in terms of pass and fail; those who scored 50 percent or above were declared passes. In the 2009/10 school year, about 62 percent of students passed: 70 percent of boys and 53 percent of girls (MOE 2010c). Because these results are norm referenced, they cannot be regarded as an absolute measure, particularly during a period of rapid enrollment expansion. Nevertheless, certain observations can be made:

- The existing policy—which predated ESDP but has been reconfirmed by it—limits access to grade 11 to 20 percent of students who pass. The remainder of this group is expected to pursue secondary TVET. Students who fail but do not wish to retake the grade 10 examination, together with those who pass but do not qualify for grade 11, can elect to join the world of work. These outcomes raise important issues of the purpose of secondary examinations—selection or certification—that are discussed further in chapter 4.
- The failure rate, although lower than in previous years, is high: about one-third of all students and almost half of all girls failed the exam.

National Grade 12 Exam Results. In the 2009/10 school year, 61 percent of students—57 percent of boys and 72 percent of girls—scored below 50 percent, based on raw scores (MOE 2010c). Given that grades 11 and 12 are preparation for higher education and the great majority of students who take this exam proceed to degree-level studies, it is significant that in 2010, close to two-thirds of students who took the exam scored below 50 percent.

These results confirm the conclusions of grade 12 NLA results discussed earlier: performance at this level is disappointingly poor, particularly because the students are a highly select group. The results also show that this level of education is dominated by male students: about 70 percent of grade 11 and 12 students are male and they tend to outperform, by a considerable margin, their female colleagues.

Improving Teaching and Learning: The Key Priority

It is clear that the poor quality of education in Ethiopia, which results in low levels of student learning, is compromising the further development of the education system through persistent high dropout and repetition rates. To remedy the weaknesses that prevent the system from delivering acceptable-quality education at the primary and secondary levels, MOE developed the General Education Quality Improvement Package in 2008 (MOE 2008b).[12] This comprehensive package of initiatives covers most of the critical components of quality improvement, including:

- Revision and upgrading of the national curriculum
- Development and provision of new textbooks across all grades and subjects (in local and national languages for primary grades), based on the new curriculum
- Improved pre-service teacher education
- Strengthening continuous professional development for serving teachers
- Capacity development for head teachers in order to improve school leadership and management
- Training for schools and education stakeholders in school improvement planning (this element will focus on four key domains: the teaching-learning process, instructional leadership and management, a conducive and attractive learning environment, and community participation)
- Training for regional and federal ministry officials to improve their planning and budgeting skills
- Development of the NLA test, particularly at postprimary levels (MOE 2008b)

Global experience has shown that bringing about improvements in teaching and learning is a long-term process, of which GEQIP, as currently designed, is only the beginning. Longer-term policy options and strategies for curricula development, teacher education, and management are discussed in chapters 4–6; these options will need to be accompanied by improvements in assessments and examinations.

Conclusion

Throughout much of the twentieth century, Ethiopia was one of the most educationally disadvantaged countries in the world. The majority of its current population has had little access to schooling, a legacy that continues to affect its current human resources. Only 39 percent of the country's adult population (aged 15 years and over) is literate (UIS 2012). While great strides have been made in expanding access to education since 1994, especially at the primary level, key challenges remain.

First, efforts to improve quality at the primary level need to be intensified and sustained. As long as only 36 percent of students who start the primary cycle graduate as a cohort from grade 8 (MOE 2010c), only a very small number of young Ethiopians will complete secondary education. This situation is likely to result in severe shortages of skilled labor as the economy grows.

Second, access to secondary education in rural areas remains limited. The East Asian development experience underscores the importance of policies and strategies that are explicitly designed to ensure that the benefits of development are widely shared. Education is a key instrument in this regard, as it promotes upward mobility and access to higher-wage jobs.

Third, the share of education in the national budget has risen from a very low level in the mid-1990s to one of the highest in the Sub-Saharan Africa region. Considering MOE's agenda of concurrently addressing access and quality challenges, especially in secondary education, it will be important to determine whether the demand for more resources for education can be met by increasing public financing alone.

Fourth, monitoring and widely sharing evidence on learning outcomes via assessments and analyses of examination data will be critically important for guiding the country's quality improvement policies and strategies.

Notes

1. This section draws heavily on Dufera 2011.
2. Derg stood for the Coordinating Committee of the Armed Forces, Police, and the Territorial Army.
3. The National TVET Qualifications Framework envisages five levels of technical and vocational education, as documented in the 2010 ECBP-TVET Reform of the Ministry of Education (MOE 2010a).
4. In 2009 the apparent grade 1 intake rate was 142 percent; the net intake rate exceeded 75 percent (MOE 2010c).
5. A *woreda* is equivalent to a district and is managed by a local government; there are about 900 woredas in Ethiopia.
6. This data is derived from the ESDP IV projection model updated by the authors in September 2011.
7. The target date is mentioned as both 2025 and 2020 in ESDP IV.
8. The gender parity index is the ratio of the number of girls to the number of boys at a given level of education.
9. Although the preliminary report on DHS 2011 has been published, the education data are not easily comparable and have not yet been analyzed in detail.
10. This section is based on Clegg 2011.

11. For the results of NLA tests published to date by the National Educational Assessment and Examinations Agency (NEAEA), see NEAEA (2004a, 2004b, 2008a, 2008b, 2010). This agency has had several incarnations. In 2004, it was known as the National Organization for Examinations; in 2008, as the General Education Quality Assurance and Examinations Agency; and in 2010, as the National Agency for Examinations. Today it is known as the National Educational Assessment and Examinations Agency (NEAEA). Its publications can be found on the agency's website at http://www.nae.gov.et/Public/MiscellaneousDownloads.aspx. For purposes of convenience, all citations for the agency in this publication use NEAEA.
12. This package of government initiatives was announced in 2008. It should not be confused with the donor-supported General Education Quality Improvement Program (GEQIP), which started in 2009 to support the government initiatives.

References

Clapham, Christopher. 1990. *Transformation and Continuity in Revolutionary Ethiopia*. Cambridge, UK: Cambridge University Press, Quoted in Dufera 2011, 2.

Clegg, Andrew. 2011. "Ensuring Relevance and Improving Quality." Background Paper Prepared for *Secondary Education in Ethiopia*. World Bank Ethiopia Office, Addis Ababa. Unpublished. (Available upon request of Rajendra Joshi, rjoshi@worldbank.org.)

CSA (Central Statistical Agency) of the Federal Democratic Republic of Ethiopia and Measure DHS/ICF Macro. 2006. "Ethiopia Demographic and Health Survey 2005." CSA, Addis Ababa, and Measure DHS/ICF Macro, Calverton, MD.

Dufera, Derebssa. 2011. "Background to the Ethiopian Education System." Background paper prepared for *Secondary Education in Ethiopia*. World Bank Ethiopia Office, Addis Ababa. Unpublished. (Available upon request of Rajendra Joshi, rjoshi@worldbank.org.)

EdStats (database). World Bank, Washington, DC. http://go.worldbank.org/85XM5TBQA0.

Ethiopia, Federal Democratic Republic of MOE (Ministry of Education). 1998. "Education Sector Development Program I (ESDP I), Five-Year Plan (1997/98–2001/02)." MOE, Addis Ababa.

———. 2002. "Education Sector Development Program II (ESDP II) 2002/03–2004/05, Program Action Plan." MOE, Addis Ababa.

———. 2003. "Education Statistics Annual Abstract (ESSA), 1995 EC (2002/03 GC)." MOE, Addis Ababa.

———. 2004. "ESSA, 1996 EC (2003/04 GC)." MOE, Addis Ababa.

———. 2005a. "Education Sector Development Program III (ESDP III) 2005/06–2009/10 (1998 EFY–2002 EFY), Program Action Plan." MOE, Addis Ababa.

———. 2005b. "ESSA, 1997 EC (2004/05 GC)." MOE, Addis Ababa.

———. 2006. "ESSA, 1998 EC (2005/06 GC)." MOE, Addis Ababa.

———. 2007. "ESSA, 1999 EC (2006/07 GC)." MOE, Addis Ababa.

———. 2008a. "ESSA, 2000 EC (2007/08 GC)." MOE, Addis Ababa.

———. 2008b. "General Education Quality Improvement Package." MOE, Addis Ababa.

———. 2009. "ESSA, 2001 EC (2008/09 GC)." MOE, Addis Ababa.

———. 2010a. "ECBP (Engineering Capacity Building Program)-TVET (Technical and Vocational Education and Training) Reform." MOE, Addis Ababa.

———. 2010b. "Education Sector Development Program IV (ESDP IV) 2010/11–2014/15 (2003 EC–2007 EC), Program Action Plan." MOE, Addis Ababa.

———. 2010c. "ESSA, 2002 EC (2009/10 GC)." MOE, Addis Ababa.

———. 2011. "ESSA, 2003 EC (2010/11 GC)." MOE, Addis Ababa.

Ethiopia, Federal Democratic Republic of NEAEA (National Educational Assessment and Examinations Agency). 2004a. "Second National Learning Assessment of Grade 4 Students." NEAEA, MOE, Addis Ababa.

———. 2004b. "Second National Learning Assessment of Grade 8 Students." NEAEA, MOE, Addis Ababa.

———. 2008a. "Third National Learning Assessment of Grade 4 Students." NEAEA, MOE, Addis Ababa.

———. 2008b. "Third National Learning Assessment of Grade 8 Students." NEAEA, MOE, Addis Ababa.

———. 2010. "First National Learning Assessment of Grade 10 and 12 Students." NEAEA, Addis Ababa.

Ethiopia, People's Democratic Republic of Derg (Coordinating Committee of the Armed Forces, Police, and the Territorial Army). 1976. "Program of the National Democratic Revolution." Derg, Addis Ababa.

Ethiopia, Transitional Government of. 1994. "Education and Training Policy." Transitional Government of Ethiopia, Addis Ababa. Quoted in Dufera 2011.

Fredriksen, Birger, and Jee Peng Tan, eds. 2008. *An African Exploration of the East Asian Education Experience*. Development Practice in Education Series. Washington, DC: World Bank.

Ravishankar, V. J., Abdulhamid Kello, and Alebachew Tiruneh. 2010. "Ethiopia: Education Public Expenditure Review." Report prepared for the Ministry of Education of the Federal Democratic Republic of Ethiopia. New Concept Information Systems, Pvt., New Delhi.

Smith, Harvey. 2011. "Governance and Management of Secondary Education: From Decentralization to School Autonomy." Background paper prepared for *Secondary Education in Ethiopia*. World Bank Ethiopia Office, Addis Ababa. Unpublished. (Available upon request of Rajendra Joshi, rjoshi@worldbank.org.)

UIS (UNESCO Institute for Statistics) (database). UIS, Montreal. http://stats.uis.unesco.org.

UIS (UNESCO Institute for Statistics). 2012. "UIS Statistics in Brief; Education (All Levels) Profile—Ethiopia." Official Source of Literacy Data webpage, UIS, Montreal. http://stats.uis.unesco.org/unesco/TableViewer/document.aspx?ReportId=121&IF_Language=eng&BR_Country=2300&BR_Region=40540.

World Bank. 2005. *Education in Ethiopia: Strengthening the Foundation for Sustainable Progress*. World Bank Country Study. Washington, DC: World Bank.

———. 2009b. "Educational Attainment and Enrollment Around the World" (updated July 8, 2009). Webpage. Data and Research, Human Development and Public Services, World Bank, Washington, DC. http://iresearch.worldbank.org/edattain/.

CHAPTER 3

The Place of Secondary Education in an Economic Transformation Strategy

Sustained economic progress is associated with a rapidly evolving skill profile of the labor force. This is a long-term process driven largely by the entrance of better-educated generations of young people into the workforce. In lower-middle-income countries, lower secondary education programs typically enroll about 80–90 percent of the relevant age group and upper secondary programs, about 50 percent. Reaching these levels in Ethiopia will require rapid improvement in primary graduation rates, sustained expansion of enrollments in lower (general) secondary education, and gradual increases in the proportion of students admitted into upper (preparatory) secondary education. Simultaneously the purpose of preparatory education needs to broaden beyond preparation for university education. A number of primary (grade 8) and, especially, general secondary (grade 10), education graduates will enter the labor market and participate in on-the-job training sponsored by employers, while others will enter vocational programs. Many of these young people can be expected to seek further education and training later in life. It is important to recognize this reality and design a number of alternative pathways to further education and training for students who do not complete general secondary education.

The primary justification for investment in secondary education lies in its contribution to economic growth and poverty reduction, as discussed in chapter 1. An important part of the projected economic growth and employment creation associated with Ethiopia's Growth and Transformation Plan (2010/11–2014/15) is expected to take place in commercial agriculture and agribusiness (that is, flower, coffee, meat, and sugar production), light manufacturing (that is, textiles and leather), and skilled services (that is, information technology, telecommunications, tourism, and retail sales). At the same time, increasing productivity will require a labor force that is increasingly skilled.

The experience of middle-income countries suggests that sustained economic progress is associated with a rapidly evolving skill profile of the labor force. For example, the Republic of Korea, between 1960 and 1985, inverted its skill-level pyramid dramatically (figure 3.1). In 1960 people with no schooling were the largest group in the population aged 15 years and over; by 1985 those with at least some secondary schooling had become the largest group. The number of Koreans who received some higher education also tripled between 1985 and 2010, from 13.5 percent to 40 percent. During each of these periods, gross domestic product (GDP) per capita (in constant won) quadrupled to reach the equivalent of almost $20,000 in 2010 (WEO).

The process of educational transformation in Vietnam—also shown in figure 3.1—is more recent, but no less dramatic. There, the proportion of the population aged 15 years and over with no schooling declined to 4.2 percent, and the proportion with secondary education, increased to more than 30 percent by 2010, while GDP increased by a factor five between 1985 and 2010 to reach $1,139 (WEO). Figure 3.2 shows a similar process in selected countries that have achieved lower-middle-income levels of GDP per capita in the last two decades.

Evolving Skill Profile

In Ethiopia the skill profile of the workforce began to transform relatively recently. Prior to 1994 the gross enrollment rate (GER) for grades 1–8 was less than 30 percent; in that year, only one-third of 13–14-year-olds had ever been

Figure 3.1. Comparison of Educational Attainment of Population Aged 15+ over Time, Korea, Rep., and Vietnam

percentage

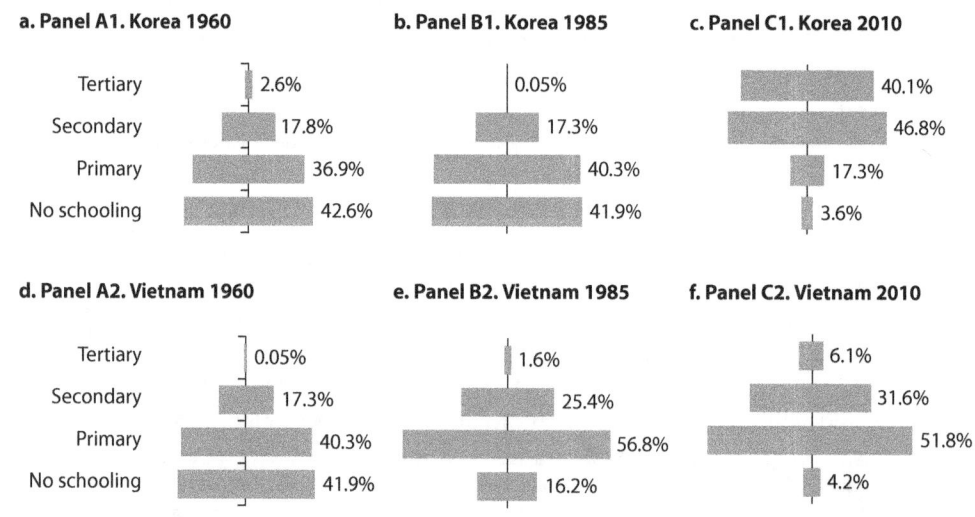

Source: Barro-Lee Dataset.

Figure 3.2 Educational Attainment of Workforce Aged 15+, Selected Middle-Income Countries, 1990 and 2010

percentage

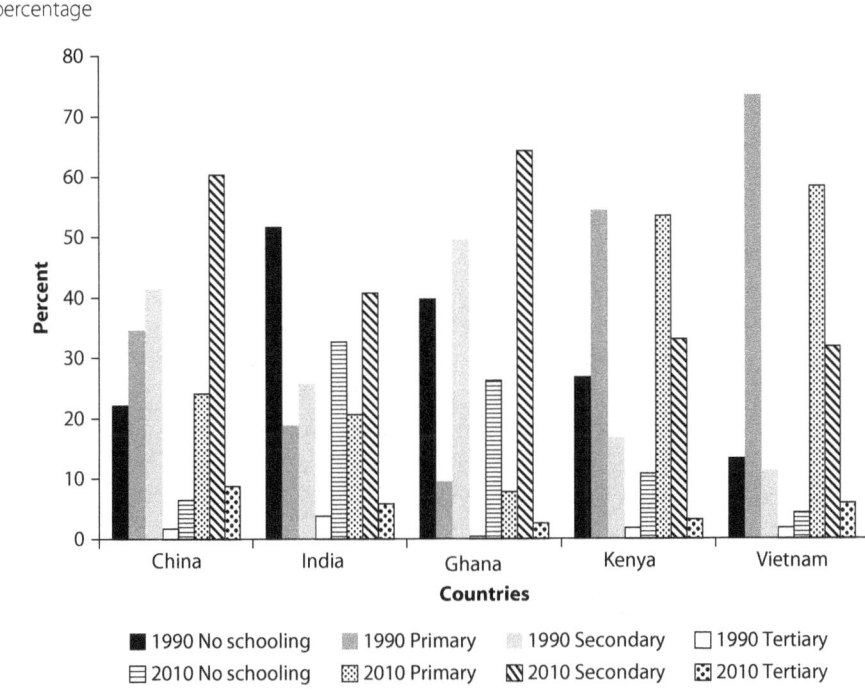

Source: Barro-Lee Dataset.

Figure 3.3 Educational Attainment of Ethiopian Labor Force, Various Years

percentage

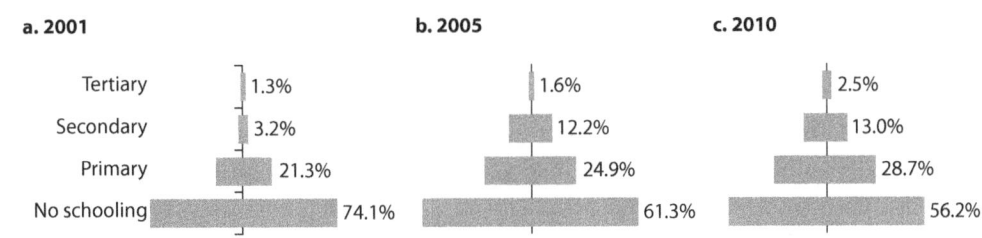

Sources: For 2001, World Bank 2005; for 2005, CSA and Measure DHS/ICF 2006; for 2010, World Bank data based on enrollment data.

to school (World Bank 2005). Figure 3.3 shows the resulting educational attainment of the labor force through 2010. Given that many of the 13–14-year-olds who never attended school remain in the labor force as agricultural workers or unskilled laborers in the informal economy, the impact of the schooling deficit in the 1980s will continue to be felt for approximately another 30 years.

Meanwhile, a better-educated younger generation is gradually making its way into the labor force. But even in 2005, 75 percent of 20–29-year-olds either had no schooling or had not completed primary education. Only 16 percent of this age group had completed secondary education (World Bank 2009). No recent data on educational attainment of the labor force is available, although enrollment data allow for a rough estimate for the year 2010 (figure 3.3).

The lessons of countries that have reached the middle-income level or higher clearly show that improving the educational attainment of the labor force is a long-term process—one driven largely by the entrance into the labor force of better-educated generations of young people. Yet with sustained effort over a period of 20–30 years, dramatic changes are possible. These changes occur to an important extent through a bottom-up sequential process, in which expansion at lower levels of the education system drives expansion at higher levels. There is considerable overlap in the process, given that growth occurs at different levels simultaneously. When students are well prepared for the next level, lower-level expansion can only drive expansion at higher levels. This trajectory suggests the importance of sustaining quality improvement and expansion policies at lower levels of the education system in Ethiopia. The issue to be considered is setting target enrollment levels for different parts of the system, based on international experience.

Enrollment Profile of Middle-Income Countries

Figure 3.4 provides a comparison of gross enrollment rates for Ethiopia and a number of lower-middle-income countries (LMICs, that is, countries with a per capita gross national income [GNI] of between $1,006 and $3,975 in 2010) and two upper-middle-income countries (UMICs)—Jordan and China.[1] At the primary level, with a GER of 96 percent, Ethiopia has almost reached the average LMIC GER of 107 percent (EdStats). However, for all other levels of education, gross enrollment rates in Ethiopia lag behind LMIC averages, including the rates reached by all other countries shown in figure 3.4. Substantially reducing this gap over the next approximately 15 years is an obvious part of achieving lower-middle-level per capita GNI.

Within the lower-middle-income group, there is considerable variation in secondary GERs. Most LMICs aim to provide universal lower secondary education and have made good progress in expanding access to this level of education. The average LMIC GER for lower secondary education is 72 percent. In this group, Guatemala has the lowest GER (just over 62 percent), and Indonesia and the Philippines, the highest (88 percent) (EdStats). China and Jordan, the UMICs, have lower secondary GERs of over 90 percent. It should be noted that even in Jordan, the total secondary GER does not reach 100 percent, but remains at 91 percent.

There is a considerable variation in GERs at the upper secondary level among the lower-middle-income countries shown in figure 3.4 (where the LMIC average is 45 percent), ranging from 38 percent in Morocco to 76 percent in the Philippines. China and Jordan have upper secondary GERs of 68 percent and

Figure 3.4 Gross Enrollment Rates by GNI per Capita, Ethiopia and Selected Middle-Income Countries, 2010 or Latest Available Year

percentage

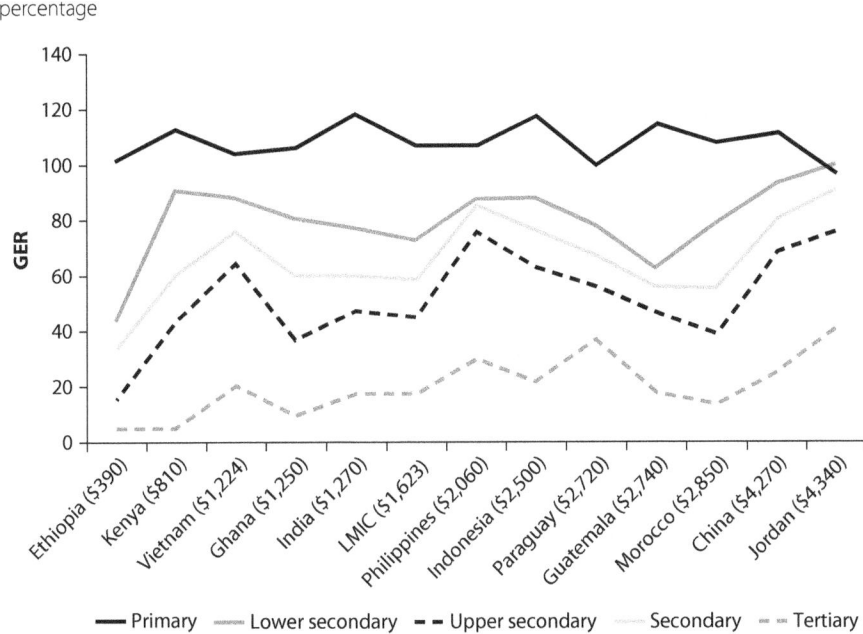

Sources: Gross enrollment rates: EdStats and UIS (Vietnam only). Gross national income: WDI.
Note: GER = Gross enrollment rate, GNI = Gross national income. LMICs (lower-middle-income countries) shown in figure: Ethiopia, Kenya, Vietnam, Ghana, India, the Philippines, Indonesia, Paraguay, Guatemala, and Morocco. UMICs (upper-middle-income countries) shown in figure: China and Jordan.

75 percent, respectively. Overall, secondary GERs for the LMIC group fall in the range of 56 percent to 76 percent, whereas the GERs for the UMICs, China and Jordan, are 80 percent and 91 percent, respectively. Vietnam stands out for a comparatively high level of enrollment in secondary education relative to its GNI per capita (EdStats). Secondary GER trends in the LMICs and in China and Jordan show that secondary education is far from universal in either LMICs or countries transitioning into higher-middle-income status, where some 20–30 percent of young people in relevant age group are not enrolled in secondary school (EdStats; UIS).

At the tertiary level the variation in GERs is very large: 41 percent in Jordan and 4 percent in Kenya, with the LMIC average 19 percent. For countries at the lower end of the LMIC range, with GNI per capita between $1,000 and $1,500, tertiary GER does not exceed 13 percent. For lower-middle-income countries with higher GNI per capita, the rate varies from 13 percent in Morocco to 41 percent in Jordan. Vietnam, with a tertiary GER of 19 percent, again stands out for a comparatively high level of enrollment in tertiary education relative to its GNI per capita. There is no obvious link between the level of tertiary enrollment and a country's GNI per capita. The picture is further clouded by variations in the level of educational quality and mismatches between higher education output and labor market demand.

In India, for example, many students graduate with skill sets that make them unemployable; unsurprisingly, some 30 percent of graduates aged 25–34 years are unemployed.[2] In Indonesia about 10 percent of tertiary graduates are unemployed, while 60 percent are employed in jobs for which they are considered overqualified. In the Philippines these rates are about 45 percent and 15 percent, respectively (di Gropello 2011). In Morocco—in spite of a relatively low tertiary GER—unemployment among the highly educated is more than 20 percent, and the average time a university graduate spends looking for employment is four years.[3] All of these experiences suggest that it is critically important to avoid excessive expansion of higher education, as well as to ensure the quality and relevance of education to labor market needs by maintaining close links between higher education programs and employers.

In Ethiopia enrollments in tertiary education increased more than sixfold over the period 2000–09, from 67,000 to 430,500, representing a rise in the tertiary GER from 1.2 percent to 4.2 percent.[4] Concurrently, the number of tertiary institutions increased from 19 to 93, of which 64 are nongovernmental accredited institutions. With more than 96 percent of enrollments in undergraduate programs, the undergraduate GER in the country today is likely greater than 5 percent. This number is expected to increase further and may exceed 10 percent by 2015. While efforts to increase the participation rate in higher education are compatible with Ethiopia's middle-income-country vision, the crowding out of public expenditures at lower levels of the education system is a matter of concern. In this context, the recent Education Public Expenditure Review (Ravishankar et al. 2010, 7) recommended "[slowing] down the pace of public investment in higher education, so as to ensure adequate space for recurrent inputs and to improve the quality of investment spending."

The Importance of Mathematics and the Sciences

The pervasive skills mismatch in many developing countries—including middle-income countries such as India, Indonesia, and Tunisia—has resulted in large numbers of university graduates remaining unemployed while shortages of skilled labor persist. A similar situation prevails in much of Sub-Saharan Africa, given that the higher education programs undertaken by a majority of African students are not in fields such as science, engineering, and technology (SET) or business—as is the case in the rapidly growing emerging economies of Korea and China—but often in the social sciences and humanities instead.

There is solid theoretical and empirical evidence that education—especially tertiary SET and business programs—has a strong positive effect on the income growth rate of all countries (World Bank 2008). Nevertheless, the quality of tertiary education, as well as the subjects studied, may be more important for growth than the quantity of people who obtain a tertiary degree. For example, a SET-based tertiary education of high quality that is grounded in empirical inquiry may contribute more to a country's growth than a social science–based education that is neither driven by relevant research nor based on local needs. The positive effect of higher SET education can include knowledge creation and spillovers, as well as the ability to borrow and adapt technologies.[5]

Figure 3.5 shows the proportion of graduates in SET disciplines in a number of middle-income countries, which ranges from 30 percent to 40 percent in most cases. In China, for example, an average of 37 percent of incoming university students are enrolled in science and engineering programs, including medicine (Weiping 2011). Ghana, on the other hand, has set an official target of 60 percent for higher education enrollments in SET disciplines, but has found it very difficult to reach this target (World Bank 2010).

The fourth phase of Ethiopia's Education Sector Development Program (ESDP IV) has set a target of 70 percent of tertiary placements in these disciplines; good progress was being made toward this goal in 2010, with 60 percent

Figure 3.5 Graduates of Tertiary Scientific and Engineering Programs, Selected Middle-Income Countries, 2009 or Latest Available Year

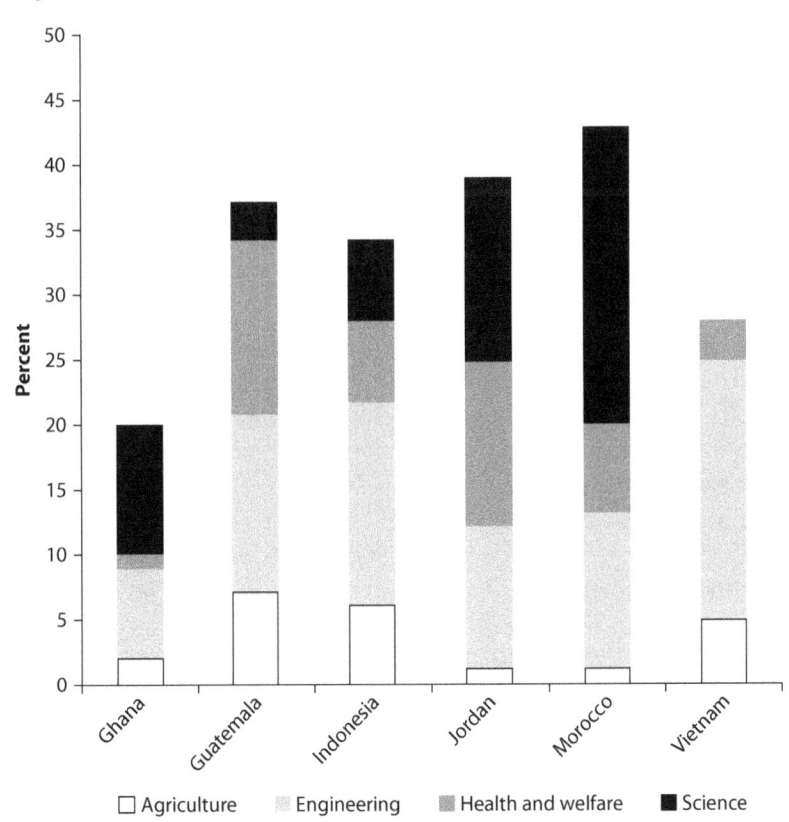

Source: EdStats.

of university students placed in SET disciplines. The quality of education in these disciplines is, however, unclear. The performance of students on the grade 12 national examinations suggests that there are indeed good reasons for university faculty to be concerned about the ability of incoming Ethiopian students to complete university SET courses at an acceptable level of quality (chapter 2).

Vocational Training: Middle-Income Country Profile

The place of technical and vocational education and training (TVET) in relation to economic development is difficult to determine; the modalities involved are very diverse, with a wide range of public and private providers offering short- and long-term programs in formal, informal, and nonformal settings. A study by UNESCO-UNEVOC (2006) of formal TVET programs found that:

- TVET programs are offered most frequently at the upper secondary and higher educational levels.
- The higher the GDP per capita of a country, the higher the degree of participation in TVET programs.
- The higher the secondary GER of a country, the higher the percentage of TVET enrollment, even after controlling for GDP per capita.

Given the diversity of TVET programs and the probable under-reporting of enrollments, it is difficult to develop benchmarks for an optimal balance between general education and TVET. Figure 3.6 shows enrollments in TVET programs at the upper secondary level in selected middle-income countries as a proportion of total enrollments (general secondary and TVET) at that level.

These figures need to be treated with considerable caution, however, as they are based on data reported by education ministries to the UNESCO Institute of Statistics (UIS) and in many instances provide incomplete coverage or under-report overall participation in TVET programs. The data reported by UIS do, however, suggest considerable variation in the share of TVET in upper secondary enrollments, with India and Kenya reporting participation of less than 2 percent and China, 44.4 percent—the high end of the range.

It is important to note that these figures are affected by the relative role of public and private TVET sectors, with participation in the latter usually significantly under-reported. Reported public provision also varies significantly, with China (85 percent public provision), Ghana (88 percent), and Vietnam (69 percent) at the high end of the spectrum, and Indonesia (33 percent) and Korea (53 percent) at the low end. In other countries, for example, the Philippines, all formal TVET programs are at the postsecondary level. Yet comparisons suggest that, especially given its current GDP per capita, Ethiopia is an

Figure 3.6 TVET as Percentage of Enrollments in Upper Secondary Education in Selected Countries, Latest Available Year

percentage

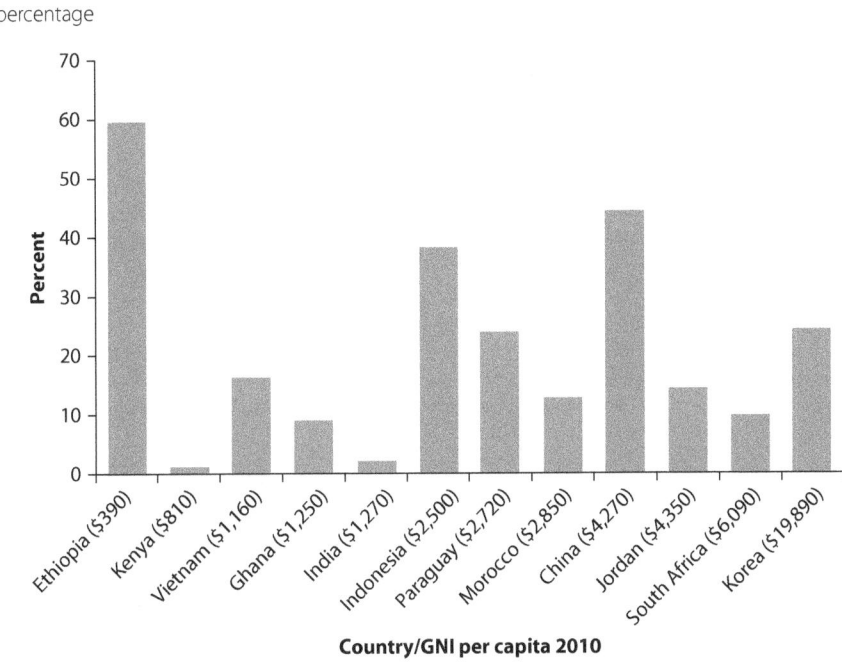

Source: UIS.
Note: GNI = Gross national income.

outlier in TVET education, with a higher proportion of all upper secondary students enrolled in formal TVET programs than in any other country in figure 3.6, including Vietnam, China, and Korea.

Education for Growth and Transformation

The evidence presented above suggests that GDP per capita does not determine the destiny of education in a country and that, conversely, educational achievement alone does not produce economic growth. In fact, countries have reached middle-income GDP per capita with different levels of educational attainment. Yet, as figure 3.7 shows, there is a broad relationship between the ability of a country to progress toward the critical threshold of development where low-cost labor is of sufficient supply and quality to manufacture low-cost products and has the potential to produce higher-quality, more sophisticated goods and services. An analysis of the Asian Development Bank (2004) concludes that in Asia, this threshold has been reached by countries where participation in the manufacturing sector exceeds 25 percent of the labor force and more than 50 percent of the population possesses a secondary education (upper-right quadrant of figure 3.7). These countries have reached a level where investments in both physical and human capital are sufficient to solidify middle-income status. As the

Figure 3.7 Percent Labor Force in Manufacturing and Secondary School Enrollment in Asia

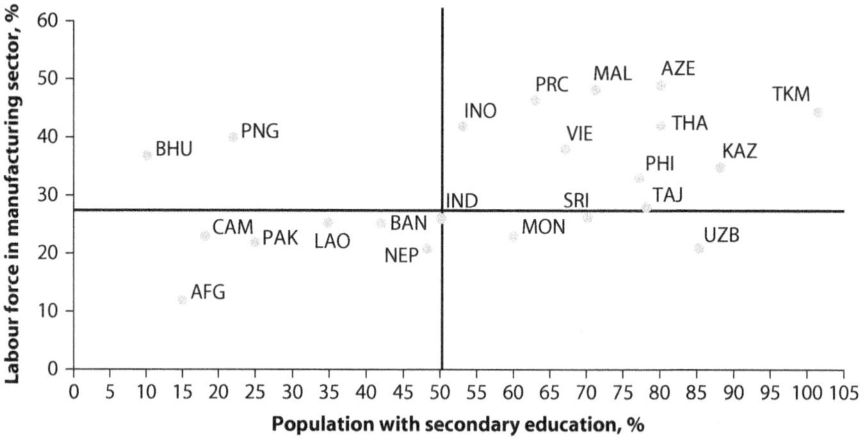

Source: Reproduced from ADB 2004, 9, figure 3.
Note: AFG = Afghanistan, AZE = Azerbaijan, BAN = Bangladesh, BHU = Bhutan, CAM = Cambodia, IND = India, INO = Indonesia, KAZ = Kazakhstan, LAO = Laos, NEP = Nepal, MAL = Malaysia, MON = Mongolia, PHI = Philippines, PRC = China, PAK = Pakistan, SRI = Sri Lanka, PNG = Papua New Guinea, TAJ = Tajikistan, THA = Thailand, TKM = Turkmenistan, UZB = Uzbekistan, VIE = Vietnam.

skill requirements of agriculture, manufacturing, and service jobs in these countries broaden and deepen, however, they will be forced to further expand relevant education and training to sustain economic growth and development.

For countries where labor force participation in the manufacturing sector is below 25 percent and less than 50 percent of the population has a secondary education, the challenge is to gradually reach the threshold levels of a middle-income economy. At this point, they will be able to take advantage of higher levels of national development and draw on advanced strategies for education and skills training. Even now, these countries can begin to develop strong programs in secondary education and technical education and vocational training that will be needed for further labor market development (ADB 2004).

According to a recent study (Fredriksen 2008), three lessons of the Asian experience stand out. First, public investments in education are critical for rapid response to the demand for skills in rapidly growing economies, such as that of Ethiopia. These investments help overcome market failures that would result in underinvestment, especially in fields with high start-up costs, by the private sector alone. Second, public education spending in Asia has been supplemented by significant financial contributions from families and government partnerships with private sector providers. Third, the sequencing of education investments is important. There can be no major expansion or improvement of higher education without first improving and expanding secondary education. And there can be no meaningful expansion of secondary education until and unless primary school graduates enter secondary school with the knowledge and skills specified in the primary curriculum.

Priorities for Educational Development in Ethiopia

Ethiopia is in the early stages of the journey toward middle-income status. It is estimated that industry currently represents only about 13 percent of the country's GDP and employs about 7 percent of the workforce. Sustained growth, as projected in the government's Growth and Transformation Plan (GTP), would increase industry's share of GDP to almost 25 percent and the share of the workforce employed in the sector, to some 15 percent, by 2025. Much of the growth in industrial production is likely to be in labor-intensive light manufacturing, which exploits a low wage-cost advantage. Increased agricultural productivity will be driven by the adoption of new technologies and the movement of people out of agriculture into other economic sectors.

This pattern of growth does not require that a large proportion of the workforce have high-level skills. It does, however, require a workforce that has strong basic skills acquired over some 10 years of basic education, including general secondary education in the case of Ethiopia. At higher levels of the education system, however, ensuring the quality of education and training and the mastery of advanced knowledge and skills, may be more important than rapidly increasing the number of graduates.

This development scenario suggests that the first priority of educational investments over the next 15 years must be the continued expansion of quality primary education. Sustained progress toward the objective of universal access to lower secondary education by 2025 within an efficient education system that provides quality instruction and appropriate levels of learning achievement will be essential. Such a system is needed to develop a labor force prepared for and capable of adopting new technologies and more productive ways of working in agriculture, industry, and services. As it progresses, Ethiopia will achieve an inversion of the educational attainment pyramid that occurred in Korea and Vietnam in the 1980s and 2000s, respectively. This will encourage investments by national entrepreneurs and help facilitate foreign direct investment. But it is worth repeating that these investments will only pay off to the extent that current efforts to improve the quality of primary and secondary education are successful and sustained.

Table 3.1 provides a perspective on the enrollment targets of ESDP IV and the forward projections for 2024/25 based on ESDP IV assumptions, by comparing these targets with current LMIC averages.

Several points can be discerned from table 3.1. First, the goal of providing all students the opportunity to complete grade 10 is well justified and consistent with both the GTP and the objective of reaching lower-middle-income status by 2024/25. But it is important to recognize that in practice, many middle-income countries have found this target difficult to realize. In most countries, some students drop out of school before completing grade 10. Consequently, lower secondary enrollment levels remain well below 100 percent in virtually every LMIC. Ethiopia should accordingly design a number of

Table 3.1 Projected Education Enrollment Targets Compared to LMIC Average

percentage

	ESDP IV 2014/15	Projections 2024/25	LMIC average (2009)
GER, grades 1–8	112	106	107
NER, grades 1–8	88	97	85
GER, grades 9–10	62	98	78
GER, grades 11–12	10	20	49
TVET (level 1–4) as share of upper secondary (preparatory and TVET)	70	75	25
GER, tertiary education	9	19	19

Source: ESDP IV; EdStats.
Note: GER = Gross enrollment rate, NER = Net enrollment rate, TVET = Technical and vocational education and training, ESDP = Education Sector Development Program, LMIC = Lower-middle-income country.

alternative pathways to further education and training for students who do not complete general secondary education.

Second, it is equally important to recognize that at the end of general secondary education (grade 10), a number of students will enter the labor market, get a job, and—whenever possible—benefit from on-the-job or in-house training offered by their employers. Other students will find jobs, but re-enter the formal education and training system at a later point in life when their career choices have consolidated. Some of this group will enter short-term TVET programs offered by public and private providers. Education and training policies need to respond to these realities accordingly and ensure the availability of alternative pathways to further education and skills acquisition. Projections of future government education expenditures also need to recognize these realities.

Third, the GER target for upper secondary (preparatory) education appears modest, while the TVET target far exceeds enrollment rates common in middle-income countries. The ratio between GERs in general upper secondary and tertiary education in LMICs is, on an average, 2.5:1, whereas it is almost 1:1 in Ethiopia. This ratio is consistent with a concept of upper secondary education that views its sole purpose as preparation for university education. At the same time, TVET in Ethiopia represents more than 70 percent of total enrollments at the post–general secondary level (that is, grades 11–12).

The experience of LMICs suggests that it may be desirable to rethink the balance between TVET and preparatory education in Ethiopia. Such a re-evaluation would most likely involve a:

- Review of the purpose of preparatory education
- Gradual increase in access to this type of education beyond the current target of 20 percent of students who pass the grade 10 national examination
- Reconsideration of the almost automatic transition from grade 12 to university
- Clear definition of the comparative advantage and purpose of publicly funded formal TVET programs vis-à-vis privately provided TVET programs

In any case, it is not clear that it would be either feasible or desirable to continue admitting virtually all grade 12 graduates to university. It may thus be important to consider policy options that create upper secondary tracks for: (1) students who wish to enter the labor market, (2) students who wish to continue their educations immediately upon graduation, and (3) students who seek to continue their education a few years later, possibly in TVET programs.

Fourth, the experience of middle-income countries suggests the importance of aligning the output of graduates—especially at upper secondary and higher levels of education—with labor market demand. Where this alignment has not been successful, graduate unemployment and social disruption have adversely affected the progress of economic development. In addition, the financial costs of too rapid an expansion of public TVET, upper secondary, and tertiary education enrollments are considerable. These costs usually affect the resources available for enhancing the quality of inputs and create a vicious cycle of low student learning throughout the system up to and including higher education, especially teacher training.

An analysis of the per student cost of education at different levels in 17 countries of Sub-Saharan Africa found that on average, unit costs at the lower secondary level are about three times greater than at the primary level, and at the upper secondary level, six times greater (table 3.2). The reasons for these disparities lie in a combination of lower pupil-teacher ratios, higher salary costs, boarding subsidies, and larger numbers of nonteaching support staff at the secondary level. Nonteaching costs at the secondary level can, for example, account for as much as 40 percent of the total cost per pupil. TVET is even more expensive on a per student basis than general secondary education. The ratio of TVET spending per student to that of general education spending per student ranges from 0.8 in Togo to 13.8 in Mozambique. In Madagascar vocational training centers cost 60 percent more per student than technical secondary schools, which themselves are four times as expensive as general secondary schools (Verspoor 2008). Table 3.3 provides the per student cost for different education levels in Ethiopia.

Fifth, the emphasis on mathematics and science education at the secondary preparatory and tertiary levels is well justified, given the evidence on the

Table 3.2 Composition of Educational Spending and Per Student Cost in 17 Countries in Sub-Saharan Africa

	Primary education		First secondary cycle		Second secondary cycle	
	Average	Variation	Average	Variation	Average	Variation
Teacher salaries (multiple of per capita GDP)	4.6	2.4–6.8	6.6	3.6–13.1	9.3	3.8–19.8
% of recurrent spending on items other than teachers	27.4	15.0–43.0	37.4	24.0–56.0	39.5	18.0–53.0
Unit cost (that is, per student cost as % of per capita GDP)	11.4	4.0–20.0	31.2	13.0–64.0	63.4	22.0–157.0

Source: Adpated from Mingat 2004, 12, table 6.
Note: GDP = Gross domestic product.

Table 3.3 Per Student Cost of Education in Ethiopia, 2009/10

multiples of primary per student cost

	Total per student cost	Total recurrent cost per student
Primary	1.0	1.0
Secondary	3.6	2.2
TVET	6.5	3.0
Tertiary	48.3	16.0

Source: Author's analysis based on ESDP IV financial projection model, as updated in September 2011.
Note: TVET = Technical and vocational education and training.

correlation among strong student performance in these subjects, the adoption of new technologies, and the rate of economic growth. In light of the poor learning achievement of the bulk of general secondary graduates in Ethiopia, however, it will be challenging to maintain educational quality at the preparatory level if the current practice of streaming 70 percent of preparatory students into the natural sciences is maintained.

The points elaborated above should guide the discussion of policy options for developing secondary education in Ethiopia, especially during the period 2015–25, as the country moves closer to becoming a lower-middle-income economy. The following chapters discuss these options with respect to specific issues. Chapter 4 analyzes the curriculum issues that need to be addressed for the education system to effectively support the country's economic transformation. Chapter 5 analyzes issues of teacher demand and supply, as well as teacher quality. Chapter 6 reviews the options for strengthening the governance and management of the secondary education system, with a particular focus on school-based management. Chapter 7 explores the options for mobilizing nongovernmental resources to help develop secondary education. Chapter 8 models a number of financing options for secondary education and assesses their implications. Finally, chapter 9 summarizes the policy options for the short, medium, and long term as part of a coherent strategy for secondary education development.

Conclusion

The data presented in this chapter demonstrates that a strong human resource base is an important foundation for progressing toward a middle-income economy. While the large majority of children in Ethiopia now have access to primary education, a major effort will be required to reach the 80 percent GER for general secondary education that is typical of LMICs. An equally significant effort will be needed to expand access to preparatory secondary education beyond the current comparatively modest target of 20 percent. Sustained progress toward these targets will entail rapid improvement in primary completion rates, careful management of the cost per secondary student, and—perhaps most important—consistent efforts to manage the quality of education, particularly that of mathematics and the sciences.

Another major consideration for the further development of secondary education is meeting the needs of students who directly enter the labor market after completing general secondary education. It is important to design a number of alternative pathways to further education and training for these students. TVET programs play an important role in developing the human capital of countries whose economies increasingly depend on manufacturing to drive economic growth. The objectives of current Ethiopian TVET policy reflect this reality; the policy both recognizes a diversity of programs and providers and stresses the critical importance of quality instruction and skills acquisition. Yet longer-term TVET education targets may overemphasize the role of formal programs provided by public institutions. ESDP IV, for example, assumes that the share of private provision of TVET will decline from more than 55 percent to 40 percent by 2014/15. This reduction may not be desirable, given that TVET programs can to a significant extent be self-financing. In the coming years, a large proportion of TVET programs will inevitably continue to be delivered by the private sector.[6] As the economy develops, companies will provide in-house training, many young people will work in formal or informal apprenticeship arrangements, and many workers already in the labor force will look for short skills-upgrading courses. An education system that accounts for these diverse pathways to education and skills acquisition will be imperative to support Ethiopia on its journey to becoming a middle-income economy.

Notes

1. The discussion in this chapter uses GDP (gross domestic product) and GNI (gross national income) interchangeably, although the value of GNI is higher than that of GDP for a particular country. The GNI values reflect the sources used in this section, but do not affect the inferences made. GNI is gross domestic product (GDP) plus net receipts of primary income (employee compensation and investment income) from abroad. GDP is the sum of the value of output of all resident producers plus any product taxes (less subsidies) not included in the valuation of output.
2. McKinsey studies show that only 10–25 percent of general college graduates in India have skills that make them suitable for employment (see Isak et al. 2007).
3. For unemployment rates among Moroccan university graduates, see Achy 2010; for the duration of university graduates' job search, see FEMISE 2010.
4. This figure is based on EdStats and a calculation of tertiary enrollment as a percentage of the 19–24-year-old age group.
5. This point is emphasized in the "Africa Competitiveness Report 2011" of the World Economic Forum (WEF (World Economic Forum) 2011).
6. The 2010 Education Public Expenditure Review (Ravishankar et al. 2010) notes that there has been a boom in private provision of TVET in Ethiopia. Private programs expanded to serve 57 percent of total trainees in fiscal 2007/08, a level that represented a 16 percent increase over the volume of private provision four years earlier.

References

Achy, Lahcen. 2010. "Trading High Employment for Bad Jobs: Employment Challenges in the Maghreb." Carnegie Paper (July), Carnegie Endowment for International Peace, Washington, DC. http://carnegieendowment.org/2010/07/15/trading-high-unemployment-for-bad-jobs-employment-challenges-in-maghreb/3b1g.

ADB (Asian Development Bank). 2004. *Improving Technical Education and Vocational Training: Strategies for Asia*. Manila: ADB.

Barro-Lee Educational Attainment Dataset. Economics Department, Korea University, Seoul. www.barrolee.com.

CSA (Central Statistical Agency) of the Federal Democratic Republic of Ethiopia and Measure DHS/ICF Macro. 2006. "Ethiopia Demographic and Health Survey 2005." CSA, Addis Ababa, and Measure DHS/ICF Macro, Calverton, MD.

di Gropello, Emanuela. 2011. "Skills for the Labor Market in Indonesia: Trends in Demand, Gaps, and Supply." With Aurelien Kruse and Prateek Tandon. Directions in Development Series. Report 60812, World Bank, Washington, DC.

EdStats (database). World Bank, Washington, DC. http://go.worldbank.org/85XM5TBQA0.

FEMISE (Forum Euroméditerranéen des Instituts de Sciences Économiques). 2010. "L'insertion des jeunes diplômés et le rendement des investissements dans l'enseignement supérieur: Cas du Maroc et de la Tunisie (The Integration of Young Graduates and the Return on Investment in Higher Education: The Case of Morocco and Tunisia)." In collaboration with Alimi Nabil, Boumeddien Jamel, Gali Sofiane, Ibourk Aomal, and Ben said Mohamed. Étude FEMISE FEM33-24. FEMISE, Marseille.

Fredriksen, Birger, and Jee Peng Tan, eds. 2008. *An African Exploration of the East Asian Education Experience*. Development Practice in Education Series. Washington, DC: World Bank.

Isak, Froumin, Shanthi Divakaran, Hong Tan, and Yevgeniya Savchenko. 2007. "Strengthening Skills and Education for Innovation." In *Unleashing India's Innovation: towards Sustainable and Inclusive Growth*, ed. Mark A. Dutz, 129–46. Washington, DC: World Bank.

Mingat, Alain. 2004. "Issues of Financial Sustainability in the Development of Secondary Education in Africa." Paper presented at the Donor Conference on Secondary Education in Africa (SEIA), Vrije Universiteit Amsterdam, The Netherlands, October 2004. SEIA Team, Africa Region Human Development, World Bank, Washington, DC. http://siteresources.worldbank.org/INTAFRREGTOPSEIA/Resources/mingat_main.pdf.

Ravishankar, V. J., Abdulhamid Kello, and Alebachew Tiruneh. 2010. "Ethiopia: Education Public Expenditure Review. Report prepared for the Ministry of Education of the Federal Democratic Republic of Ethiopia." New Concept Information Systems, Pvt., New Delhi.

UIS (UNESCO Institute of Statistics) (database). UIS, Montreal, Canada. http://www.uis.unesco.org.

UNESCO-UNEVOC. 2006. *Participation in Formal Technical and Vocational Education and Training Programmes Worldwide: An Initial Statistical Study*. Bonn: UNESCO-UNEVOC.

Verspoor, Adriaan M. 2008. *At the Crossroads: Choices for Secondary Education in Sub-Saharan Africa*. With the SEIA Team. Africa Human Development Series. Washington, DC: World Bank.

WDI (World Development Indicators) (database). World Bank, Washington, DC. http://data.worldbank.org/data-catalog/world-development-indicators.

WEF (World Economic Forum), World Bank, and AfDB (African Development Bank) 2011. "The Africa Competitiveness Report 2011." WEF, Geneva.

Weiping, Wu. 2011. "Higher Education and Skills for China." PowerPoint presentation made at the World Bank, Washington, DC, March. http://siteresources.worldbank.org/INTINDONESIA/Resources/226271-1170911056314/3428109-1300348698455/Weiping-Wu.pdf.

WEO (World Economic Outlook) (database). IMF, Washington, DC. http://www.econstats.com/weo/V011.htm.

World Bank. 2005. *Education in Ethiopia: Strengthening the Foundation for Sustainable Progress*. World Bank Country Study. Washington, DC: World Bank.

———. 2008. *Acceleration Catch-Up: Tertiary Education for Growth in Sub-Saharan Africa*. Directions in Development Series. Washington, DC: World Bank.

———. 2009. "Educational Attainment and Enrollment around the World." Data and Research, Human Development and Public Services, World Bank, Washington, DC. http://iresearch.worldbank.org/edattain/. Accessed July 8, 2009.

———. 2010. "Republic of Ghana: Education in Ghana—Improving Equity, Efficiency and Accountability of Education Service Delivery." Report 59755-GH. Africa Region Education Unit (AFTED), World Bank, Washington, DC.

CHAPTER 4

Curriculum: Quality and Relevance

The current general secondary curriculum in Ethiopia was not designed with universal access in mind; it is academically demanding and closely tied to university entry requirements. This type of curriculum is no longer appropriate because progress toward universal secondary education will result in a student body with a much wider range of abilities and aspirations than has been the case so far. To provide all students the opportunity to succeed and develop the human resources necessary for a rapidly growing economy, the next round of curriculum revision should give priority to content differentiation. This change would allow students to study subjects at different levels of depth and choose electives that prepare them for different career options. Secondary education differentiation should start in grades 9–10 and become increasingly pronounced in grades 11–12, where some students will prepare for university entrance, some for postsecondary nonuniversity technical and vocational education and training programs, and others for the world of work (and on-the-job training provided by employers). In addition, curriculum content needs to be relevant to a labor market where metacognitive skills are at a premium, while providing schools the flexibility to create an instructional environment suited to local conditions.

While countries have reached middle-income status without first achieving universal lower secondary education (chapter 3), in virtually all cases their economic growth has been accompanied and supported by a rapid increase in the proportion of young people with secondary education.[1] This increase signals a transition from a system designed to prepare the elite for higher education to a system able to offer effective secondary education to a large majority of the relevant age cohort. A middle-income economy requires a large proportion of workers who have completed 10 years of education, many of whom will be expected to perform tasks that use metacognitive skills, defined as the ability to use higher-order thinking by actively controlling the cognitive processes that are engaged during learning. In this environment learning to think and learning to learn become priorities.

With a better-educated labor force, middle-income countries have been able to achieve levels of productivity that support sustained economic development.

In these countries, the secondary curriculum must adequately serve the needs of two masters: learners and the economy. The demands of both will be much more varied in the future than they have been in the past, when the main concentration of secondary education was producing a small cadre of highly qualified secondary school-leavers for a small modern economic sector.

Current Curriculum

The current curriculum will be appropriate only as long as secondary education is selective and designed to prepare a limited number of students for higher education. But for a secondary system with middle-income country enrollment rates, it is too difficult and too academic. That is, the curriculum is not designed to meet the demands of students who are not destined for higher education. It is also overly costly. At current participation rates these issues are already an important reason for ineffective instruction and low student performance on both national examinations and learning assessments at the general secondary level (chapter 2); their impact may become even more significant as enrollments increase rapidly in coming years.

Difficult and Academic

The current Ethiopian curriculum has evolved from a more conventional 6-2-4 structure, in which the middle two years were the lower secondary program. The 1994 Education and Training Policy (ETP) revised the curriculum to become an 8-2-2 structure, with grades 11 and 12 reserved for preparatory schooling for a three-year university undergraduate program.[2] This change meant that many topics previously taught in the first year of undergraduate programs were moved down to grades 11–12 and, consequently, topics from grades 11–12 were moved down to grades 9–10. The overall result of the change was to increase, sometimes greatly, the overall difficulty of grades 9 through 12. The general secondary curriculum (grades 9–10) became, in effect, equivalent to the curricula typical of grades 11–12 in many countries worldwide. The current national grade 10 examination in Ethiopia is aligned with this curriculum and designed to select students for grade 11.

The demanding nature of general secondary education in Ethiopia is borne out by table 4.1, which compares grades 10 and 12 in the Ethiopian system to the corresponding grades and pupil age in a number of education systems worldwide. As can be seen, the grade 10 curriculum in Ethiopia is equivalent to that of grade 11 or 12 in almost all other countries shown. An interesting exception is Singapore, where the O-level (after 10 years of education) is equivalent to Ethiopian grade 10. But this specific curriculum is followed by only a small, highly academically select minority in Singapore. The majority of students in the city state opt for one of two lower-level streams that lead to "normal academic" or "normal technical" examinations, which are easier than the O-level exams.

Table 4.1 Comparison of Educational Systems, Various Countries

Normal starting age (years)	Ethiopia	United Kingdom	United States	Singapore	Ethiopia International School, Addis Ababa	Botswana	South Africa	Namibia	Uganda
4	ECE				K				
5	ECE	Reception (K)	K	K	K			K	
6	Grade 1	Year 1	Grade 1	P1	Year 1	P1	P1	Grade 1	P1
7	Grade 2	Year 2	Grade 2	P2	Year 2	P2	P2	Grade 2	P2
8	Grade 3	Year 3	Grade 3	P3	Year 3	P3	P3	Grade 3	P3
9	Grade 4	Year 4	Grade 4	P4	Year 4	P4	P4	Grade 4	P4
10	Grade 5	Year 5	Grade 5	P5	Year 5	P5	P5	Grade 5	P5
11	Grade 6	Year 6	Grade 6	P6 PSLE	Year 6	P6	P6	Grade 6	P6
12	Grade 7	Year 7	Grade 7	S1	Year 7	S1	GET 1	Grade 7	P7 PSLE
13	Grade 8	Year 8	Grade 8	S2	Year 8	S2	GET 2	Grade 8	S1
14	Grade 9	Year 9	Grade 9	S3	Year 9	S3 JSE	GET 3 JSE	Grade 9	S2
15	Grade 10 Exam*	Year 10	Grade 10	S4 O level*	Year 10	S4	FET 1	Grade 10 JSE	S3
16	Grade 11	Year 11 GCSE*	Grade 11*	S5	Year 11 IGCSE*	S5	FET 2	Grade 11	S4 O level*
17	Grade 12 Exam**	Year 12	Grade 12	S6 A level**	Year 12 IB (ord)**	S6 O level*	FET 3 (ord)*	Grade 12 CSE* (ord)	S5
18	Year 1	Year 13 A Level**	Year 1**	Year 1		Year 1**	Year 1**	Year 1**	S6 A level**
19	Year 2	Year 1	Year 2	Year 2		Year 2	Year 2	Year 2	Year 1
20	Year 3 BS	Year 2	Year 3	Year 3 BS		Year 3	Year 3	Year 3	Year 2
21		Year 3 BS	Year 4 BS			Year 4 BS	Year 4 BS	Year 4 BS	Year 3 BS
22							Year 5 Honors		

Source: Reproduced from Clegg 2011.

Note: Ethiopian grade-level estimates are based on the syllabi for physics, chemistry, biology, and mathematics. * = ordinary leaving examination, equivalent to Ethiopian grade 10. ** = higher leaving examination, equivalent to Ethiopian grade 12.

Most abbreviations used in this table are those used in the countries concerned: A = advanced; BS = Bachelor of Science; ECE = early childhood education; FET = further education and training; (G)CSE = (General) Certificate of Secondary Education, often offered at the O (ordinary) and A (advanced) levels; GET = General Education and Training; IB = International Baccalaureat; IGCSE = International General Certificate of Secondary Education; JSE = Junior Secondary Examination; K = kindergarten; ord or O = ordinary level; PSLE = Primary School-Leaving Examination; S = secondary; UK = United Kingdom; USA = United States of America.

A further difference between Ethiopia and the majority of other countries shown in table 4.1 is that in most cases, examinations in the latter are appropriate for testing a wide range of abilities. The clear conclusion is that the Ethiopian curriculum is difficult and highly academic compared to most other countries, even those where teaching is in students' mother tongue.[3] The poor performance of Ethiopian students on the national examination and National Learning Assessment for grade 10 is perhaps therefore unsurprising.

The difficulty of the academic content of the Ethiopian curriculum is exacerbated by the switch to English as the medium of instruction in grade 9 because the English-language competency of both teachers and students remains limited. In primary education the medium of instruction is the mother tongue, or home language, of students, although some regions or areas have recently introduced English as the medium of instruction for science and mathematics starting in grade 5 or 7. A comprehensive study of the medium of instruction in Ethiopian primary schools carried out in 2006 showed that mother-tongue learners consistently outperformed English-language learners in national tests in science, mathematics, and English (Heugh et al. 2007). Unsurprisingly most teachers frequently resort to code-switching—that is, the concurrent use of more than one mother tongue and English—to ensure better student understanding of a given topic.

Not Designed for Universal Education

The Ethiopian secondary curriculum (like those of many African countries) remains essentially "one-size-fits-all" curriculum, with the "size" designed to fit more academic learners best. Individual differences between learners become increasingly significant and problematic as students grow older; some of these differences are due to identifiable learning problems that may be amenable to solution, while others are simply evidence that children mature at different rates and differ in intellectual capacity. A universal education curriculum must accommodate these differences; it must be learner centered rather than subject centered and incorporate strategies to cope with differences in learners' needs. It must neither brand slower learners failures, nor put a brake on the progress of the most able. Progress in this direction will require dealing with the issues of overload, misplaced topics, learning gaps, and repetition.

Overload. It is easy to add elements to a curriculum, but very difficult to remove them. As a consequence, all curricula tend to become sclerotic (and increasingly dull) over time because of the pressure to add new elements.[4] Many examples from the Ethiopian science syllabi typify how this "overload" has arisen over time. First, many topics that have long since disappeared from school curricula elsewhere (box 4.1) remain in the syllabi, despite revisions. Second, many topics (particularly in physics) are covered in much greater detail than is required for an understanding of a given concept, leaving the learner "unable to

Box 4.1

Types of Chemical Reaction Taught in Grade 9

The grade 9 chemistry syllabus in Ethiopia has an extensive section (4.5) entitled "Types of Chemical Reaction," which identifies four kinds of reaction: combination, decomposition, single displacement, and double decomposition. These ideas arose in the nineteenth century when scientists were primarily preoccupied with classifying the vast amount of information that their research was producing. This particular classification has long since disappeared from scientific discourse, replaced by one based on the knowledge of how atoms change during reactions—knowledge that was not known until the early twentieth century (and is part of other sections of the syllabus).

School science curricula in the country are, however, very conservative; such elements of outdated nineteenth-century science are not uncommon. This example is only one of many in current science syllabi in Ethiopia. Such material takes up much unnecessary teaching time, many textbook pages (because of the extensive minutiae listed in the curriculum, all of which must appear in the books), and lends itself to a multiplicity of examination questions based on recall. Removing these elements is the first step toward a twenty-first-century science curriculum centered on the learner.

Source: Clegg 2011.

---

see the forest for the trees." The syllabi also tend to be overprescriptive, thus becoming work plans rather than curricula.

Finally, there are examples of repetition between curricula years. While it is educationally desirable that learning area curricula be spiral in nature, this design can result in a more detailed treatment of a topic when it is first introduced than is either appropriate or desirable (except perhaps for the most able learners)—a trend very evident in Ethiopian science subjects.

Misplaced topics. The conceptual demands of a curriculum and the conceptual ability of intended learners should match, but in Ethiopia this is often not the case. The grade 10 curriculum, for example, contains abstract topics that make demands on learners that would not normally be made until grade 11 or 12 in many developed countries, and then only in the academic stream of upper secondary education.

Misplaced topics were also found in the primary mathematics curriculum (table 4.2). As can be seen, Ethiopian grade 1 and 2 mathematics contain number concepts that are typically not introduced until a grade or two later in developed countries that perform relatively well on international learning assessments. This pushes Ethiopian learners into using algorithms and mathematical routines before they have an understanding of the concept of the

Table 4.2 Comparison of Mathematics Curricula in Five Countries

Topic	Ethiopia	England	Singapore	United States (California)	Japan
Addition and subtraction up to 20	Grade 1[a]	Year 3	P1	Grade 1	Grade 2
Multiplication of whole numbers (product/dividend < 30)	Grade 1	Year 2	P1	Grade 2	Grade 2
Fractions (of shapes and objects)	Grade 1	Year 3	P2	Grade 2	Grade 3
Multiply/divide a two-digit number by a one-digit number	Grade 2	Year 4	P3	Grade 3	Grade 3
Counting in multiples (tables)	Grade 2	Year 5	P3	Grade 3	Grade 2

Source: Reproduced from Clegg 2011.
a. *Grade level or year indicates when key concepts are first introduced.*

number, with significant adverse consequences for basic numeracy that are very difficult to correct later. This is a significant issue throughout Africa, where curricula have been designed as selective tools to identify and encourage fast learners rather than as mechanisms to help the greatest number of students achieve the highest possible levels of numeracy.

Emerging gaps. Curriculum development is a dynamic process that needs to keep up with new knowledge areas and emerging demands for skills and competencies. While secondary curricula in Ethiopia are being revised in five-year cycles, they have not always been able to keep up with rapid changes in science, technology, and the economy.

- *Missing topics.* While the curriculum framework refers to the idea of knowledge areas (see Ethiopia 2009), curriculum details are not written in terms of these areas. Rather, the details consist of traditional subject syllabi, with several subjects in each learning area. This convention has led to significant gaps, as important topics emerge over time that do not fit neatly into conventional syllabi. Some of these gaps are covered in part by cross-cutting elements of the curriculum, such as environmental education, but many remain.
- Particularly significant gaps exist in earth sciences, space science, and climatology. Box 4.2 shows how these gaps were addressed during a recent revision of the science curriculum in Qatar. The revision used a typical methodology of first developing a curriculum for an entire learning area, then basing teaching plans and examination syllabi on it.
- *Mastery of skills.* A significant gap in the existing Ethiopian secondary curriculum is skill mastery. While introductory paragraphs in each subject often refer rather generally to the importance of mastering skills appropriate to the relevant subject, these skills tend to be rather loosely defined and are seldom named in the subsequent list of competencies. Of particular note is the science learning area, for which the government's science

> **Box 4.2**
>
> ## New Science Curriculum in Qatar, 2004
>
> Schools in Qatar are all independent of the state, which pays them a per capita fee. They are at liberty to organize their own teaching programs and even to select external examination providers. However, all schools must follow the national curriculum. The national science curriculum has a number of elements, each with its own subdivisions (table B4.1). How this material is taught and by whom is left to the schools.
>
> **Table B4.1 Elements of Science Curriculum in Qatar**
>
> | Elements (grades 5–9) | Subdivisions |
> |---|---|
> | Scientific enquiry | Methods of scientific investigation, how scientists work, processing and communicating information, handling equipment and making measurements |
> | Life sciences | Diversity and variation in living things, living things and their environment, life processes, humans as organisms, health and hygiene, green plants as organisms, microorganisms |
> | Materials | Changing materials, matter and energy, patterns in reactivity |
> | Earth and space | Earth sciences, space |
> | Physical processes | Forces and movement; matter and energy; waves, light, and sound; electricity and magnetism |
>
> *Source:* Adapted from Clegg 2011, 31.

education concept paper emphasizes the importance of skills (MOE 2010a). However, these skills are not developed in the curriculum details or assessment instruments, and elements that are not assessed tend not to be well taught.

- Yet lack of skills is perhaps the most significant indicator of the low quality of high school graduates. Particularly absent from the curriculum are higher-order thinking skills, a gap that is probably generated as much by the way many subjects are assessed as by the way in which they are taught. This issue is addressed at more length later in this chapter.
- *Preparing for technical and vocational education and training (TVET) and the world of work.* Current policy is to stream 80 percent of grade 10 graduates toward TVET and the labor market. The Ethiopian TVET subsector is currently in the middle of a significant revolution that is replacing the traditional (and long) general technical training programs typically offered by government training institutions with short, competency-based modular programs offered by a wide variety of government and private providers. There has been little discussion, however, of how secondary education should evolve to create the kind of school-leaver who will fit naturally into the new TVET system. This is a debate that must take place.

- The traditional technical subjects taught in TVET schools in the past, such as technical drawing, are expensive, unpopular, and increasingly irrelevant to a modern economy. More relevant subjects that have taken their place elsewhere, such as design and technology, tend to be expensive and require highly trained teachers.
- The issue of technology in the curriculum is very much under debate internationally (see, for example, Fensham 2008) and a variety of possible avenues are emerging. These alternatives involve both changes within traditional subjects, particularly science, and the introduction of new subjects, such as entrepreneurship. Similarly, mechanisms to guide students toward career choices and further training remain underdeveloped in the country.

High cost. As already noted, Ethiopia has a high-cost secondary curriculum. Although the curriculum is organized into just five learning areas, teachers are trained to teach only specific subjects within each area and typically have only a single major. This means that overall, the teaching force cannot be deployed flexibly—something particularly important in small schools, especially those with less than two sections per grade. Worldwide, the sciences and humanities, for example, are increasingly being taught as single subjects up to grade 9 or 10, particularly to lower-ability children. This change has been driven, in the main, not by economic but by pedagogical and epistemological factors that emphasize the essential unity of a learning area. In some areas, the change has led to a misalignment of secondary coursework with subsequent higher education programs but, in general, the gains of broader understanding have offset the loss of depth that might occur.

A second significant cost is incurred by examining a large number of subjects that are taught only a few periods a week, compared to examining a small number of subjects that are taught more intensively. The high cost of teaching certain subjects, particularly science, is an additional cost element. Modern science curricula, which put greater emphasis on skill mastery than the acquisition of detailed knowledge, need expensive facilities and equipment far less than do traditional curricula, largely because they focus on the relevance of subject matter to everyday life, rather than treating science as an esoteric subject that can only be studied in a special environment.

Finally, resources have not always been invested with due regard for cost effectiveness. This is most obvious in the case of information and communication technology (ICT), on which Ethiopia has spent considerable amounts of money to support curriculum delivery. This delivery has mainly taken the form of radio and television programs broadcast directly to the classroom on flatscreen plasma televisions via a one-way satellite link (known as the "plasma program" in Ethiopia). Its purpose has mainly been to improve student achievement by countering the effect of large classes, inadequately trained teachers, and shortages of basic teaching and learning materials.

Box 4.3

The Disappointment of the Plasma TV Learning Program

The Ministry of Education (MOE) cites a number of reasons for the inability of the plasma program to influence learning outcomes:

- The language level is too difficult.
- The lessons proceed too quickly.
- Interaction is not possible.
- Teachers have little time to discuss lesson points with their students.
- Learning is passive.

Moreover, as teachers cannot view lessons prior to broadcast, they are unable to integrate them into their own programs. This in turn undermines their authority. The MOE concept paper on mathematics and science teaching concludes that the problem lies, in the main, not with the technology, but with the way in which it is used.

It is likely that the underlying reason for the apparent failure of the plasma program, like so many other information technology initiatives in Africa (including the One Laptop Per Child Program attempted in Ethiopia), is that it was not driven by demand. Instead it was thrust on a reluctant teaching force; unfortunately, it does not easily integrate with normal teaching styles based on textbooks. Teachers have had little or no training in how to make the best use of the program, which leads to insecurity because they feel that they are not in full control.

The Ministry of Education has recently modified the plasma program to correct these weaknesses.

Source: MOE 2010a.

In addition, the nongovernmental organization (NGO) Schoolnet Ethiopia has been active in bringing affordable Internet access to schools. Most grade 11–12 preparatory schools, for example, have both plasma TV receivers and Internet access; most grade 9–10 general secondary schools have plasma TV receivers, but their installation in new schools is limited by budget constraints and can often take some years.

It is anticipated that in the future, the two delivery channels will be combined and video content streamed or downloaded as podcasts or supplied on DVDs. However, it can only be seen as disappointing that the grade 10 and 12 National Learning Assessments of 2010 failed to detect any significant contribution to the variance in achievement resulting from the regular use of the plasma program (box 4.3). Similarly, independent monitoring of Internet use in schools found no significant influence on student learning outcomes (Bass 2011).

International Trends in Curriculum Reform

Over the last several decades two broad waves of educational reform can be identified. Both have been influenced by concerns that the education system was not properly serving national needs. A significant trend that emerged in the first wave of reform in the 1960s was to place the child, rather than the teacher, at the center of all education activities. Nevertheless the teacher remained in full control of the teaching and learning process and the class remained the teaching unit. This trend was influenced primarily by the need to increase the pool of high-level expertise in the labor force and therefore tended to focus on superior academic achievers (Ware 1992). The current Ethiopian curriculum is a characteristic product of this wave of reform.

This first wave, with its academic emphasis and selective practices, was superseded by a second wave some 30 years later, which shifted the emphasis of education toward educational equality and the goals of the Education for All movement. The shift continued the process of handing responsibility for learning from the teacher to the learner. It was in part driven by a change in pedagogical emphasis from Piagetian interpretations of the learning process toward more constructivist interpretations, which tend to support the view that Education for All is an achievable goal.

The second wave of reform initially focused on primary education, but has evolved to include basic education of a 9–10-year duration. Table 4.3 contrasts the main emphases of the two reform waves. As with other broad observations on education, these waves should not be interpreted too rigidly. The essentials of both have, of course, been around for centuries and sound educational reformers are careful to emphasize that new ideas should build on, and not displace, the best of an existing education system. The table also indicates the broad directions in which the Ethiopian curriculum can be expected to evolve in order to meet the challenges of universal general secondary education. These second-wave changes have had important consequences for the purposes of curricula and assessment; they have also made keeping students in school a key priority.

Table 4.3 Some Characteristics of Curriculum Reform, 1960s–2010s

First wave	Second wave
Preparation for a career or higher education	Education for All
Focus on understanding	Focus on skills as well as understanding
Acquisition of knowledge	Application of knowledge
Broad coverage of detailed content	Less content, making for more effective learning
Mastery of subject content	Ownership of content
Teacher as originator of knowledge	Teacher as manager of learning process
Whole class working as a unit	Individual or group work
Examinations select students for a higher level	Examinations provide a certification
Exclusive: pass and fail are important concepts	Inclusive: pass and fail cease to exist
Curriculum is subject centered	Curriculum is learner centered

Source: Adapted from Ware 1992, 12, table 1.4.

Purpose of the Curriculum

An important feature of the second wave of curriculum changes in industrialized and middle-income countries was the transformation of exclusive secondary education systems (which focused on the selection of students for a higher level of education) into systems whose purpose is certification, not selection. In the latter systems, the concept of pass and fail ceases to exist and all learners emerge with some kind of certification. These systems are inclusive, with a flexible curriculum that caters to all students. A universal education curriculum must therefore be learner centered to allow learners to proceed at a speed determined not only by subject content, but their own aptitude. There are many examples of how this is done in countries around the world. Three differing models are briefly described below and compared to the current Ethiopian model.

Singapore: Four Distinct Secondary Tracks

After the initial foundation stage (primary grades 1–4) of education, three core subjects are taught according to student ability. Each core subject is offered to students at either the foundational or standard level in primary grades 5 and 6. This means that teachers take into account the ability of their students in designing lessons and assessments. Students thus learn at a pace that suits them. At the end of primary (grade 6), all students sit for the Primary School Leaving Examination, which assesses their abilities for placement in a secondary school course or track that suits their leaning pace and aptitude. The first track—which continues through integrated secondary education and a junior college program—leads to a General Certificate of Education advanced-level (GCE-A) qualification after four to six years of study. Students in this track proceed to preuniversity training without sitting for the GCE O (ordinary)-level examination; they use the time that would otherwise have been devoted to preparing for that examination to study a curriculum of greater academic and nonacademic breadth. Most students in this track continue to university.

The second track, the Secondary Express Course, leads to a GCE O-level qualification after four years of study. These graduates are eligible for admission, among others, to GCE A-level courses. Students on this track receive a GCE A-level qualification after two to three years of additional study. About one-fifth of all learners follow the first two tracks, which are, in principle broadly equivalent to the existing preparatory qualification of the Ethiopian secondary education system. The remaining group of secondary students in Singapore—about 80 percent—follow one of two other tracks: Normal Academic or Normal Technical. Both of these tracks lead to a GCE N (normal)-level qualification after four years of study. Some GCE-N graduates go on to the O-level after an additional year of study, but many leave for TVET programs.[5] Most European countries follow a similar multitrack curriculum model (although they do not necessarily offer segregated schooling). In contrast, a comprehensive model that addresses the diverse interests and abilities of learners through a single flexible curriculum track has evolved in North America and Nordic Europe (Benevot 2006).

Table 4.4 Comparison of Five Syllabi: "Physics—The Study of Movement"

Topic	Ethiopia grade 10	Singapore O-level	Singapore N-level		CIE IGCSE[a]	
			Academic	Technical	Core	Supplemental
	All learners	About 20% learners[b]	About 40% learners	About 40% learners	About 50% learners	About 50% learners
Calculate speed and acceleration	X	X	X	X	X (speed)	X (acceleration)
Distance/time and speed/time graphs	X	X	X	X	X	—
Acceleration under gravity	X	X	X	—	X	—
Terminal velocity	X	X	—	—	—	X
Using the five equations of motion	X	—	—	—	—	—
Relative velocity	X	—	—	—	—	—

Source: Reproduced from Clegg 2011.
Note: X = included in syllabi, — = not included in syllabi.
a. *The IGCSE examination is offered by the U.K.-based examination company, Cambridge International Education. It is usually taken in grade 11.*
b. *This percentage excludes students in the Secondary Express track.*

Table 4.4 compares how these three tracks and the Ethiopian grade 10 syllabus handle the physics topic of "movement." For comparison's sake, the International General Certificate of Secondary Education (IGCSE) is also included. The table clearly illustrates two issues with respect to the Ethiopian grade 9 and 10 science curriculum: not only is it difficult by international standards, it fails to differentiate between the varying needs of learners. The five equations of motion, a unique feature of the Ethiopian syllabus, represent a typically misplaced topic (see discussion above). These equations are abstract and mathematical, whereas all other topics have a concrete element that makes them more intuitively understandable, which is important at this level. In most curricula, equations of motion are typically not introduced until grade 12 physics.

International General Certificate of Secondary Education (IGCSE): Differentiated Content. In this model there is a single curriculum within which topics are delineated according to the level of difficulty. After about grade 9 (broadly equivalent to grade 8 in Ethiopia), all learners follow the basic core curriculum; faster learners take, in addition, an "extended" or "supplemental" curriculum. The core and extended curricula are assessed by different tests within the same examination system; the core test differentiates the lower grades and the extended test, the upper grades. In some countries (for example, Namibia, South Africa, and Scotland), a small proportion of learners also opt to take a separate, more advanced set of tests based on a third, "higher" level of difficulty.[6] Variants of this model are found in many countries, including the United States, Canada, Australia, England, and Nordic Europe (Clegg 2011).

England and Australia have taken the differentiated content model one useful stage further by assigning a level of difficulty to each topic. This practice is applied to the whole curriculum, from grades K to 12, with difficulty levels typically ranging from 1 to 8. These ratings give teachers important information about how difficult each topic will be to teach. While they must ensure that most learners master topics at lower levels, they expect only a few to master higher-level topics in any particular year. Attainment levels also provide useful information for those devising achievement tests, the results of which provide both national and school information on average student learning levels.[7]

Purpose of Assessment

Changes in the purposes of education must be accompanied by changes in the objectives of assessment. A recurrent complaint of higher education teachers in Ethiopia is that students leave grade 12 with underdeveloped skills and a limited ability to apply what they have learned to novel situations. This is an issue that should be explicitly addressed by the next curriculum revision, which raises the question of how to assess skills. Table 4.5 shows South African assessment objectives for three subjects. These objectives indicate, for example, that 30 percent of the final assessment in physical sciences must, by some means, address skill mastery. Innovative evidence-based assessment techniques will ultimately emerge to assess skills; however, many skills can be assessed today by means of a conventional pencil-and-paper examination.

The current Ethiopian curriculum does not indicate assessment objectives in an adequate way.[8] An analysis of grade 12 tests in physics and chemistry for 2010 shows that 94 percent of the test scores in physics and 90 percent of those in chemistry were based on questions that tested knowledge and understanding.

Table 4.5 Guidelines for Three Grade 12 Examinations by Topic, South Africa, 2005

Assessment exam/topic	Percentage of subject material (%)
Home language	
Language and text interpretation	23
Literature	27
Writing	33
Oral tasks	17
Mathematics	
Knowledge	25
Routine procedures	30
Complex procedures	30
Problem solving	15
Sciences	
Enquiry skills	30
Knowledge and its application	40
Nature of science and its relationship to society	30

Source: South Africa 2005.

Box 4.4

Counseling Support Groups in Namibian Schools

As one element of a strategy to address the ramifications of human immunodeficiency virus/acquired immune deficiency syndrome (HIV/AIDS), each school in Namibia has established a small group of volunteer teachers to spearhead counseling services in the school. Although the initial driver was HIV, group members have gradually been given training in various counseling skills and encouraged to develop outreach services with the goal of ensuring that the school becomes acquainted with all parents and caregivers. The goal is to address in a timely manner problems that could potentially impact academic performance or lead a student to drop out. The support groups are, in turn, themselves supported by a cluster system.

Source: Clegg 2011.

The remaining percentages of the scores were based on questions that tested higher-order capacities, such as the application of knowledge. No questions tested the application of scientific skills, yet close to half of grade 12 curriculum objectives for both subjects are concerned with higher-order capacities and skills.

Keeping Students in the System

Access, transition, and retention policies in a learner-centered curriculum should focus on keeping students in the system rather than selecting them out, particularly at phase changes in the education system. Repetition practices should gradually be replaced by inclusive practices in which, increasingly, learning difficulties are diagnosed early and addressed. Reduction in dropout rates should accordingly become a significant school performance indicator. A key element in reducing this rate is a broadly based inclusion policy that addresses such issues as advice and support, particularly for girls who are in danger of dropping out. A second element is designing an advice and support system (that is, pastoral care) that ensures schools are made aware of any social or academic difficulties experienced by their students. Box 4.4 outlines a system that is being put in place in Namibia to address such issues.

Priorities of Ethiopian Curriculum Reform

In order to sustain the growth and transformation of Ethiopia's economy with a better-educated and more productive labor force, the main priority of the next curriculum revision must be to meet the needs and aspirations of all general secondary school-age youngsters, including those who need extra support in learning, those who will leave secondary education to enter the job market with or without additional technical training (probably the majority of learners), and those who have the potential to reach the very highest levels of academic achievement. The revision must also ensure that the conceptual demands of the curriculum match the conceptual ability of a wide range of learners, making it possible for all students to realize their potential and complete at least 10 years of education.

Achieving these goals necessitates a number of decisions at the policy as well as the technical level. The most important goals of the future curriculum revision should be to:

- Ensure an enabling environment
- Redefine the purpose of the curriculum for successful learning
- Adapt assessment and examination systems
- Provide opportunities for students to develop metacognitive skills
- Use ICT to improve teaching
- Ensure equitable access to the curriculum for girls and ethnic minorities
- Make the curriculum more cost effective

To support these changes it would be helpful to improve curriculum documentation (appendix A). The current curriculum is a multipurpose document: a curriculum, a work plan, and an examination syllabus, all in one. More focused documents may better support instructional effectiveness.

Ensuring an Enabling Environment

In order to implement a curriculum effectively, certain minimum conditions that enable learning should be in place. When they are not, educational quality cannot be achieved. These minimum conditions include competent teachers, sufficient textbooks and other instructional materials, and an adequate number of classrooms.

Teachers are, of course, the backbone of any strategy for curriculum implementation. Strategic options for increasing teachers' instructional competence are discussed in chapter 5. At this point it suffices to note that the challenge of teaching an academically demanding curriculum to students, many of whom are being taught in English for the first time in grade 9, are daunting. Improving student academic performance will require that teachers continuously improve their own subject-matter and pedagogical content knowledge, as well as their English-language competency, thus developing the capacity to provide effective instruction while minimizing the language burden.

Textbooks are a critical requirement of effective instruction. They currently dominate teaching in Ethiopia because a great many teachers have not yet reached the professional level at which they can regularly conduct lessons without one. If textbooks are not available, teachers often spend time dictating key passages, or writing them on the board, which takes up most of their contact time with students. It is vital that textbooks be available, of good quality, and readable. The procurement of new textbooks has therefore been a major component of the General Education Quality Improvement Program (GEQIP). The new textbooks are of good quality and represent a significant improvement over the previous ones. They have also been procured at a very reasonable price; the new full-color physics books for grades 9–12, for example, cost an average of $2.59.

Yet, challenges remain. A Fry readability test applied to the new grade 10 physics textbook suggests that while the book is appropriate for readers whose native language is English, students with limited English will find it difficult.[9] As more students with limited English enter secondary education, these issues will become increasingly important. Given that the next round of secondary curriculum revision is expected to focus on flexibility and differentiation, thought must be given to how the curriculum strategy can be reflected in textbooks and how these textbooks can be made more accessible to students with a limited mastery of English.

Instructional materials other than textbooks are also important in secondary education, especially for science education. Experiments conducted by students are an important part of quality instruction in the sciences. In addition, ICT skills acquisition requires equipment. School libraries will also need to include access to books and reference materials. Appendix B provides details on the equipment required for effective science instruction at the secondary level, as well as suggestions for cost-effective alternatives to fully equipped, freestanding laboratories.

Similarly, ICT does not necessarily require specialized infrastructure. Technology can, in fact, provide lower-cost solutions as devices become smaller, e-readers become cheaper, and mobile phone networks provide low-cost Internet access. In many cases, moreover, DVDs offer much more flexible local access to learning materials and information than does the Internet. Any ICT-based instructional materials should, moreover, reflect the lessons learned from the plasma TV program, with development driven by teacher need, not technology availability. In addition, teacher training institutions should be in the forefront of such developments and provide their trainees both the knowledge of how to use ICT effectively and the skills to do so.

Physical infrastructure. Expanded secondary education requires the construction of additional classrooms, laboratories, workshops, and new schools; furniture, equipment, and learning materials; and supporting infrastructure. Costs associated with design criteria and specifications can vary over a wide range, but are often high. It is important to manage the cost of infrastructure development with care. The key challenge is to provide the number of classrooms necessary to keep class sizes at a reasonable level.

Low-cost design and construction are essential, given the number of new places needed in Ethiopia over the next decade. Developing strategies for a more intensive use of buildings is also important: double-shift use of buildings, if well organized, can result in significant cost savings. Singapore is an example of a high-income country that ended double-shift use of school buildings only in 2000. Simple, standardized classroom and school designs, strategic construction of specialized facilities, and school mapping can help control costs. Extending existing primary schools rather than building new secondary schools is another important way to minimize costs.

Most important, community involvement in the development of educational infrastructure can play a significant role in controlling costs. Here, the central or regional government can provide technical support while recognizing the limitations on what the poorest communities can contribute. In Kenya, for example, the government has rarely provided financial support for infrastructure development. Rather, the Harambee movement motivated parents and communities to take the lead in this area (Verspoor 2008). Many communities in Ethiopia are already supporting the development of school infrastructure (MOE 2010b). Expanding formal support to these efforts may be worth considering, for example, by providing support for design and construction, especially of specialized facilities (for example, laboratories and information technology facilities; see appendix B). But it is important to realize that improvements in special-purpose infrastructure will have little impact unless teachers, particularly school managers, are fully versed in how to make best use of these improvements—a process that experience suggests does not happen automatically and often requires carefully designed and targeted training inputs.

Redefining the Purpose of the Curriculum

As noted earlier, the poor performance of learners on national examinations and national learning achievement tests in Ethiopia cannot be attributed only to poor teaching; it is also a function of the difficulty of the curriculum. These challenges are likely to become even more severe as the number of lower-ability students in grade 9 increases, as will inevitably happen as Ethiopia progresses toward the objective of universal access to 10 years of education. To achieve progress toward universal general secondary education and successful learning on the part of all students, a number of issues must be addressed, as discussed below.

The Difficulty of Grade 9–12 Curricula Must Be Recognized and Addressed

The comparison of syllabi presented in table 4.1 above shows that the content of the preparatory cycle in Ethiopia is roughly equivalent to A-level studies in countries such as Singapore, England, and Uganda. Similarly, the cycle is roughly equivalent to the first year of university in the United States, Botswana, South Africa, and Namibia. In most countries, the majority of subjects taught in Ethiopian grades 11–12 are usually only tested after a student has had roughly 13 years of school; moreover, examinations in these countries typically cover between 3 and 6 subjects, not 10, as in Ethiopia.

Flexibility and differentiation need to be introduced into the curriculum. The curricula for grades 9 and 10 should be reviewed to ensure that they cater not only to the needs of students who will pursue further academic studies, but also to those of the 80 percent of students who will pursue TVET programs and/or enter the labor market. Curriculum changes thus need to introduce some form of differentiated program, content, or attainment levels similar to those instituted in Singapore, England, Australia, and the IGCSE.

The purpose of grades 11 and 12 should be reconsidered, with a related redefinition of the curriculum. As has happened in most lower-middle-income countries (LMICs), the number of students entering this level should be growing faster than the number entering higher education. Current enrollment targets for this level in Ethiopia are far below the LMIC average (chapter 3), with an increasing proportion of graduates leaving grade 12 to look for opportunities other than university entrance. The curriculum should be adjusted to respond to the aspirations and competencies of these students.

An evolving qualifications framework is needed for the changing TVET system. Changes in TVET systems in countries across the globe are creating a very different post–general secondary school educational environment from that which previously existed. These changes have a number of significant implications for the secondary curriculum. TVET systems are, for example, demanding students who have an increasingly strong foundation in general academic subjects, especially mathematics and the sciences. In a number of countries, entry into many TVET programs is being postponed until after completion of 11 or 12 years of general education. And almost everywhere the general academic content of TVET programs is being strengthened.

At the same time conventional degree programs at the tertiary level have been widened, the distinction between degree and nondegree programs has become increasingly blurred, and many new avenues of higher and further education and training—particularly technical avenues—have been opened (Atchoarena 2001). Throughout the world, secondary education has had to respond to these challenges (box 4.5).

Adapting Assessment and Examination Systems

To be effective, curriculum change and assessment and examination change need to go hand in hand; a curriculum is almost always heavily driven by examinations, particularly when high-stakes exams determine access to the next level of education. Progress toward a secondary curriculum that reflects the needs of students with a wide range of abilities, as well as changing labor market demands, will require moving toward standards-based assessments and examinations (appendix C); shifting from selection to verification (accompanied by the elimination of the pass-fail concept); and changing a system that tests predominantly only recall to a system that increasingly tests higher-order skills.

Developing Metacognitive Skills

Metacognition refers to learners' awareness of their own knowledge, that is, their ability to assess their knowledge, identify gaps in it, address these gaps, and, generally, control their own cognitive processes.[10] In today's world, learners must learn how to learn. This is especially important in rapidly developing economies

Box 4.5

Responses to the Changing TVET Environment

Emergence of new subjects. New technology-based subjects have emerged to replace older craft-based subjects, such as technical drawing and home economics. The purpose of the new subjects is to provide a broader, more flexible base on which students can build (and rebuild) careers and programs of further study. Examples range from fibers and fabrics to food science, design, technology, and ICT. Another important emerging subject is entrepreneurship.

Changes within existing subjects. Existing, more traditional, subjects have changed by incorporating new, modern elements and skills. Examples are the use of ICT across the curriculum and the emergence of technology as the application of science in existing science curricula.

Career guidance in schools. The rapid expansion of a job market that requires specific knowledge skills has replaced an earlier market for which few skills were needed. This change has increasingly meant that learners have had little knowledge of job market requirements when making subject choices in school. This lack of alignment between schooling and the job market has led to the creation of career guidance programs that link up-to-date information on available careers with the results of self-analysis questionnaires.

Source: Clegg 2011, based on learning materials produced under the auspices of the South African Institute for Entrepreneurship (www.entrepreneurship.co.za, accessed May 2012), as well as the careers list used by the Vocational Counseling Services division of the Ministry of Labour of Namibia (http://www.schoolnet.na/ICS/careers/index.html, accessed May 2012).

(with rapidly changing production technologies), where workers' skills and lifelong learning are critical for a productive labor force.

The curricula at both the general secondary and preparatory level in Ethiopia must therefore lay the foundations for and promote lifelong learning, which will improve graduates' skills and continued employability. Although the ability to learn is a critical issue, it is very difficult to implement within a curriculum. It involves, for example, recognition of the importance of metacognitive skills and how to lay the foundations for the development of such skills in curricula and teaching methodology.

Simple to describe but difficult to translate into curriculum elements, it is even more difficult to translate metacognitive skill requirements from the curriculum to classroom activities. Many elements are already present in some form in the intended Ethiopian secondary curriculum; however, there is little focus on these elements in the existing intended curriculum and they are almost entirely absent from the implemented curriculum (the distinction between the intended and implemented curriculum is well known.) Box 4.6 shows examples of curriculum elements that promote metacognition.

Box 4.6

Curriculum Elements that Develop Metacognitive Skills

Reading meaningfully. Learners with poor metacomprehension skills often read passages without really understanding them. Simple activities such as following written instructions (particularly important in science lessons, for example) and using the information gained to solve new problems can help develop this skill.

Learning how to learn. Learners need the ability to make adjustments to their own learning processes in response to feedback that reflects the current status of their learning. While this is mainly a methodological issue, a carefully and logically developed curriculum can greatly help teachers assist learners in mastering this skill. Activities and questions in teacher materials and textbooks must always build on existing knowledge to help students become aware of their own knowledge and its limitations; teachers should then direct them in how to address these limitations and build new knowledge on top of what they already know.

Communal activities that lead to more effective learning. Children never have to be taught how to use a cell phone; it is a skill developed communally and then through practice. Modern curricula increasingly emphasize the skill of working in groups to solve problems communally, prompting students to discuss their learning with each other, develop their own understanding of a given problem, and encode the process of reaching this understanding.

Real understanding. Most metacognitive skills are learned while a student is learning something else. Mastery of a topic that is sufficient to allow a learner to answer a recall question is often insufficient to promote adequate metacognitive reflection; the learner will not know that he or she has not fully understood the topic. Existing curricula in Ethiopia promote the learning of factual data rather than the understanding of underlying concepts, leaving learners little or no time to practice or develop metacognitive skills. Crucially, examinations in the country must reduce their emphasis on simple recall in favor of testing the ability to apply knowledge to new situations.

Cognitive restructuring. This metacognitive skill involves the internalizing, reinstating, and restructuring of information that a student is trying to process. The skill is already an element of many aspects of the secondary curriculum—paraphrasing in language, for example—but is seldom given the focus it deserves. For example, the translation of information from one form to another in science, such as descriptive to numerical to graphical, is a very important scientific skill. However, this skill is only taught in passing in current Ethiopian science syllabi and then is not tested.

Information retrieval skills. The ability to apply knowledge to a new situation is fundamental to learning, particularly in subjects like mathematics and science. In mathematics, for example, teachers often report that learners have the mathematical ability and knowledge to solve problems, but are often unable to access and retrieve this knowledge in an appropriate way. Such processes can be helped with carefully guided practice, which can—and often is—recognized as a specific curriculum objective.

Source: Clegg 2011.

Using ICT to Improve Teaching, Learning, and ICT Skills
ICT in schools is commonly used to support teaching and learning, teach ICT skills, and improve the efficiency of educational planning and administration.

Improving Teaching and Learning
ICT developments in education throughout the world, such as the Ethiopia plasma TV program described earlier, have been largely driven by technology. ICT projects are done because they can be done, not because evidence indicates that they will improve learning or there is established demand for them. Teachers are not simply asked to make use of a new and troublesome teaching aid, but to make wholesale changes to their teaching styles. Only a highly professional teacher is able to do this easily; ironically, a highly professional teacher would not necessarily need the assistance that a TV program can offer.

The difficulty of persuading teachers to make use of science equipment and the disappointing impact of the Ethiopian plasma program (see box 4.3 above) are illustrative in this regard. The most important lesson here is that for any education technology program to be effective, it must respond to demand. However, long experience with education technology demonstrates that creating this demand is not a simple matter (Cuban 1986, 2001).

One way to create this demand is to establish an online virtual resource center for teachers, while circulating DVDs to schools with poor connectivity. Professional teachers will always find a virtual resource useful, but some kind of bait will be needed to attract their less-skilled colleagues. Useful bait can take the form of materials needed by this type of teacher—materials that do not demand significant changes to their teaching styles, such as something that reduces their workloads (for example, good test items or answers to textbook questions). Once the bait is taken, teachers may be attracted to try other resources (for example, TV podcasts) that can lead to improvements in teaching practices. One proven attraction is a "listserve" (available for free on websites such as Google) linked to a resource site, which both permits professional discussion between teachers and allows the site manager to advertise new content.

Given the substantial sunk investments in the plasma program in Ethiopia, it may be difficult to discontinue in the short term. In the medium and long term, however, it should be replaced by more cost-effective technologies, such as, possibly, the next generation of "smart" mobile phones. At this point ICT strategy should recognize the difficulties encountered to date and modify and integrate existing programs into a larger teacher support package, made available both online and on DVD.

While broadcast media are likely to play a role in any ICT strategy in the foreseeable future, the teaching-learning process can be made more interactive by making materials accessible in the form of podcasts, which would also permit their more selective use by teachers. Eventually, podcasts will become part of a larger repertoire of useful Internet browser- and Java-based materials, such as applets (now widely available and freely downloadable, particularly for the sciences) and on-screen tests.

The small individual WiFi receivers that are currently emerging, in addition to existing plasma TVs in classrooms, offer an opportunity to make the TV program more learner-centered. In addition, the plasma program could become a powerful tool for teaching languages. Use of ICT by both teachers and learners, probably with a heavy presence of mobile devices in the classroom, is likely to become routine over the longer term. But this development needs to be conceptualized as a long-term process that includes training and technical and pedagogical support to help teachers exploit the potential of ICT in instructional strategies.

A useful way to encourage the use of ICT in teaching is to provide lists of possible "ICT opportunities" in curriculum documents, particularly in sample work plans. These moments can range from (critically) gathering information from the Internet, to the use of applets to demonstrate concepts (particularly in science), to using applications as tools. It can also include students' use of computers for conducting and producing work, incorporating other digital technologies such as cameras. Using ICT as a tool in evidence-based assessments is another emerging area, particularly given that digital movie photography using cheap mobile phones has become so simple.

Teaching ICT Skills

Second to the plasma learning program, using computers to teach ICT skills is the main educational application of ICT in Ethiopia. This practice will continue and evolve as the labor market evolves. One issue of significance is the concept of a "computer lab." As devices shrink in size, the conventional fixed computer lab (which has taken valuable space out of optimal use in many schools) is rapidly becoming archaic, except for courses that teach students how to use a keyboard. WiFi connectivity and laptops have made the computer lab mobile, meaning that it can be taken to the classroom rather than vice versa. This change makes the use of computers (and, increasingly, other mobile devices) more flexible, allowing for individual study and the use of ICT in parts of lessons rather than comprising whole lessons.

To support the adoption of ICT in teaching and learning, all teachers should, as soon as possible, become computer literate. A minimum standard could be prescribed, but initially it should be very basic. Training programs should include use of existing TVs in teaching. More advanced uses of ICT in teaching and learning should be supported in a manner that is selective, intensive, and demand driven.

In-service education and training programs should also be developed to take advantage of existing teacher support structures. These programs should then be concentrated in schools where teachers seek to improve their ICT skills and develop strategies for integrating ICT into their teaching. The goal of training programs should be the gradual creation of schools in all regions that are centers of ICT competence from which good practices can spread. Although top-down mass promotion of ICT among teachers may be appealing, long experience in promoting the use of practical science facilities has shown that such an approach is largely ineffectual, and even counterproductive.

Improving the Efficiency of Educational Planning and Administration

The presence of computers and Internet connectivity is opening up opportunities to enhance the efficiency of educational administration, including planning and scheduling. Computers are increasingly used, for example, for school personnel and financial management, inventory, data collection, and analysis. At the school level, ICT can be used to compile individual student data (including learning achievement scores) and conduct school improvement planning, provided that links to local demographic data and a national education management information system have been established. This use of ICT would allow schools to plan for enrollment expansion and benchmark their performance against regional data and data from other woredas.

These data systems are not yet fully developed in Ethiopian schools, but as Internet connectivity spreads and teachers and administrators become computer literate, the use of ICT for planning and administration will expand rapidly. In fact, these technologies have the potential to further improve both the School Improvement Plan process and decentralized financial management systems in the country.

Improving Access to the Curriculum

Affordable general secondary education in grades 9 and 10 must, of necessity, often be provided on a small local scale. This means that the curriculum must be sufficiently flexible in design to cater to the needs of a wide variety of sites, from schools with a few additional classrooms to rural primary schools to large urban schools. This type of design requires separating the details of *what* is taught (the curriculum) from *how* it should be taught (the work plan); what is taught will be common to all schools, how it is taught will depend on local circumstances (appendix A). Currently both these elements are prescribed in the same document; countries needing to improve access in a variety of settings have separated the two. The issue of "how to teach" is usually best addressed with work plans designed at the regional or school level, where variations in local context can best be identified.

Students enter schools with different kinds of backgrounds and knowledge. Effective instruction connects to the local environment, culture, and language. As more students from rural areas and ethnic minorities enroll, these challenges will become increasingly important. In virtually all countries most educational content is defined nationally, but a number of countries allow districts and schools to add some local content to the curriculum to increase the local relevance of the curriculum (box 4.7). As the student body becomes more diverse,

> **Box 4.7**
>
> ## Local Content in Secondary Education Curricula
>
> *Indonesia.* Local curriculum content is an independent subject that represents more than 20 percent of the curriculum. The minimum educational standard contains a core curriculum, which must be implemented nationally, and local curriculum content, which can be modified by each district according to perceived need. Schools may add courses of local interest so long as they do not reduce the time allotted for the national curriculum.
>
> *Vietnam.* The formal school system has adopted a unified curriculum for all types of schools in the whole country. However, provinces can base their implementation of the curriculum on the specific circumstances and conditions of different kinds of students. About 15 percent of the national curriculum is allocated to local content (for example, local history, geography, traditions of production and culture).
>
> *The Philippines.* Individual schools may enrich the national curriculum by including locally relevant subjects, as the country has a very diverse culture with a number of languages spoken across its 16 regions.
>
> *South Africa.* A characteristic feature of South African secondary education is the wide range of secondary school facilities, from the luxurious to the basic. The national curriculum is written in terms of broad outcome targets, rather than content. Teachers and curriculum specialists are currently working together in the regions to develop different ways of achieving these outcomes in ways appropriate to local circumstances.
>
> *Sources:* Gregorio and Tawil 2003; personal communication of authors with Andrew Clegg, independent curriculum specialist, UK.

instructional strategies will also need to become differentiated. For example, girls often face special problems with regard to curriculum delivery, which has traditionally not taken into account differences in the way students learn and the biased messages conveyed by curriculum materials.

A gender-responsive pedagogy that pays attention to the specific learning needs of girls and boys calls for teachers to embrace an all-encompassing gender approach to the processes of lesson planning, teaching, classroom management, and performance evaluation. For example, in planning practical science lessons, a teacher has to take into account the specific instructional needs of girls and boys. And he or she must ensure that boys do not dominate learning processes in order to demonstrate their superiority in the presence of girls. It is also important that teachers be aware that the language they use in the classroom can reinforce negative gender attitudes. Again, these challenges will become increasingly important as more girls and students from rural areas and ethnic minorities enroll. Curriculum materials should accordingly be designed to include positive role models for both genders and avoid stereotypes.[11]

The expansion of access to general secondary education in Ethiopia will require the development of small schools in sparsely populated rural areas that do not yet have a secondary school. In many cases these schools will be extensions of or affiliated with existing primary schools. The major constraint on how the secondary curriculum will be taught in these schools is the number of teachers available to teach it, which in a small local school may be very few. In such circumstances one teacher may be required to cover an entire learning area (for example, science), rather than one subject within a learning area. It follows that the secondary curricula should be written in terms of learning areas rather than the subjects within them. Larger schools will still be able to develop work plans based on conventional subjects within a learning area, should they so wish.

Making the Curriculum more Cost Effective

The resources required to achieve secondary enrollment targets while delivering education of acceptable quality will be considerable (chapter 8). Making the curriculum more cost effective can contribute in important ways to reaching the goals that Ethiopia has set for itself. The cost of a curriculum is influenced by a number of factors, including the number of teachers required to teach it; the cost of learner materials, facilities, and equipment; efficient use of facilities; and the cost and effectiveness of the support system needed by teachers. There are cost-effective options for each of these areas, discussed below.

Number of Teachers

A curriculum with a large number of different subjects requires more teachers than one with a just a few subjects. While large schools may be able to accommodate such a curriculum in a cost-effective manner, with all teachers having a full workload, this type of curriculum adds significantly to the unit cost of schooling if a given school is small or certain subjects are minority subjects with small classes. In such circumstances teachers may be called on to cover subjects in which they have little or no training, a practice that lowers the effectiveness of teaching.

The minimum number of teachers required to manage a curriculum can be lowered by using such strategies as:

- Ensuring that all teachers can teach at least two subjects, perhaps with major and minor qualifications (this requirement will be especially important as the system expands via small schools in rural areas)
- Reducing the number of subjects taught
- Increasing the number of grades that teachers teach

Combining the three physical sciences (biology, chemistry, and physics) and combining the humanities (history, geography, and civics) is now common practice in many countries worldwide for all students up to grade 9 or 10; often the practice continues at higher levels for students in less academically focused streams. As noted earlier, these subject combinations have usually emerged for sound academic and pedagogical reasons. Lower costs have been a useful additional benefit. This benefit is particularly common in the sciences, where combining subjects has enabled an emphasis to be placed—without unnecessary repetition—on elements common to all sciences, such as the concept of scientific enquiry. The practice has also facilitated the inclusion of emerging subject areas, such as earth, climate, and space science.

Cost of Textbooks

The number of textbooks required is directly related to the number of subjects in a curriculum. Combining subjects (for example, reducing science subjects from three to one) reduces the number of textbooks required, although the size of the books will increase somewhat. The new grade 9 and 10 science textbooks in Ethiopia are large and although individually cheap, their overall cost is still significant. Length is directly related to the way syllabi are constructed because authors are under an obligation to cover every point mentioned in a syllabus, however trivial.

Reducing the content of syllabi by removing much of the secondary illustrative material would give authors the freedom to cover the main concepts in an effective way without having to include material that they find unhelpful. This change would reduce the size of books without making them less effective; in fact, experience suggests that leaner textbooks that are more to the point are often more effective. They are certainly less threatening for students!

Cost of Teaching Science

Science subjects are often expensive to teach because they require practical work, which is conventionally interpreted as requiring elaborate laboratories and equipment. However, there is currently a global move away from expensive equipment for teaching science skills, particularly at the primary and lower secondary levels. The purpose of laboratory work has always been twofold: to improve understanding of science concepts by demonstrating them directly and to teach scientific skills. The latter requires little more than a room with a source of water and some basic equipment, while the equipment demands of the former depend directly on the requirements of the syllabus. These requirements, particularly at the level of grades 9 and 10, can often be considerably reduced without significant sacrifices in educational quality. Expensive teaching materials and facilities should thus not be a requirement in these grades. Appendix B provides suggestions for cost-effective strategies for managing the cost of science equipment and specialized infrastructure.

As noted earlier, the current Ethiopian science curriculum is heavily biased toward knowledge acquisition in the three traditional subject areas. As a result, it is expensive to teach well because the practical work required is intended to help students understand abstract concepts and requires expensive facilities and materials. The next curriculum revision offers an opportunity to put much greater emphasis on skills acquisition, as well as to streamline and better focus the knowledge acquisition element (as illustrated in box 4.2) while better aligning it with students' differing interests and abilities. This would not only provide a more effective foundation for modern tertiary and TVET courses, it would also make good science teaching cheaper.

Cost-Effective Use of Space
Many Ethiopian secondary schools are managed as though they were primary schools, with classes visited by teachers. This means that teachers tend to use few aids beyond those they can easily carry to a lesson. With the exception of science laboratories, few schools have departmental bases where teaching materials are kept and that are visited by learners. This system has worked well in the past, given an academic curriculum that makes the textbook the main teaching aid. An expanded curriculum, particularly one that places greater emphasis on skills and "learning by doing," will make demands on both teaching and learning. These demands will be impossible to meet without the establishment of subject departments where materials can be kept and displays maintained, allowing for the development of student work environments that have an abundance of environmental, print, oral, and written language materials.

In the current system, there is a tendency for rooms like laboratories and information technology (IT) rooms to be used outside of a regular timetable; they are visited by learners and teachers alike only when a teacher wishes to use them—a practice that tends to lead to significant underutilization of the spaces.

Conclusion

The educational transformation that must accompany Ethiopia's progress toward a middle-income economy includes a revision of its general secondary and preparatory curricula. New curricula will need to cater to the needs of a much more diverse group of students and prepare them for participation in a more diverse, complex economy. These conditions suggest that *content differentiation* and *relevance* and *flexibility* in implementation are key priorities.

Differentiation
As noted at the outset of this chapter, the current general secondary curriculum was not designed with universal access in mind. Comparative analysis suggests that the Ethiopian curriculum at this level is academically demanding and aligned mainly with the demands of university entrance. It may be appropriate for the most academically able students, who aim to continue their educations in preparatory and university programs. But it is unlikely to serve the needs of the increasingly large group of students who will enter TVET programs or the world of work upon graduation.

As the general secondary education system evolves from an elite to a universal system, it is expected to enroll at least 80–90 percent of the relevant age group, with a target date of 2025 or thereabouts.[12] In order to successfully educate this larger student body, the general secondary system will need to respond to a much wider range of student abilities and aspirations, a larger share of girls, and an increased number of students—many from ethnic minorities—learning in small schools in sparsely populated rural areas.

Given these conditions, a "one-size-fits-all" curriculum will not enable students to learn to their maximum potential. At grade 9 the abilities and aspirations of students are already so diverse that teaching the same content to a single group of students—some academically gifted, others with more aptitude in applied subject matter—will not be in the interest of either. For this reason, the expansion of access to secondary education has been accompanied everywhere in the world by a differentiation in content that allows students to pursue specific interests and succeed at different levels. In many countries this differentiation starts at the lower secondary level (grades 7–9) and becomes more pronounced at the upper secondary level (grades 10–12), where students prepare for different career paths, including university education, postsecondary TVET programs, and the labor market (often followed by on-the-job training).[13]

At the lower secondary level students typically study a common core content. Differentiation occurs because students either elect to study subjects at different levels of depth or subjects that are not included in the core curriculum, but that help them prepare for the job market and explore career options.

In middle-income countries access to upper secondary education (typically grades 10–12) has increased rapidly over the past two decades, with the GER reaching 45 percent in lower-middle-income countries and 70 percent in upper-middle-income countries. At the same time the purpose and content of the curriculum has evolved to offer students choices in academic and career preparation, as well as educational value to students who are not admitted to higher education. In some countries this has been done through the creation of different academic and career-oriented tracks in the same or different institutions. In others the choice is more subject-specific, with electives enabling students to study subjects at a level of depth that corresponds to their abilities and career aspirations.

Three reasons have driven the increase in access to upper secondary education beyond the level required to produce a cohort of higher education students. First, grade 10 may be too early to identify students with the greatest potential for higher education. Second, in most middle-income countries many TVET programs demand an increasingly solid foundation in academic subjects; in fact, many TVET programs have moved into the nonuniversity postsecondary sector as an attractive alternative to university education for secondary school graduates. Third, as employers increasingly demand employees with advanced generic competencies (for example, analytical, problem solving, and communication skills, together with the ability to work in teams) for entry-level jobs, complete upper secondary education has become an increasingly important preparation for the world of work.

To be successful, secondary curricula need to encourage a range of instructional strategies and be connected to the local context, especially for the teaching of science and local language and culture. In addition curriculum design will need to take into account that many secondary students will be in small schools where, due to staffing constraints, it may be difficult to implement a highly differentiated curriculum. Under those conditions electives may have to be limited, natural sciences and social sciences taught respectively as integrated subjects, and instructional strategies more individualized.

The experience of middle-income countries thus suggests that the next round of curriculum revision in Ethiopia should consider content differentiation options that will allow students in grades 9–10 to pursue electives beyond the common core curriculum for each subject. These electives should enable learners to pursue a subject at different levels of depth or explore different areas of interest; helping them specifically prepare for secondary preparatory education (grades 11–12), TVET programs, or the job market, according to their interests and abilities. In addition the purpose of grades 11–12 should be broadened beyond university preparation by creating specific tracks or electives, together with content differentiation, for students wishing to join the workforce or pursue nonuniversity TVET programs.

Relevance
The second curriculum challenge in Ethiopia is responding to the demands of a rapidly growing economy that uses increasingly complex methods of production (in industry and services, as well as in agriculture), which put a premium on metacognitive skills. This implies the need to:

- Emphasize instructional methods that promote and enhance metacognitive skills
- Prepare students for lifelong learning in a rapidly changing economy
- Recognize that preparation for the world of work will become a progressively more important objective of the secondary curriculum as an increasing number of students do not immediately pursue further education and training[14]
- Provide content that is aligned with the increasingly applied academic foundation requirements of TVET programs, including ICT skills.

This is a formidable agenda that will affect decisions on content, structure, and teaching methods of the curriculum. It will also have a profound impact on the quality of the labor force for the next several decades.

Flexibility
The real impact of curriculum change will be seen at the school level, where its success will ultimately be determined. In a country as vast as Ethiopia, schools

operate in different environments, making a number of specific initiatives necessary. It is essential, for example, that the education system continues to intensify GEQIP efforts to promote effective instruction adapted to local conditions. This goal requires sustained efforts to decentralize in-service teacher support and supervision (chapter 5), as well as ensure that necessary equipment and infrastructure are in place.

Efforts are also needed to improve the teaching of mathematics, science, and IT. The emphasis in science should be on providing students the opportunity to carry out simple experiments, possibly using micro-equipment that can be used in ordinary classrooms in schools that do not have specialized facilities. For IT, it is important to review the effectiveness of the plasma program learning strategy and assess its longer-term potential in the light of emerging Internet-based, DVD, and mobile alternatives. In addition, flexibility in curriculum implementation should allow for the introduction of adequate local content, while avoiding the biases of stereotypes and employing a range of instructional strategies to reach girls and ethnic minorities. Finally, it is crucial to deliver equivalent content in small schools by means of a streamlined curriculum and flexible staffing arrangements.

Notes

1. This chapter is based on Clegg (2011).
2. Prior to 1994, the duration of the standard undergraduate program was four years.
3. A recent report on national examinations in Ethiopia (Gregory 2011, 12) comes to a similar conclusion, noting:

    Year 10 mathematics and physics examinations were especially challenging and a review of the national curriculum may be warranted to ensure that the learning expectations were age appropriate. There was substantial agreement from a number of sources that present classroom experiences were generally unlikely to provide the learning opportunities necessary to acquire the knowledge to answer many of the questions on the examinations.

4. Larry Cuban of Stanford University has counseled curriculum developers to be wary of social demands that lead to an unnecessarily cluttered curriculum (Cuban, 1992).
5. See "Secondary School Courses," webpage of the Ministry of Education of Singapore, http://www.moe.gov.sg/education/secondary/courses/ (accessed June 2012).
6. See the website of UCIE (University of Cambridge International Examinations) at http://www.cie.org.uk/ (accessed June 2012).
7. See the websites of the U.S. Department of Education ("Secondary Curriculum Subjects" webpage, http://www.education.gov.uk/schools/teachingandlearning/curriculum/secondary) and the Australian Curriculum, Assessment, and Reporting Authority (www.acara.edu.au) (both URLs accessed June 2012).
8. The level of detail specific to a subject area, and frequently, changes from grade to grade, are absent from assessment objectives. The result is that elements such as higher-order thinking skills, science enquiry skills, mathematics problem-solving

skills, and generic skills—although mentioned in passing as desirable in curriculum documents—are neither taught nor assessed in a significant manner. The idea that a test can provide some indication of how well learners of a particular chronological age are likely to understand the textbooks written for them should be used with caution, however, as many factors can influence students' understanding that are not taken into account by most test formulae.

9. The Fry Readability Formula assigns an approximate grade reading level to a passage of text by plotting the average number of sentences and syllables in a sample text passage on the Fry Readability Graph.

10. A recent World Bank publication (2005, 80) defined metacognitive skills as the abilities to:

    integrate formal and informal learning, declarative knowledge ("knowing that"), and procedural knowledge (know-how);
    access, select, and evaluate knowledge in an information-soaked world;
    develop and apply forms of intelligence beyond strictly cognitive processes;
    work and learn effectively and in teams;
    face, transform, and peacefully resolve conflict, which involves participatory and active citizenship skills;
    create, transpose, and transfer knowledge;
    deal with ambiguous situations, unpredictable problems, and unforeseeable circumstances; and
    cope with multiple careers by learning how to locate oneself in a job market and to choose and fashion the relevant education and training.

11. Addressing these shortcomings requires sensitization, understanding, and training—not only for teachers and textbook writers, but for the entire education system. A training program in gender-responsive pedagogy is, for example, offered by UNESCO through its Regional Centre for Guidance, Counseling, and Youth Development for Africa in Lilongwe, Malawi. The Forum for African Women Educationalists (FAWE) has also developed useful materials on gender-responsive pedagogy (see FAWE 2011).

12. This projection assumes a primary education completion rate of 95 percent and a primary-to-secondary transition rate of 80 percent.

13. In certain countries, Germany and Singapore among them, content differentiation starts even earlier than grade 7.

14. Preparing for work is a stated objective of both the first and second cycles of secondary education, as indicated in the curriculum framework for Ethiopian education (Ethiopia 2009), but to date this objective has not been addressed effectively.

References

Atchoarena, David, and André Marcel Delluc. 2001. "Revisiting Technical and Vocational Education in Sub-Saharan Africa: An Update on Trends, Innovations and Challenges." Final Report (November). IIEP/Prg.DA/01.320 Rev, IIEP (International Institute for Educational Planning), UNESCO, Paris, for the World Bank.

Bass, Julian M. 2011. "An Early-Stage ICT Maturity Model Derived from Ethiopian Education Institutions." *International Journal of Education and Development Using Information and Communication Technology (IJEDICT)* 7 (1): 5–26.

Benevot, Aaron. 2006. "The Diversification of Secondary Education: School Curricula in Comparative Perspective." IBE Working Paper on Curriculum Issues 6. International Bureau of Education (IBE), UNESCO, Geneva.

Clegg, Andrew. 2011. "Ensuring Relevance and Improving Quality." Background paper prepared for *Secondary Education in Ethiopia.* World Bank Ethiopia Office, Addis Ababa. Unpublished. (Available upon request of Rajendra Joshi, rjoshi@worldbak.org.)

Cuban, Larry. 1986. *Teachers and Machines: The Classroom Use of Technology since 1920.* New York: Teacher's College Press.

———. 1992. "Curriculum Stability and Change." In *Handbook of Research on Curriculum,* ed. Phillip W. Jackson, 216–47. New York: Macmillan Library Reference.

———. 2001. *Oversold and Underused: Computers in the Classroom.* Cambridge, MA: Harvard University Press.

Ethiopia, Federal Democratic Republic of MOE (Ministry of Education). 2009. "Curriculum Framework for Ethiopian Education (KG–Grade 12)." MOE, Addis Ababa.

———. 2010a. "Concept Paper and Strategies for Improving Science and Mathematics Education in Ethiopia." MOE, Addis Ababa.

———. 2010b. "Education Sector Development Program IV (ESDP IV) 2010/11–2014/15 (2003 EC–2007 EC), Program Action Plan." MOE, Addis Ababa.

FAWE (Forum for African Women Educationists). 2011. "Improving the Quality of Teaching and Learning: FAWE's Gender-Responsive Pedagogy Model." FAWE, Nairobi. http://www.fawe.org/resource/focus/gr-pedagogy-september-2011/index.php.

Fensham, Peter J. 2008. "Science Education Policy Making: Eleven Emerging Issues." "Report commissioned by Section for Science, Technical, and Vocational Education, UNESCO, Paris.

Gregorio, Lucille C., and Sobhi Tawil, eds. 2003. "Building the Capacities of Curriculum Specialists for Educational Reform." Final Report of the Regional Seminar, Vientiane, Lao PDR. UNESCO Asia and Pacific Regional Bureau for Education, Bangkok, September 9–13, 2002.

Gregory, Kelvin. 2011. "National Examinations." Paper prepared for the General Education Quality Improvement Program, MOE, Ethiopia, Addis Ababa. Unpublished.

Heugh, Kathleen, Carol Benson, Berhanu Bogale, and Mekonnen Alemu Gebre Yohannes. 2007. "Final Report: Study on Medium of Instruction in Primary Schools in Ethiopia." Study commissioned by MOE, Federal Democratic Republic of Ethiopia, Addis Ababa.

South Africa, Republic of Department of Basic Education. 2005. "Curriculum 2005." Department of Basic Education, Pretoria.

Verspoor, Adriaan M. 2008. *At the Crossroads: Choices for Secondary Education in Sub-Saharan Africa.* With the SEIA Team. Africa Human Development Series. Washington, DC: World Bank.

Ware, S. 1992. "Secondary School Science in Developing Countries: Status and Issues." Document 17347 (PHREE/92/53). PHREE Background Paper Series. World Bank, Washington, DC.

World Bank. 2005. *Expanding Opportunities and Building Competencies for Young People: A New Agenda for Secondary Education.* Directions in Development Series. Washington, DC: World Bank.

CHAPTER 5

Teacher Preparation and Development

Recent changes in pre-service training for secondary teachers in Ethiopia have made supply issues appear manageable, although it may be challenging to recruit teachers in subject areas with high external demand (for example, physics), as well as to staff small schools. The principal challenge of teacher policy will be to implement a quality-focused teacher development strategy that emphasizes student-centered learning and reflective teaching. These objectives require a strategy designed to improve teachers' instructional competence through pre- and in-service programs. In parallel, the strategy needs to establish a policy framework for teacher management, with clear standards for teacher performance and incentives for teachers to reach these standards.

The current Education Sector Development Program (ESDP IV; MOE 2010a) lists the development of teachers and school leaders first among its priorities for improving the quality of primary and secondary education.[1] This priority is consistent with international experience and evidence. It is also a task that has often been more difficult and challenging than expected. But it must be addressed successfully if the education system is to effectively support the growth and transformation of the economy, as teacher performance is one of the major determinants of student learning achievement.

The Teacher Training System

The teacher training system in Ethiopia is divided into two parts, one for primary and one for secondary teachers. Colleges of Teacher Education (CTEs) train teachers for the first (grades 1–4) and second (grades 5–8) cycles of primary education. While training for the first cycle concentrates on preparing teachers for an integrated curriculum, the second cycle prepares teachers for a subject-based curriculum. Until academic year 2009/10 the qualification required for the first cycle was a one-year certificate in teachers' training upon completion of grade 10 and for the second cycle, a three-year diploma upon completion of grade 10.

Secondary teachers in Ethiopia have traditionally been trained at universities in four-year degree programs, which combined educational coursework and practicum experience with academic courses in various disciplines. Educational coursework was conducted by members of the faculties of education. Qualification requirements were raised in 2010 and the first-cycle primary school teacher training was changed from a one-year certificate to a three-year diploma program. Secondary teacher training changed from an integrated four-year educational bachelor's degree to a three-year degree course in a major field, plus an additional year of professional teacher training to obtain a Post-Graduate Diploma in Teaching (PGDT). The one-year professional education program consists of training in educational foundations, pedagogy, and school-based practicum experience. In addition, English teachers receive additional language training and a Higher Diploma Program (HDP) is available to teacher educators at CTEs and universities. On the job, teachers participate in continuous professional development (CPD) programs.

To date, there is no differentiation between teachers preparing to teach the general secondary (grades 9–10) and preparatory secondary (grades 11–12) levels. The Ministry of Education (MOE) is, however, considering raising the qualification requirement for the preparatory level to a master's degree.

Despite significant efforts to promote active learning, continuous assessment, reflective teaching, the development of higher-order thinking skills, and action research, studies and observations indicate that Ethiopian classrooms at all levels remain primarily teacher centered. Teachers use didactic instruction—there is little evidence of the use of inquiry processes, the development of metacognitive skills, or enhanced creativity (see, for example, Hailegiorgis 2010).

PGDT is designed to confront several problems of the old teacher training program, including:

- Inadequate subject-matter competence on the part of teachers
- Insufficient and improper active learning methods in the classroom
- Insufficient professional commitment and work ethic among teachers
- Lack of teacher interest in following up and assisting students
- Poor school-community relationships.

It is important that PGDT not prepare teachers for traditional schools and classrooms, but to become the vanguard of a new teaching approach that imparts the scientific method and creative, higher-order (metacognitive) skills, as discussed in chapters 1 and 4. The program emphasizes that teacher training programs model strategies for both dealing with variations in students' individual learning styles and promote active learning and reflection. Different instruments will be used to assess student learning progress than in the past, with regular monitoring, recording, and feedback provided to students and parents. Teachers will learn to identify their own learning needs, manage their professional development, and continuously update their subject-matter knowledge.

Given that educational policies and curriculum frameworks underpin this process, teachers will also be prepared to participate in curriculum development. Finally, the program underscores the importance of establishing and maintaining partnerships between schools and their surrounding communities.

In addition to the reorganization of pre-service training by PGDT, teacher management issues are being addressed as part of the General Education Quality Improvement Program (GEQIP). Recent reforms include new teacher candidate selection processes, practicum experiences, mentoring, career ladders, licensing and relicensing procedures, and CPD.

Teacher Demand and Supply

The number of secondary teachers has grown rapidly in the country, from 28,183 (3,008 females) in 2006/07 to 52,731 (9,690 females) in 2010/11. This increase reflects the continued growth of secondary student enrollment in recent years. Between 2006/07 and 2009/10, enrollment in grades 9–10 grew at an annual rate of almost 6 percent, while the number of students in grades 11–12 grew at an annual rate of almost 12 percent. Table 5.1 shows the secondary education enrollment targets set for 2014/15 in ESDP IV, as well as the enrollment targets implicit in its longer-term policy objectives.

Estimating teacher demand entails not only estimating the total number needed, but also analyzing subject requirements. The rapid overall increase in teacher requirements in ESDP IV results from several factors shown in table 5.1: (1) very rapid enrollment growth; (2) a projected decrease in class size (that is,

Table 5.1 Actual and Projected Enrollment and Teacher Requirements, 2009/10–2024/25

	2009/10 (actual)	2014/15 (projected)	2019/20 (projected)	2024/25 (projected)
Grades 9–10				
Enrollment	1,414,797	2,108,193	3,185,892	4,427,991
Nongovernment enrollment (% of total)	5.2%	10.0%	10.0%	10.0%
Students per section	64.2	50	50	50
Teacher-section ratio	1.6	1.6	1.6	1.6
Total number of teachers	31,984	60,716	91,754	127,526
Student-teacher ratio	41.9	31.3	31.3	31.3
Grades 11–12				
Enrollment	241,068	431,316	669,507	1,154,138
Students per section	48	40	40	40
Teacher-section ratio	1.66	1.66	1.66	1.66
Total number of teachers	7,671	16,110	25,006	43,107
Student-teacher ratio	28.9	24.1	24.1	24.1
Grades 9–12				
Total number of teachers	39,656	76,826	116,760	170,633
% of teachers who left in previous year	2.6	2.6	2.6	2.6
New teachers to be recruited annually		8,263	15,718	12,107

Sources: MOE 2010b; financial projection model of ESDP IV (MOE 2010a), as updated by World Bank in September 2011.

> **Box 5.1**
>
> ### Calculating the Number of Required Secondary Teachers
>
> The number of teachers that need to be recruited in year t_1 (R_{t1}) will be:
>
> $$R_{t1} = ((E_{t1}/SS_{t1}) \times RTS_{t1}) - T_{t0} + TL$$
>
> Where E = enrollment
> SS = section (class) size
> RTS = ratio of teachers to sections
> T = Number of teachers in place
> TL = Number of teachers who have left the teaching profession
>
> The principal policy targets that determine the number of teachers required are: (1) the number of pupils per class (section), that is, class size, and (2) the ratio of full-time teacher equivalents per section. The latter is the number of teachers required to deliver 30 periods of 40 minutes, or 1,200 minutes, of instruction each week in grades 9 and 10. With a weekly teacher workload of 22.5 hours, or 1,350 minutes, this ratio works out to be 0.9. At the preparatory level, the ratio slightly exceeds 1.
>
> *Source:* ESDV IV Simulation Model (MOE 2010a).

students per section); and (3) an increase in the number of teachers per section. EDSP IV projections would require graduating an average of more than 10,000 teachers every year for the next 15 years, compared with a past annual output of some 3,000–4,000 from the 3-year degree program.[2] Box 5.1 describes the method for calculating teacher requirements used by the EDSP IV financial projection model.

The teacher requirement calculated on the basis of ESDP IV parameters most probably represents a high-end estimate for at least three reasons. First, the objective of 100 percent gross enrollment rare (GER) in grades 9–10 may be difficult to achieve by 2024/25; the average for lower-middle-income countries is 72 percent. Second, the teacher-section ratio is high; teachers are officially expected to have 22.5 contact hours, but a ratio of 1.5 teachers per section in grades 9–10 means that teachers would teach only 20 periods, or 13.3 hours per week. The projected 1.8 ratio for grades 11–12 would mean a teaching load of 17 periods, or 11.1 hours. Third, the plan to decrease class size to 50 students in grades 9 and 10 may seem a reasonable objective at first glance, but it is not clear that decreasing it to 40 students in grades 11 and 12 would be justified, given that this decrease may not have a measurable impact on student learning. In fact, research evidence suggests that investments in improving teacher competence may have a larger impact on student learning than decreasing class size (Wößmann 2006).

The number of teachers required is further affected by the efficiency of their deployment by school size (that is, number of students enrolled), while meeting the timetable prescribed in the curriculum. Teacher requirements by subject for each school will obviously vary depending on the grades and number of sections per grade that are offered. The first issue here is that the current large number of subjects (14) at the secondary level requires the recruitment of 14 teachers with different specializations, as teachers are typically qualified to teach only one subject.

The second issue is the wide variation in the number of periods of instruction projected for different subjects, ranging from 4 periods for general business and 6 for technical drawing in preparatory schools, to 90 periods of mathematics and 84 periods of English for a school with 12 sections each in grades 9 and 10, 2 sections each in grades 11 and 12 for natural science, and one section each in grades 11 and 12 for social science (see table 5.2). Such a school would have 1,440 students and allow for 20 percent of grade 10 students to continue to grade 11.

These requirements will make it challenging to reach the ESDP IV goal of increasing general secondary education in rural areas from 20 percent to 35 percent (30 percent in Afar and Somali) unless a model for staffing small rural schools is developed that stresses the importance of encouraging teachers to acquire qualifications via "minors" in second or even third subject areas. For example, a school offering only grades 9 and 10 with 4 sections of 50 students each (400 students total) would provide a full teaching load of 20 hours (30 periods of 40 minutes each) only to mathematics and English teachers; Amharic, ICT, history, and geography teachers would have only 16 hours (24 periods) and the physical education teacher, only 5 hours and 20 minutes

Table 5.2 Teacher Requirements by Subject in Grade 9–12 School of 1,440 Students

Subject	Grade 9	Grade 10	Natural sciences Grade 11	Natural sciences Grade 12	Social sciences Grade 11	Social sciences Grade 12	Total number of periods	Periods per teacher	Number of teachers	% of teachers for each subject
Amharic	2	2	3	3	3	3	66	33	2	5.9
English	4	4	6	6	6	6	132	26	5	14.7
Mathematics	5	5	5	5	5	5	150	30	5	14.7
ICT	2	2	3	3	3	3	66	33	2	5.9
Physics	3	3	4	4	n.a.	n.a.	88	29	3	8.8
Chemistry	3	3	4	4	n.a.	n.a.	88	29	3	8.8
Biology	3	3	4	4	n.a.	n.a.	88	29	3	8.8
Technical drawing	n.a.	n.a.	2	2	n.a.	n.a.	8	8	1	2.9
Civics	3	3	3	3	3	3	90	30	3	8.8
Geography	2	2	n.a.	n.a.	4	4	56	28	2	5.9
History	2	2	n.a.	n.a.	4	4	56	28	2	5.9
Economics	n.a.	n.a.	n.a.	n.a.	4	4	8	8	1	2.9
General business	n.a.	n.a.	n.a	n.a.	2	2	4	4	1	2.9
Physical education	1	1	1	1	1	1	30	30	1	2.9
Total	30	30	35	35	35	35	930	27.4	34	100

Source: MOE 2010a, as updated by World Bank in September 2011; World Bank data.
Note: Projections assume 12 sections each for general instruction in grades 9 and 10, with 50 students in each section; 2 sections each in grades 11 and 12 for natural science and one section each for social science, with 40 students per section. The average workload per teacher is assumed to be 30 periods, with possible supplementary hours of 10 percent. ICT = Information and communication technology, n.a. = Not applicable.

(8 periods). To recruit 400 students, moreover, the school would need to be accessible to students in a catchment area with a population of more than 7,000 people. Yet 84 percent of the Ethiopian people live in rural areas with settlements of 2,000 people (Ethiopia 2010), which could provide, at most, 100 students for grades 9 and 10. The large majority (83.2 percent) of secondary schools are currently located in urban areas.

The ESDP IV simulation model also includes a projection of university enrollment targets in the third year of study by academic field through 2024/25 (table 5.3). These targets include streaming 20 percent of grade 10 graduates into grade 11 and assigning 70 percent of them to natural science-related fields.

Based on the third-year enrollment projections in table 5.3, the relationship between secondary teacher requirements by subject cluster and the size of the potential teacher candidate pool are estimated in table 5.4. That table suggests that in all subject clusters except for Amharic, English, civics, history, and geography, the new PGDT program will be able to select from among a large group

Table 5.3 Projected Third-Year University Enrollments by Field of Study, Selected Years

Academic field of study	Target share of enrollment in first year of study (%)	Number of students enrolled in third year			
		2009	2014	2019	2024
Engineering and technology	40	5,517	3,0240	80,565	139,350
Natural and computational sciences	20	6,850	13,079	35,807	61,933
Medicine and health sciences	5	5,064	5,686	8,952	15,483
Agriculture and life sciences	5	4,601	4,554	8,952	15,483
Business and economics	20	8,726	13,648	35,807	61,933
Social sciences and humanities	10	8,499	8,527	17,903	3,0967
Total	100	39,257	75,734	187,986	325,149

Source: MOE 2010a, as updated by World Bank in September 2011.

Table 5.4 Estimated Teacher Demand and Supply by Subject, 2019

Subject clusters in curricula of grades 9–12	Estimated number of third-year university students in relevant field	Teachers required by subject		
		As a % of total number of teachers required	Number	As % of all third-year students in relevant academic field
Mathematics, ICT, physics, chemistry, technical drawing	116,372	41.1	6,460	5.6
Biology	17,904	8.8	1,383	7.7
Economics, general business	35,807	5.8	912	2.5
Amharic, English, civics, history, geography	17,903	41.2	6,476	36.2
Physical Education	—	2.9	456	—
Total	187,986	100	15,718	8.4

Source: Financial projection model of ESDP IV (MOE 2010a), as updated by the World Bank in September 2011.
Note: — = Not available.

of university students. For a more accurate picture of teacher demand and supply, analysis would need to be conducted by subject, but enrollment projections are not available for individual subjects.

But these calculations do not adequately reflect actual available teacher supply, as they do not account for differential employment opportunities available to graduates of bachelor-degree university programs. In fact, contrary to the estimates in table 5.3, the experience of the first year of PGDT recruitment suggests a large number of candidate social science teachers are available, but that candidate physics teachers with sufficiently high grade point averages may be difficult to find.[3] It will be important to monitor whether this trend persists.

Overall, analysis of teacher demand and supply issues in this section suggests that:

- The challenges of secondary teacher education are not so much challenges of quantity, but rather of quality. The rapid expansion of university enrollment should ensure an adequate supply of qualified candidates for teacher training, but it may be difficult to recruit high-quality candidates in certain disciplines, such as physics.
- Staffing small schools deserves special attention. Although it may be possible to combine certain teaching assignments (for example, an economics teacher should be able to teach general business, and a physics teacher might be able to teach mathematics), it will be important to encourage and provide teachers opportunities to acquire qualifications in "minors" in second and even third subject areas.

Improving Teacher Effectiveness

Teacher education is best conceived of and organized as a seamless continuum with three stages:

- *Initial teacher training and education:* a pre-service course before entering the classroom as a fully responsible teacher
- *Induction:* the process of providing training and support during the first few years of teaching or during the first year in a particular school
- *Teacher development* or *continuing professional development:* support for practicing teachers.

Becoming an accomplished, effective teacher involves completing quality pre-service training and a career-long process of professional growth in which instructional strategies are updated and new skills acquired. Ethiopia launched the PGDT program to improve the pre-service phase of teacher education. Yet the country will also need to develop robust induction programs, followed by enhanced continuous professional development. To bring about desired improvements in teacher performance, teacher education programs will, moreover, need to be complemented by a teacher management system that recognizes and rewards good teacher performance and enhances teacher motivation.

One important distinction between teacher policies in developing and developed countries is that developing countries have tended to focus more on the supply side (teacher preparation and development), while developed countries have focused on both the demand (teacher motivation) and supply sides (Lynd 2005). The critical challenge for countries on the path from a low- to middle-income economy is establishing a robust demand-side system for improving teacher performance.

Improving Pre-Service Teacher Training: PGDT

The first class of students to participate in the PGDT program began their postgraduate training in September 2011. It is far too early to make any judgments about how successful it will be in practice. The challenge will be implementing PGDT in such a way that it has a tangible impact on classroom instructional practice. Potential actions and policy changes to achieve this goal may include:

- Developing new training modules to enhance the ability of teachers to teach higher-order (that is, metacognitive) skills
- Enhancing the capacity of university staff to model and teach PGDT instructional methods and supervise the teaching practicums of their students
- Tightening selection criteria by introducing a basic skill test for admission into teacher training programs, with the aim of recruiting the top 60 percent of students completing a bachelor's degree.

Developing New Training Modules

At the moment universities are using the teacher education curricula to produce their own teaching modules. These modules guide the delivery of courses and serve in the place of textbooks in subjects where no textbooks exist. This ad-hoc approach has resulted in variable standards, duplication of effort, and inefficiencies in reproduction.

GEQIP aims to centralize and standardize the development of teacher education modules in the interest of ensuring quality across universities, aligning teacher education more closely with the new curricula, and benefitting from economies of scale. Impact studies have shown that there is presently a poor fit between the teaching methods encouraged by locally produced modules, which tend to be traditional in style, and the expected outcomes of teacher education foreseen in the PGDT (Kraft 2011b). The Ministry of Education accordingly intends to develop a total of 45 new modules that will be piloted during spring term 2012 (table 5.5). It goes without saying that the design of these modules will need to reflect the instructional approaches of PGDT.

Table 5.5 Content of MOE Teacher Education Modules

• Background (conceptual base)	• Content and skills
• Program (content) standards	• Instructional materials
• Benchmark	• Materials and resources
• Performance indicators	• Core activities
• Planned course	• Assessment
• Course standards	• Enrichment
• Unit standards	• Re-teaching
• Lesson standards	

Source: Kraft 2011b, 17.

Enhancing the Capacity of University Teaching Staff

The quality of university instruction will ultimately determine the quality of teacher graduates and the extent to which changes in instructional practice and student learning performance meet PGDT objectives. Many university instructors are unfamiliar with student-centered teaching strategies; few practice interactive methods or are capable of modeling instructional approaches that develop metacognitive skills. Nor do many have first-hand experience of secondary school teaching.

The PGDT program reflects the goals and practice of the Higher Degree Program (HDP) of the MOE, in which most current teacher educators at the university level received their training. It is not evident however, that HDP has had the desired effect on university teacher educators, nor has it had much impact on teacher graduates in secondary schools. Measures that may be considered to address university staff capacity include:

- Reviewing the results of HDP and implementing changes in its design to correct weaknesses and align it more closely with PGDT content and methods
- Making teaching experience in a secondary school a criterion for the recruitment and promotion of university staff
- Encouraging university staff to take sabbatical leave for teaching assignments in secondary schools
- Assessing whether the incentive system for university instructors needs to be modified to achieve the objectives of the PGDT program.

Tightening Selection Criteria

Different countries use different combinations of mechanisms to screen teacher candidates, attempting to ensure that the best candidates actually become employed in the profession (appendix D). Essentially, three mechanisms are used—often in combination—to screen teachers: (1) marks and/or grades at the qualifying level of education; (2) interviews; and (3) examinations. Interviews are typically used to ascertain a future teacher's true interest in the profession and the suitability of their personality for teaching, as well as their communication skills and other factors. Examinations are organized to ensure that university graduates with a major or minor in their intended teaching field have sufficient subject-matter knowledge to teach at the appropriate level.

Whether a screening device should be of low, medium, or high significance generally depends on supply and demand, not the quality of teacher candidates. Working conditions of teachers, as well as alternative employment opportunities, will affect the number of applicants for teacher training in important ways. Entry into a teacher education program is highly competitive in Japan, the Republic of Korea, The Netherlands, and Singapore—where the teaching profession is prestigious and well rewarded—hence only the better students are admitted. England and Singapore even require an examination for entrance into a postgraduate teacher education program. In contrast, selection policies for teaching programs in the United States are considered medium stakes, as future teachers seldom have difficulty entering a program and neither professional salary nor prestige is considered very high, although teacher salaries are competitive with a few professions in the country.

In countries where a significant proportion of the students who apply to teacher training programs come from the lower-achieving half of the university cohort or significant achievement problems exist in schools, some form of basic skills testing in reading and mathematics is often used as an admission criterion (ETS 2003). Given the significant student achievement problems highlighted by different national learning achievement tests in Ethiopia and the rapidly increasing supply of university graduates—especially from natural sciences and economics programs—it would appear that high-stakes selection policies would be appropriate and feasible for the country.

Where there is ample supply of qualified applicants, admission criteria can be tightened. If the rate of growth of university admissions in Ethiopia comes close to the projections presented earlier in this chapter, it may be possible to institute a series of high-stakes filters in certain disciplines in order to assure that the best and brightest candidates enter teacher training programs, graduate, and are employed as secondary teachers.

Continuous Professional Development

There is a consensus in the literature that initial teacher training is just the first step on the road to becoming a competent teacher. Even under the best circumstances, changes in initial teacher training will only gradually affect what happens in schools and classrooms. New teachers need to be supported as they enter the profession. Longer-serving teachers need to improve and update their professional knowledge and skills. Effective programs for the continuous professional development of existing teachers are thus critical to bringing about desired changes in instructional practices and, consequently, measurable improvements in student learning. Good CPD plans exist in Ethiopia, but as in the case of pre-service training, effective implementation remains a challenge. It is critical that the country use a decentralized system to deliver training support and supervision to schools and teachers.

Box 5.2

Induction Programs for Beginning Teachers

Induction programs for new teachers are gaining in popularity as a tool to help decrease new teacher turnover, strengthen teacher practices, and improve student learning. Switzerland, Japan, France, New Zealand, and the city of Shanghai, China, have well-established programs to support teachers. These well-funded programs support all beginning teachers, incorporate multiple sources of assistance, typically last at least two years, and go beyond mentoring and survival skills. In Switzerland, new teachers are involved in practice groups where they network to learn effective problem solving. In Shanghai, new teachers join lesson-preparation and teaching-research groups. New teachers in New Zealand take part in an advice and guidance program for two years. Lesson study groups are the mode of induction support in Japan, while in France, new teachers work for an extended time with groups of peers who share their experiences, practices, and tools. While there are considerable differences among the approaches of these countries, their induction programs have three major similarities: they are highly structured, focus on professional learning, and emphasize collaboration.

Source: Wong et al. 2005.

Support for Beginning Teachers

The change in the duration of teacher education programs from three to one years under PGDT makes effective professional support for beginning teachers important. Such programs have been identified as particularly effective for promoting instructional effectiveness, student learning, and teacher retention (Thompson et al. 2005). Box 5.2 provides examples of beginning teacher induction programs from several industrialized countries and the city of Shanghai.

Support for Longer-serving Teachers

Much of GEQIP was designed to address the professional development needs of teachers by enhancing continuing professional development at the school level and providing English-language training for all teachers who use English as the language of instruction, including teachers of English. The goals of CPD in Ethiopia are shown in box 5.3. Strengthening professional development as part of an integrated teacher education program involves addressing both short- and medium-term priorities, including:

- Developing additional CPD modules with a special emphasis on pedagogical content knowledge (see below).
- Targeting mathematics, science, and English for special attention
- Institutionalizing CPD as a permanent, integral feature of teacher education.

Box 5.3

Goals of CPD in Ethiopia

- Assessing and reporting student learning
- Making teachers capable of managing their own CPD
- Mastery of curriculum
- Forming partnerships with local school communities

Source: MOE 2009a

Developing CPD Modules

Most of the professional development effort to date has involved running workshops on the CDP Framework established by MOE (2009a) and reviewing its CPD Practical Toolkit. Teachers all over the country have conducted needs assessments, but have tended to come up with the same list of requested training topics: active learning, action research, teaching large classes, classroom management, and occasionally, reflective teaching.

Two national-level CPD modules were produced on teacher portfolios and mentoring. These modules were trialed in 2009 and 2010, but so far there is little evidence that they have been widely used in CPD trainings. Development of further modules could be supported by the creation of registries at the national, regional, and woreda levels to keep track of outstanding classrooms and schools (for observation); talented university instructors; helpful workshops, courses, and instructional videos; available NGO and volunteer resources; and new instructional materials and assessments. These materials could then be accessed at the school or cluster level.

It will be important to continue to develop training modules that address teachers' subject-matter knowledge, instructional practices, and ability to teach higher-order skills. Several countries, Indonesia among them, have discovered serious problems with teachers' subject-matter knowledge (Kraft 2011a).[4] The disappointing performance of Ethiopian students on learning assessments and national examinations suggests that Ethiopia faces a similar problem. In addition, there is growing awareness throughout the world that effective instructional practices complement subject-matter knowledge in what is termed pedagogical content knowledge (PCK).

PCK is a form of *practical* knowledge that is used by teachers to guide their actions in classroom settings. It consists, among other things, of knowing: (1) how to structure and identify academic content in order to teach students; (2) understanding the common conceptions, misconceptions, and difficulties that students encounter when learning particular content; and (3) specific teaching strategies that can be used to address students' learning needs in particular classroom circumstances (appendix E). Finally, given the increasing importance of metacognitive skills (chapters 1 and 4), it is important that teachers be able to help students develop these skills, enabling them "to learn how to learn."

Supporting Science, Mathematics, and English
Given the policy choices of (1) making English the language of instruction at the secondary level and higher and (2) streaming 70 percent of secondary graduates into natural science disciplines, improving the professional competence of teachers should be a CPD priority for many years to come, especially in light of the poor performance of Ethiopian students on national learning assessments and examinations (chapter 2). At the top level, strategies exist to create centers that specialize in mathematics, the sciences, and English to meet the emerging demand for teacher support and good teaching materials. The proposed model for science and mathematics is to create a National Science and Mathematics Center with a small number of regional campuses.

A continentwide survey of science, mathematics, and information and communication technology (ICT) education in Africa at the secondary level, carried out under the auspices of the World Bank, highlights a number of teacher support centers established over the last 30 years or so (Ottevanger et al. 2005). Many of these centers were set up explicitly to support science and mathematics, usually with donor assistance, and were apparently effective for a time, but generally fell into disuse after donor funding dried up or key staff members left. If the proposed center in Ethiopia is not to suffer the same fate, it will require a long-term financial commitment, continual staff training, and a degree of immunity from budget cuts. It will also need to satisfy a demonstrable need of science and mathematics teachers. Ultimately it may move toward being self-sustaining. Careful consideration should be given to its governance in order to allow and encourage the center to attract private funding. South Africa provides an interesting example of a public-private partnership in this regard (box 5.4).

Considerable evidence from research and classroom observation in Ethiopia strongly suggests the need for continuing professional development interventions to ensure that English teachers in the country are proficient in the language and have up-to-date pedagogical skills (see, for example, MOE 2010a; Kraft 2011b). English teachers are not the only instructors who need this support. Vast numbers of teachers of other subjects must also improve their English-language skills because, depending on the region, English becomes the medium of instruction starting in grade 5, 7, or 9. An English-Language Quality Improvement Program (ELQIP) has accordingly been launched and its implementation needs to be monitored closely. It is expected that the program will need to endure for a considerable period of time, expanding coverage to include teachers of subjects other than English who use English as the language of instruction at these grade levels and above.

> **Box 5.4**
>
> **South African Science Centers**
>
> South Africa has in recent years developed a remarkably effective network of Science Centers, a development driven in part by private sector funding (particularly from the mobile telephone company MTN) and in part by the government requirement that all national science facilities (for example, museums, the Sutherland Telescope, Koeberg Nuclear Reactor) have an outreach arm. Many of the centers were developed to support teachers and classes that are bussed into the facilities. In other instances, staff from the centers do outreach work in schools. Some centers are even science or science education departments of universities.
>
> While the network of Science Centers is not officially part of an organized teacher support system in the country, good centers provide considerable support to teachers and schools in their areas. A key goal of all centers is to ultimately become self-sustaining through the services that they offer.
>
> *Source:* Clegg 2011, 38.

Lasting improvement in instructional effectiveness will require the institutionalization of continuous professional development. CPD needs to be conceptualized and funded as a part of the teacher education system that is considered at least as important as pre-service training. For this purpose a combination of the following interventions could be considered:

- Establishing a mandate for and developing the capacity of universities to actively support teacher induction and CPD programs (university staff would be expected to work collaboratively with teachers to improve their instructional practices and themselves be exposed to the realities of classroom teaching)
- Strengthening decentralized support structures by developing a cadre of CPD counselors and instructors at the regional and woreda levels, as well as experienced lead teachers and mentors for all subjects at the school and cluster levels
- Linking the CPD program to standards-based licensing and relicensing programs not only to encourage teacher participation on a regular basis, but to make this participation part of their professional responsibilities.

Teacher Management

Managing teachers' performance and development is a critical component of improving the quality of teaching. Well-organized teacher education programs are an essential first step toward this goal. In addition, evidence shows that motivation is an equally important factor in teacher performance. Financial incentives, professional recognition, career prospects, and supportive working conditions have all been identified as having a positive influence on teacher job satisfaction and performance (Bennell 2007; Fry 2010).

In many middle- and high-income countries teacher demand drives teacher development, as teachers are motivated to improve their knowledge and skills—often in response to job performance evaluations. The supply of training opportunities is designed to respond to this demand. Conversely, many low-income countries have top-down approaches to teacher development; teacher job satisfaction in these countries has also not been adequately addressed by educational quality improvement programs.

Although considerable progress has been made in developing teacher education programs in Ethiopia, less progress has been made in addressing issues of teacher motivation. Unless addressed, these issues may become a major obstacle to improving classroom instruction and student learning achievement. In well-performing education systems, improvements in teacher effectiveness have been complemented by teacher management systems that:

- Establish clear standards for teacher performance.
- Provide for accreditation of teacher education programs and institutions.
- Ensure career growth opportunities for teachers.
- Develop school principals as instructional leaders.

Establishing Standards

Teacher standards define the range of skills, knowledge, and values that all teachers are expected to master during pre-service training and continuous professional development programs. Standards are now found in almost all countries of the world. England, for example, has established teacher standards for beginner through advanced teachers. Box 5.5 provides an example of standards that have been adopted throughout most of the 50 states of the United States.

Standards are the foundation of effective teacher management. They should clearly reflect defined professional responsibilities and be accompanied by performance indicators. These indicators should provide examples of observable, tangible behaviors that indicate the degree to which teachers meet each standard. Without standards and indicators it is difficult to distinguish between poor, average, good, and excellent teachers. This has significant adverse effects on teacher performance because excellence is not recognized, poor performance is not addressed, and priorities for professional development are not identified.

Ethiopian teaching standards for secondary education list only five categories, but include within them almost all standards found throughout the world. However, the Ethiopian standards are less specific. The categories are:

- Facilitate student learning.
- Assess student learning and use the information to improve teaching practices and student learning.

Box 5.5

Teaching Standards in the United States

The Council of Chief State School Officers (CCSSO) in the United States, through its Interstate Teacher Assessment and Support Consortium (InTASC), has prepared a set of model core teaching standards. These standards, summarized below, outline what teachers should know and be able to do to ensure that every K–12 student reaches the goal of being ready to enter college or the workforce in today's world. These standards were released in April 2011; they outline the common principles and foundations of teaching practice that cut across all subject areas and grade levels and are necessary to improve student achievement.

The Learner and Learning

Standard #1: Learner Development. The teacher understands how learners grow and develop, recognizing that patterns of learning and development vary individually within and across the cognitive, linguistic, social, emotional, and physical areas, and designs and implements developmentally appropriate and challenging learning experiences.

Standard #2: Learning Differences. The teacher uses understanding of individual differences and diverse cultures and communities to ensure inclusive learning environments that enable each learner to meet high standards.

Standard #3: Learning Environments. The teacher works with others to create environments that support individual and collaborative learning, and that encourage positive social interaction, active engagement in learning, and self-motivation.

Content

Standard #4: Content Knowledge. The teacher understands the central concepts, tools of inquiry, and structures of the discipline(s) he or she teaches and creates learning experiences that make the discipline accessible and meaningful for learners to assure mastery of the content.

Standard #5: Application of Content. The teacher understands how to connect concepts and use differing perspectives to engage learners in critical thinking, creativity, and collaborative problem solving related to authentic local and global issues.

Instructional Practice

Standard #6: Assessment. The teacher understands and uses multiple methods of assessment to engage learners in their own growth, to monitor learner progress, and to guide the teacher's and learner's decision making.

Standard #7: Planning for Instruction. The teacher plans instruction that supports every student in meeting rigorous learning goals by drawing upon knowledge of content areas, curriculum, cross-disciplinary skills, and pedagogy, as well as knowledge of learners and the community context.

(box continues on next page)

Box 5.5 Teaching Standards in the United States *(continued)*

Standard #8: Instructional Strategies. The teacher understands and uses a variety of instructional strategies to encourage learners to develop deep understanding of content areas and their connections, and to build skills to apply knowledge in meaningful ways.

Professional Responsibility

Standard #9: Professional Learning and Ethical Practice. The teacher engages in ongoing professional learning and uses evidence to continually evaluate his or her practice, particularly the effects of his or her choices and actions on others (learners, families, other professionals, and the community), and adapts practice to meet the needs of each learner.

Standard #10: Leadership and Collaboration. The teacher seeks appropriate leadership roles and opportunities to take responsibility for student learning; to collaborate with learners, families, colleagues, other school professionals, and community members to ensure learner growth; and to advance the profession.

Source: Reproduced from CCSSO 2011.

- Engage in continuous professional development.
- Understand national education policy and strategies and participate in curriculum and other program development.
- Establish and maintain partnerships with the local school community.

For these standards to work as an effective tool of teacher management, they need to become more concrete. In addition, measurable performance indicators need to be linked to each standard in order to guide teacher evaluations and performance improvement plans. Eventually, a fair evaluation process will contribute to providing teachers the support, recognition, and guidance that they need to sustain and improve their efforts.

Accreditation of Pre-Service Training Programs

In many countries the state, province, and/or nation have adopted policies to ensure that teacher education programs are of high quality and produce graduates with the competencies needed for effective instruction. International experience suggests that the most effective way to achieve this objective is through some type of formal accreditation of teacher training faculties and programs.[5]

International Trends in Accreditation

Accreditation agencies initially assessed a wide range of criteria related to teacher education programs, such as the number of professors with advanced degrees, class sizes, existence and quality of laboratories, number and employment of graduates, and a range of other "quantitative" measures. As a result, the accreditation process became little more than filling out checklists every 5 or 10 years.

More recently, accreditation systems have become much more aligned with "qualitative" and outcome-based measures. Many now assess teacher education programs by what graduating teachers actually know and how well they put their knowledge of pedagogy and academic content into practice. The relationships of teaching programs with schools and practicing teachers are also measured, not just the participation of future teachers in practicum experiences. The ability of teacher graduates to work with multicultural, special-needs, gifted, and other specific student populations have also become important in the accreditation of education programs. The standards that were recently adopted in Australia (box 5.6) are now typical of education systems throughout the world. Quality assurance of teacher education qualifications and teacher education programs are increasingly being managed by independent state agencies and professional bodies. This trend reflects a global shift toward a model that has long existed in the United States and is now being implemented in much of Europe.

Managing Accreditation

Management models for quality assurance and accreditation differ according to specific national conditions; however, standards and accreditation agencies worldwide share several common features:

- They link institutional accreditation closely to the implementation of standards for teacher registration and teacher licensing.
- They are responsible for setting standards for the outcomes of teacher education programs and teacher licenses.
- They are independent of both the government and universities, but have strong representation of teachers and teacher educators. These organizations are, in fact, self-regulating professional bodies.
- They are funded by registration and accreditation fees.

Several examples of the responsibilities, organizational arrangements, and funding mechanisms of such agencies in different countries are presented in appendix F.

In Ethiopia, reaching the PGDT objectives will require changes to and improvements of university teacher training programs. The Ethiopian MOE is attempting to "harmonize" both academic and professional courses across all universities as a means to this end. But this alone will be insufficient to improve the quality of teacher preparation. The government responded to the need for quality assurance in higher education by establishing the Higher Education Relevance and Quality Agency (HERQA) in 2003 to provide an accreditation system for higher education programs. However, the experience of HERQA to date indicates that creating an accreditation agency is not an easy task, especially if it does not have the resources, drive, independence, and clout to issue the kind of verdicts on public universities required to implement teacher standards and accreditation policies.

Box 5.6

Australia: National Program Standards for Accreditation of Initial Teacher Education Programs

Standard 1. Program outcomes: Providers must show that graduates of their programs will meet the graduate career stage of the National Professional Standards for Teachers, as well as how this will be demonstrated.

Standard 2. Program development: Programs take account of contemporary school and system needs, current professional expert knowledge, authoritative educational research findings, and community expectations.

Standard 3. Program entrants: Applicants' levels of personal literacy and numeracy should be broadly equivalent to those of the top 30 percent of the population; applicants should also possesses a discipline-specific qualification relevant to the Australian curriculum or other recognized areas of schooling provision. For secondary teaching the requirement is at least one *major* in a teaching area and, preferably, a second teaching area comprising at least one *minor*.

Standard 4. Program structure and content: Undergraduate programs for secondary teachers must provide sound depth and breadth of knowledge appropriate for the teaching area(s) their graduates intend to teach. As noted above, these programs should provide at least one *major* in a teaching area and, preferably, a second teaching area comprising at least one minor.

Standard 5. School partnerships: Teacher education providers have established enduring school partnerships to deliver their programs, particularly the professional experience component. Through these partnerships, programs provide students professional experience that enables them to work with learners at a variety of school-year levels and learn to appreciate the diversity of students and communities served by schools. Providers and their school partners also ensure that teachers who supervise students' professional experience (in particular, supervised teaching practice) are suitably qualified and registered. These supervisors should have expertise and be supported in coaching, mentoring, and making judgments about whether students have fulfilled the Graduate Teacher Standards.

Standard 6. Program delivery and resourcing: Programs must use effective teaching and assessment strategies (linked to intended learning outcomes) and provide sufficient resources, including staff, facilities, and embedded information and communication technologies.

Standard 7. Program information and evaluation: Providers must use a range of data, such as student assessment information, destination surveys, employer and other stakeholder feedback to drive improvements and periodic formal evaluations of their teacher education programs.

Source: Adapted from AITSL 2011, 12–16. Author: AITSL. Copyright holders: Standing Council on School Education and Early Childhood, and Education Services Australia.

Because of similar problems, many countries have moved toward the creation of independent accreditation agencies with the strong participation of professional teacher organizations. This has rarely been an easy task and often requires several years of study and consultation with stakeholders. Yet without an effective accreditation mechanism, it can be difficult to prepare quality teachers. In Ethiopia, the MOE may therefore want to consider phasing in a process that will ultimately result in the establishment of an independent standards and accreditation agency.

Establishing a Framework for Career Growth

Many teachers lose their motivation over time and feel frustrated by the typical flat career trajectory of the teaching profession. In response to this problem, many countries have adopted policies that provide a framework for career growth opportunities, ranging from a series of advancement opportunities for teachers both inside and outside the classroom, as well as tiered approaches to licensure. Such a framework defines teacher standards, career development opportunities, and procedures for evaluation, licensing, and relicensing. It often implies a move toward performance-based rewards and away from seniority-based pay increases (see Ingvarson et al. 2006).

Effective education systems have standards and conditions that recognize excellence and encourage good teachers to build lifelong careers in the classroom, with explicit standards for different categories of teachers, such as:

- *Intern teachers:* teachers engaged in initial training or teaching during a probationary school period
- *Newly qualified teachers:* interns deemed professionally qualified, perhaps after a probationary year
- *Qualified teachers:* teachers deemed fully qualified and experienced
- *Master teachers:* highly professional teachers who not only produce good classroom results, but also train their junior colleagues.

The licensing and re-licensing program now being designed in Ethiopia should establish standards and performance criteria for promoting teachers to each subsequent category. It should also be linked to a professional development program that provides teachers opportunities to maintain and update their knowledge and skills for career development, similar to programs found in medicine, law, and other professions. Points or credits in such a program would be awarded for such activities as module completion, face-to-face courses, distance-learning activities, mentoring, presentations at cluster and regional events, local research projects, and other "creditable" activities. A system must also be created to record participation and credit, as well as enforce mechanisms that ensure teachers participate in such activities on a regular basis. A similar system should be developed for principal and cluster supervisor positions.

Preparing Principals for Instructional Leadership

The Leadership and Management Program (LAMP) in Ethiopia aims to improve the capacity of educational leaders and managers to improve school quality. Training courses are designed based on needs assessments and capacity analyses of primary- and secondary-school management and supervisory positions in a decentralized education system. These courses emphasize the management responsibilities of principals, reflecting growing recognition of their role not only in managing schools, but also in providing instructional leadership. This latter element may need to be developed as a priority of LAMP training programs, including training principals in standards-based teacher evaluation and the development of teacher performance improvement plans.

Conclusion

Teacher supply and demand issues are likely to be manageable in Ethiopia, even if secondary enrollment expands as rapidly as planned. But staffing smaller schools in rural areas is likely to be a challenge. Many of these schools will initially offer only grades 9 and 10, often in association with existing primary education programs. Meeting their staffing needs will require a combination of the following options:

- Developing a streamlined curriculum that reorganizes subjects into clusters (that is, integrated natural science and/or social science subjects), reducing the need for specialist teachers in all subjects (chapter 4)
- Offering the opportunity to student teachers to qualify in more than one subject or in clustered subjects, possibly through additional subject-matter training with an associated salary premium (alternatively, the structure of PGDT and bachelor's degree programs could be redesigned to include a required minor)
- Encouraging grade 7 and 8 teachers to acquire the qualifications for teaching grades 9 and 10.

Improving teacher performance in the country requires a two-pronged strategy. The first prong is the development of teachers' instructional competence through pre- and in-service programs. The second is the implementation of a policy framework that establishes clear standards for teacher performance and provides incentives for teachers to reach these standards. Implementation of both will need to proceed in parallel.

Enhancing Teachers' Instructional Competence

Ethiopia has paid considerable attention to strengthening teacher preparation and development. The shift away from the three-year bachelor's degree program in education to a Post-Graduate Diploma in Teaching is aimed at strengthening teacher preparation, specifically, content mastery and first-hand teaching experience (through practicums). Yet the PGDT program alone may not be sufficient to achieve desired results. A comprehensive teacher education effort is needed that conceptualizes teacher education as a lifelong process and aligns the PGDT program, beginning teacher induction support, and continuous professional development for teachers. Priorities for action include:

- Improving the effectiveness of university teacher education programs, where implementation of new teaching modules is accompanied by intensive efforts to help university staff master new approaches and model desired instructional behaviors
- Supporting new PGDT graduates through broad-based induction programs for beginning teachers
- Developing a CPD system that can support schools and teachers at the regional and woreda levels to design and implement school-based teacher support (possibly via teacher support centers or school clusters, with key resource teachers available to support beginning teachers, model innovative approaches to the use of technology, and demonstrate practice improvement strategies, including the lesson-study approach)
- Having principals and lead teachers provide continuous school-based support and supervision to longer-serving teachers to ensure that they acquire the necessary pedagogical content knowledge and can apply it in their classrooms.

Strengthening Teacher Management

As noted earlier, there is considerable evidence that teacher motivation may be the most critical element in effective teacher performance (Bennell 2007). This is partly a function of salary and working conditions, but also of selection procedures and criteria that emphasize the longer-term interests of teacher candidates. In many countries, teachers receive rewards and recognition for exceptional performance and the acquisition of additional professional qualifications.

Ethiopia needs to strengthen its teacher management framework if teachers' instructional performance and student learning are to improve. This will require policy adjustments in several areas, but the starting point is the definition of standards and indicators of expected teacher performance. These standards and indicators will be the foundation of a fair and forward-looking teacher evaluation system that helps teachers prepare performance improvement plans. Standards will also provide the basis for accreditation of university teacher education programs, the licensing and re-licensing of teachers, and the implementation of a merit-based career progression system.

Perhaps most important, international experience suggests that successful implementation of standards-based teacher management systems ultimately requires an administrative body independent of both the Ministry of Education and universities, governed by a board with broad representation of all major stakeholders. This suggests several priorities for action:

- Establishing an independent professional body for standards development, teacher registration and licensing, and the accreditation of teacher education institutions
- Creating a career structure for teachers that allows them to progress based on demonstrated performance
- Linking pre-service (PGDT) and in-service programs explicitly to standards-based teacher career development
- Monitoring and accreditation of university teacher education programs based on (1) their record of graduating teachers whose teaching meets established standards, (2) the subject matter and pedagogical content knowledge of their teacher educators, and (3) educators' ability to model effective classroom practices and support the practicum and induction training of their students
- Strengthening the capacity of principals to become instructional leaders and effective school managers (see chapter 6) through short courses and decentralized support systems
- Gradually strengthening incentives for the professional development of teachers in order to create an environment where incentives become the main driver of their professional development, as opposed to a system where professional development efforts are mainly focused on the supply side.

It is important to realize that changes in teachers' instructional behavior occur only gradually and require not only well-designed initial training, but also continuous professional development, support, and supervision (see, for example, Hopkins 2001). Most importantly, it will require effective teacher management. Changing instructional practices involves training, supporting, and supervising teachers over a sustained period of time—a decade or more—which in turn involves an integration of initial teacher training and continuous professional development.

Notes

1. This chapter is based on Kraft 2011b.
2. Total enrollment in universities in 2008/09 was 9,496 students, of which 3,193 were in their third year of study (MOE 2009b).
3. This information was shared with the authors by Ministry of Education officials at a meeting in Addis Ababa in 2011.
4. The SACMEQ (Southern and Eastern Africa Consortium for Monitoring Educational Quality) and PASEC (Programme d'Analyse des Systèmes Educatifs; Program on the Analysis of Education Systems) assessments, the main regional evaluations of basic education achievement in Sub-Saharan Africa, have also identified problems with teacher subject mastery in several countries.

5. Formal accreditation means that an external agency endorses a professional preparation course as adequate for the purposes of a particular profession. That is, the program is able to produce graduates who meet the profession's standards for entry and are competent to begin practice.

For information on teaching standards and accreditation in the United States, see the websites of the National Council for the Accreditation of Teacher Education (NCATE)—www.ncate.org; the National Board for Professional Teacher Standards (NBPTS)—http://www.nbpts.org; and the Teacher Education Accreditation Council (TEAC)—www.teac.org. For similar bodies in other countries, see the Victorian Institute of Teaching in Australia—http://www.vit.vic.edu.au/Pages/default.aspx; the Ontario College of Teachers in Canada—http://www.oct.ca/home.aspx; and the Teachers' Council (KHURUSAPHA) of Thailand—http://www.ksp.org.th/Khurusapha/en (all URLs accessed May 2012).

References

AITSL (Australian Institute for Teaching and School Leadership). 2011. Rev. ed. *Accreditation of Initial Teacher Education Programs in Australia: Standards and Procedures.* Carlton South, Victoria, Australia: Education Services Australia. May. http://www.aitsl.edu.au/verve/_resources/Accreditation_of_initial_teacher_education.pdf.

Bennell, Paul, and Kwame Akyeampong. 2007. "Teacher Motivation in Sub-Saharan Africa and South Asia." DFID Educational Paper. Researching the Issues 71. Department for International Development (DFID), London. http://www.dfid.gov.uk/r4d/pdf/outputs/policystrategy/researchingtheissuesno71.pdf.

CCSSO (Council of Chief State School Officers). 2011. "Interstate Teacher Assessment and Support Consortium (InTASC) Model Core Teaching Standards: A Resource for State Dialogue." CCCSO, Washington, DC, April. http://www.ccsso.org/Documents/2011/InTASC_Model_Core_Teaching_Standards_2011.pdf.

Clegg, Andrew. 2011. "Ensuring Relevance and Improving Quality." Background paper prepared for *Secondary Education in Ethiopia.* World Bank Ethiopia Office, Addis Ababa. Unpublished. (Available upon request of Rajendra Joshi, rjoshi@worldbank.org.)

Ethiopia, Federal Democratic Republic of CSA (Central Statistical Agency). 2010. "Census Summary Final Report: 2007 Population and Housing Census of Ethiopia." CSA, Addis Ababa.

———. MOE (Ministry of Education). 2009a. "Continuous Professional Development for Primary and Secondary School Teachers, Leaders, and Supervisors in Ethiopia: The Framework." MOE, Addis Ababa.

———. 2009b. "Education Statistics Annual Abstract (ESSA), 2001 EC (2008/09 GC)." MOE, Addis Ababa.

———. 2010a. "Education Sector Development Program IV (ESDP IV) 2010/11–2014/15 (2003 EC–2007 EC), Program Action Plan." MOE, Addis Ababa.

———. 2010b. "Education Statistics Annual Abstract (ESSA), 2002 EC (2009/10) GC." MOE, Addis Ababa.

ETS (Educational Testing Service). 2003. "Preparing Teachers around the World." Policy Information Report, ETS, Princeton, NJ.

Fry, Lucia. 2010. "What Makes Teachers Tick." Rev. ed. VSO, London. http://www.vso.org.uk/Images/What_Makes_Teachers_Tick_tcm79-21000.pdf.

Hailegiorgis, Terefe and Anthony Dewees. 2010. "TPD1 Completion Report." Draft. Report prepared for Ministry of Education of the Federal Democratic Republic of Ethiopia, Addis Ababa, April. Unpublished.

Hopkins, David. 2001. *School Improvement for Real.* London: Routledge/Falmer Press.

Ingvarson, Lawrence, Alison Elliott, Elizabeth Kleinhenz, and Phil McKenzie. 2006. "Teacher Education Accreditation: A Review of National and International Trends and Practices." ACEReSearch report, ACER (Australian Council for Educational Research), Camberwell, Victoria, Australia.

Kraft, Richard J. 2011a. "Expanding Opportunities and Building Competencies for the Young Indonesian: An Agenda for Senior Secondary Education." Report prepared for World Bank Indonesia Office, Jakarta. Unpublished.

———. 2011b. "Teacher Preparation." Background paper prepared for *Secondary Education in Ethiopia*. Unpublished. World Bank Ethiopia Office, Addis Ababa. (Available upon request of Rajendra Joshi, rjoshi@worldbank.org.)

Lynd, Mark. 2005. "Fast-Track Teacher Training: Models for Consideration for Southern Sudan." Paper written for the American Institutes of Research and the Sudan Basic Education Program. Available on the website of the University of Massachusetts, Amherst, MA. http://courses.umass.edu/educ870/teacher_education/Documents/Lynd%20-%20Fast-track%20Southern%20Sudan.pdf.

Ottevanger, Wout, Jan van den Akker, and Leo de Feiter. 2005. *Developing Science, Mathematics and ICT (SMICT) in Secondary Education: Patterns and Promising Practices.* Africa Human Development Series. Washington, DC: World Bank.

Thompson, Marnie, Pamela Paek, Laura Goe, and Eva Ponte. 2005. "The Impact of New Teacher Induction on Teacher Practices and Student Learning." Paper presented at the Annual Meeting of the American Educational Research Association, Montreal, April 13, 2005. Available on the website of ETS, Princeton, NJ. http://www.ets.org/Media/Resources_For/K-12_Education/pdf/AERA_2005_Thompson.pdf.

Wößmann, Ludger W. 2006. "Class-Size Effects in School Systems around the World: Evidence from Between-Grade Variation in TIMSS." With Martin R. West, *European Economic Review* 50 (3): 695–736.

Wong, Harry K., Ted Britton, and Tom Ganser. 2005. "What the World Can Teach Us about New Teacher Induction." *Phi Delta Kappan* 86 (5): 379–84.

CHAPTER 6

Strengthening Governance and Management

Decentralization has been a key education reform in Ethiopia, with important responsibilities already having been transferred to the regional, woreda, and school levels. Ethiopia aspires to further deepen its decentralization policies by expanding the scope of school-based management (SBM). This type of management involves the gradual transfer of academic, financial, and human resources management to School Management Committees. Using a phased approach accompanied by capacity building for stakeholders at all levels, the transition toward full SBM is expected to lead to more efficient utilization of resources, improved teacher performance, and increased levels of student learning.

Changes in the curriculum content and learning environment, as well as the way in which resources are mobilized and deployed, are major elements of the secondary education agenda in Ethiopia.[1] But without an improved institutional environment, desired outcomes will not materialize. Improving the way secondary education is governed and managed is thus essential to ensuring broad access to quality secondary education, which is needed to support Ethiopia's drive to become a middle-income country.

Decentralization is perhaps the most ubiquitous governance reform currently taking place in the education sectors of developing and developed countries alike. International evidence supports these reforms, suggesting that a judicious combination of central direction and local autonomy can create an environment in which resources are most effectively deployed to support student learning.

Hanushek and Wößmann (2007) identify three governance- and management-related variables that affect learning outcomes: choice and competition, school autonomy, and school accountability. Demand-side pressure on schools from parents and communities can improve the performance not just of the schools to which parents send their children, but all schools that want to compete for students. Similarly, school- and community-level decision making and fiscal decentralization can positively affect school outcomes, such as examination results, because schools become accountable for the "outputs" that they produce. Good-quality and timely service provision can be ensured if service providers are held accountable to their clients; in the case of the education sector, these clients are students and their parents. Further, if schools are managed more transparently, opportunities for corruption are reduced and the likelihood increases that funds will be used efficiently for the purposes intended.

The *World Development Report 2004* argues convincingly that the effectiveness of service outcomes can be increased by strengthening the "short" accountability route, that is, by increasing clients' power over providers and separating the policy maker from the service provider organization (figure 6.1) (World Bank 2003). Short-route accountability does not replace the long route, as improving services also requires stronger accountability mechanisms, with operational actions linked to long-run institutional strategies and goals.

Decentralization affects both the nature of planning and the instruments of policy implementation in an education system. Top-down planning and command-and-control implementation give way to bottom-up participatory planning and incentives-based implementation strategies. Most importantly, a tradition of one-way upward accountability to central authorities is replaced by processes of reciprocal accountability between all stakeholders (Elmore 2004). In this environment the role of the central government evolves, but remains crucial. The government focuses on setting policy, establishing and monitoring performance standards, and supporting capacity building and policy implementation at all levels of the system.

A popular decentralization strategy in many countries is school-based management (SBM), defined as the systematic decentralization of authority to the

Figure 6.1 Increasing Accountability: The Short Route

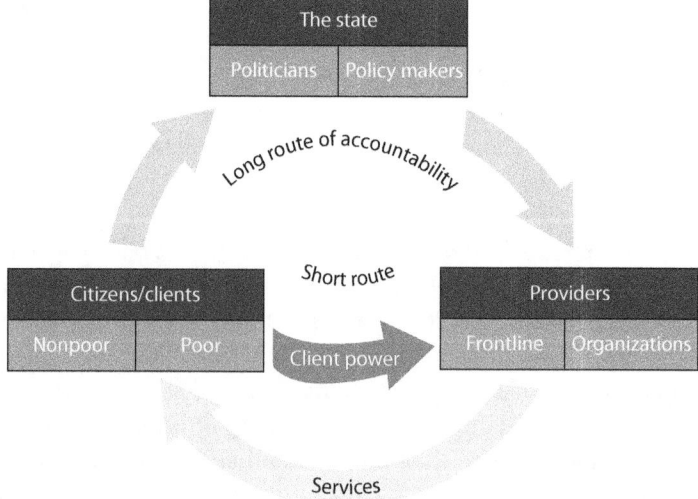

Source: Adapted from World Bank 2003, 65, figure 4.1.

school level—including responsibility for decisions on significant matters related to school operations—within a framework of centrally determined goals, policies, curricula, standards, and accountability (Caldwell 2005).

Decentralization has been a key school reform in Ethiopia for the last two decades; important responsibilities have already been transferred to the regional, woreda, and school levels. Implementation has been supported by considerable investments in capacity building and community engagement in the managing and financing of school education has notably increased. The country now aspires to further deepen its decentralization policies by expanding the scope of SBM.

This chapter starts with a summary of international experience with school-based management, followed by a review of decentralization in the Ethiopian system, with a particular focus on this type of management. Based on this review, a possible road map for expanding SBM is presented, together with capacity-building measures.

School-Based Management: International Experience and Approaches

School-based management has been introduced in a wide range of countries—high income, middle income, and low income—among them, Australia, New Zealand, the United States, the United Kingdom, The Netherlands, China, Thailand, Ghana, Rwanda, El Salvador, Nicaragua, and Guatemala. The model used in each has been different, as this type of management encompasses a wide variety of approaches (box 6.1).

Fundamentally, approaches to SBM differ in the "who" (that is, to whom decision-making authority is devolved) and the "what" (that is, the degree of autonomy that is devolved) (World Bank 2008). In terms of the "who," some programs transfer authority only to principals or teachers, others mandate the participation of parents and community members—often via school committees (or school councils or School Management Committees). In terms of the "what," the authority transferred may concern budget allocations, the hiring and firing of teachers and other staff, curriculum development, the procurement of textbooks and other educational materials, infrastructure improvements, and/or the monitoring and evaluation of teacher performance and student learning outcomes.

Figure 6.2 provides a classification of SBM reforms according to how "strong" they are in relation to the degree and scope of the authority delegated to individual schools. Some countries have decentralized to this level decisions related to the allocation of more than 90 percent of the state budget for public school education (Caldwell 2005). Others have gone less far, delegating responsibility to the school level only for decisions on nonsalary expenditures and/or capital investments.

School-based management allows national and local governments to focus on policy making, setting standards, and monitoring progress, rather than trying to micromanage service delivery. School leaders focus the attention of staff and the wider school community on improving student learning outcomes. In return for

Box 6.1

Types of Control in School-Based Management

- *Administrative-control SBM:* authority is devolved to the school principal.
- *Professional-control SBM:* teachers hold the main decision-making authority so that they may use their knowledge of the school and its students.
- *Community-control SBM:* parents have the major decision-making authority.
- *Balanced-control SBM:* decision-making authority is shared by parents and teachers.

Source: Barrera-Osorio et al. 2009.

Figure 6.2 Classification of SBM Reforms Implemented in Various Countries

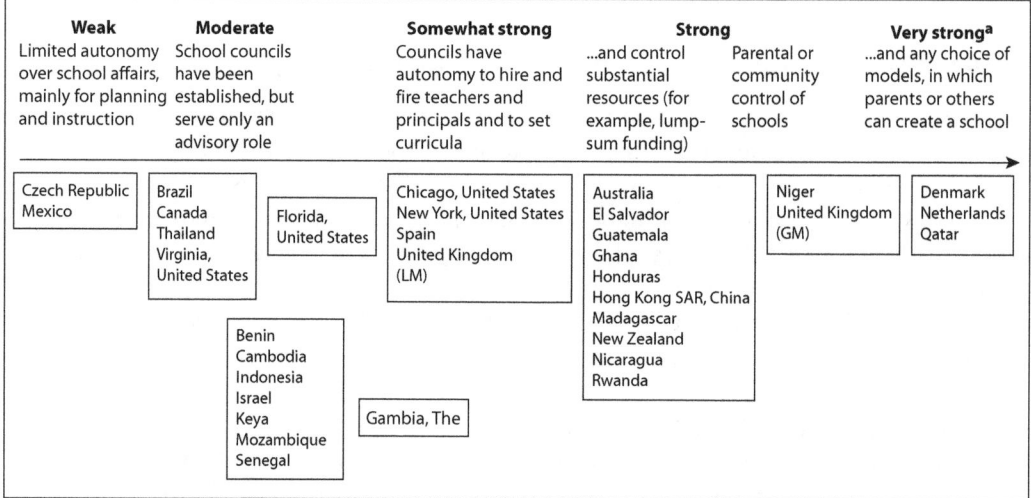

Source: Reproduced from Barrera-Osorio et al. 2009, 22, figure 1.1.
Note: For the United Kingdom, LM (locally managed schools) and GM (grant-maintained schools) are two slightly different school-based management models implemented there.
a. These terms represent ratings in the continuum of autonomy and authority vested in schools by the various types of school-based management (SBM) reforms.

gaining greater authority to manage their own affairs, schools are expected to meet the goals of the education system. Benchmarking the performance of schools in similar socioeconomic circumstances is common practice in systems where SBM has been introduced.

A qualitative study of schools with outstanding results in seven Latin American countries concluded that their success was underpinned by the quality of school-level management and the effectiveness of classroom teaching practices. The schools attributed a good part of their success to their autonomous operations, as trends at the central level enabled them to move toward increasingly decentralized administrative and pedagogical models (Caldwell 2005).

Experience with school-based management indicates that it takes many years for decentralization to have an impact on student outcomes (World Bank 2007b). Passing legislation that shifts power, authority, responsibility, and influence from one level to another in a school system does not in itself produce the desired impact on learning or change the management culture at all levels. Even when institutions are in place and operational, it may take time for changes to translate into test scores and examination results. Studies have shown that SBM reforms need at least five years to bring about fundamental change at the school level and about eight years to yield significant changes in student test scores (Bruns et al. 2011). However, the changes required by SBM can make the use of resources more efficient and improve accountability much earlier. This finding suggests that capacity building in these areas should be an early priority.

Leaders at the central level need to have a full understanding of the purpose and nature of SBM, its expected learning outcomes, and how it can most easily be implemented. Box 6.2 identifies six principles drawn from international experience that should be considered when putting school-based management into place.

Empirical Evidence of the Impacts of School-Based Management

The tradition of local communities establishing and operating schools exists or has existed in many countries, including Ethiopia. Such schools were once managed by the local community, which is a form of school-based management; however, the terminology of SBM was coined *after* governments transferred the management of schools to the schools themselves. These reforms started in Australia in the 1960s and spread to the United States, Canada, the United Kingdom, and many other countries (World Bank 2007a).

Rigorous evaluation of the impact of SBM is difficult; much remains to be learned. Existing evaluations deal with two different contexts, evaluating the experience either of developed or developing countries. In developed countries, these evaluations concern primary and secondary schools, whereas in developing countries, the bulk of impact evaluations focus on primary schools (largely because the latter were associated with donor-assisted primary education projects). The bulk of school-based management programs that have been evaluated follow the community control model (box 6.2).

A number of impact studies of SBM have been conducted in the United States. A study in Boston demonstrated, for example, that charter schools raised mathematics scores by more than half a standard deviation per year in middle school (Abdulkadiroglu et al. 2011).[2] Findings from evaluations in Chicago and New York were more modest, but still statistically and economically significant (Hoxby and Murarka 2009; Hoxby and Rockoff 2005). A study of the Harlem Children's Zone,[3] a program that focuses on the poorest minority students in that neighborhood, found that students enrolled in grade 6 gained more than one standard deviation in mathematics, and up to half a standard deviation in

> **Box 6.2**
>
> **Guiding Principles for Implementing School-Based Management**
>
> - Establish the program's scope and structure.
> - Adjust institutional structures at the central and regional level to support SBM and define clear roles and responsibilities for the school governance structure.
> - Promote the development of school plans that translate school decisions into tangible improvements in school performance.
> - Improve financing mechanisms and instruments for transferring resources to schools.
> - Establish sound procedures for ensuring schools' accountability for their individual resources and decisions.
> - Ensure that all participants understand the SBM program and have the skills needed to implement it.
>
> *Source:* World Bank 2007a.

English by grade 8 (Dobbie and Fryer 2011). The authors of the latter study argue that these effects are sufficient to reverse the black-white achievement gap in mathematics. Another charter provider in the United States, the Knowledge is Power Program, which also focuses on low-income and minority students, produced gains of 0.1 standard deviations a year, with larger gains for special-education and limited-English students—in the range 0.3–0.4 standard deviations a year (Angrist et al. 2010).

In England, a 1980s reform allowed state high schools to opt out of local control. These "grant-maintained schools" became autonomous, funded directly by the central government. Schools seeking autonomy had only to propose and win a majority vote among current parents. Almost one in three high schools voted in favor of autonomy between 1988 and 1997. Clark (2009) finds large achievement gains at schools in which the vote barely won, compared with schools in which it barely lost.

An early experiment with school-based management in the developing world took place in El Salvador in the early 1990s (Jimenez and Sawada 1999). Evaluations have since shown that schools that introduced this type of management increased parental participation and efficiency (by raising resources and reducing repetition and dropout rates). They may even have improved learning outcomes, as measured by standardized tests. In Kenya, parental oversight of teachers has led to significant gains in test scores (Duflo et al. 2011).

Recent rigorous impact evaluations of randomized trials in Mexico examine the impacts of two relatively limited autonomy programs. In terms of student achievement, preliminary analysis suggests that test scores increased overall for both treatment and control schools, although the differences were small. When disaggregated by grade, however, the cohort that was exposed to school autonomy the longest experienced the largest gains. These students' scores increased by a 0.5 standard deviation between third and sixth grade if they were in treatment schools, while those in control schools increased by a 0.34 standard deviation, with a difference-in-differences estimated program impact of a 0.16 standard deviation (Gertler et al. 2012).

A randomized trial of Mexico's School Management Support Program found that doubling resources and, hence, the responsibilities that parent associations are given, improve learning outcomes by almost a quarter of a standard deviation (Gertler et al. 2010; Gertler et al. 2012). This evaluation examined programs in highly disadvantaged rural communities located in four high-poverty states of southern Mexico that have high concentrations of indigenous peoples. Again, there were especially strong effects in standardized test scores for third-grade students.

In Nicaragua, de facto autonomy had positive effects on student promotion and student achievement in mathematics and language in primary schools, and in language in secondary schools (Bruns et al. 2011). An increase in schools' influence over teacher-related decision making was the area of decentralization that appeared to have had the largest impact on student achievement (King et al. 1999).

Decentralization in Ethiopia

In the 1990s the government of Ethiopia embarked on a far-reaching decentralization of the education system. This involved changes in policy making, public service delivery, and regulation, as well as the establishment of a fiscal transfer system for annual nonearmarked "block" grants to the regions. The implications of these reforms have profoundly affected the management of the education sector, which has devolved decision making and specific functions from the federal to the regional level, from the regional to the woreda level, and to some extent, from the woreda to the school level.

Successive Education Sector Development Programs (ESDPs) have placed increasing emphasis on strategies that strengthen capacity at lower levels of the system, including those that improve school-level management, accountability, transparency, and community participation. A component of the government's General Education Quality Improvement Program (GEQIP), which aims to enhance the quality of general education (including secondary education), also focuses on management and administration.

The regulatory framework for governance and management of the school system is outlined in several government documents, including Education and Training Policy (Ethiopia 1994), Strengthening of the Management and Administration of Schools (Amendment) Proclamation 217/2000 (Office of the President 2000), Directive for Educational Management, Organization, Public Participation, and Finance (MOE 2002), and various letters (that is, directives) issued from time to time by Regional Education Bureaus.

> **Box 6.3**
>
> **Ethiopian Policy on Educational Organization and Management**
>
> - Clear guidelines, stating the rights and duties of all stakeholders involved in education, will be issued to ensure participatory and proper professional relationships in their activities.
> - Educational management will be decentralized to create the necessary conditions to expand, enrich, and improve the relevance, quality, accessibility, and equity of education and training.
> - Educational management will be democratic, professional, coordinated, efficient, effective, and encourage the participation of women.
> - Educational institutions will be autonomous in their internal administration and in designing and implementing education and training programs, with overall coordination and democratic leadership by boards or committees consisting of members from the local community (society), development and research institutions, teachers, and students.
> - The management of teachers and other educational personnel will be organized on the basis of professional principles, including a professional code of ethics, salary schedule, working conditions, incentives, professional growth opportunities, and overall rights and duties.
>
> *Source:* Ethiopia 1994.

The "Education and Training Policy" (ETP) states that education management will be decentralized in order to improve educational relevance, quality, access, and equity (box 6.3).

Proclamation 217/2000 moved the education decentralization agenda forward by: (1) transferring the power to issue regulations with respect to administration, management, curricula, and the employment of teachers in public schools, as well as to supervise the implementation of these regulations, from the federal level to regional governments or city administrations; (2) giving the education bureaus of regional governments or city administrations the power to issue directives to implement regulations issued by their respective councils; and (3) declaring that public schools shall be accountable to the appropriate education bureaus of their respective regional government or city administration.

The 2002 "Directive for Educational Management," popularly known as the "Blue Book," sets out the duties and responsibilities of the various bodies responsible for educational management: the Ministry of Education (MOE); the Regional Education Bureaus; the Zonal Education Office; the Woreda Education Office; schools (at each level); education and training management boards at the woreda, *kebele* (a subdivision of a woreda), and urban area levels;[4] and parent-teacher associations (PTAs). It also defines the major functions and responsibilities of the following positions: supervisor, principal, vice-principal, teachers, and students, as well as the functions in which community participation is deemed imperative.

The directive further specifies the main responsibilities and duties of schools, defining the latter as the creation of competent citizens who develop knowledge and talent and implement educational programs, as well as support and supervise teachers. Two further duties of schools are defined as: "To enhance their internal income by various means, to use the income generated for expanding and improving quality education" and "To coordinate and facilitate the community and parents around where a school is established so that they can jointly own it, administer it, and give financial assistance" (MOE 2002, section 1.1.5). Regarding community participation, the directive advocates "the creation of a situation where the community will exercise full control over the school through its active participation in school administration, budget allocation, and implementation" (MOE 2002, part three, preamble) and requires "the participation of the community, fully empowered to set up and run the schools, as the ultimate owner" (MOE 2002, section 3.1).

Decentralization from the Federal to Regional and Woreda Governments

Ethiopia is a federal state, with elected subnational governments at the regional and woreda levels. The big regions are divided into administrative areas, called zones. Zones comprise a number of woredas. Two city governments in Ethiopia have the status of regions.

The strength of the legal framework for decentralization in Ethiopia lies in the simultaneous transfer of funds, functions, and staff. Decentralization has been challenging in many countries because of the difficulty of transferring functions and resources simultaneously. An assessment of the progress of decentralization from the federal to the regional and woreda levels is presented in table 6.1. This assessment is based on measures of progress defined in the table as "strong," "moderate," and "weak," depending on the depth of decentralization.

Remarkable progress has been made in decentralizing fiscal, staffing, and legal functions to the regional and woreda levels. Nonearmarked and nonsector-specific block grants are now transferred from the federal to regional governments. These governments in turn transfer nonearmarked and nonsector-specific block grants to woreda governments. Woredas have full authority to allocate these grants, which are merged with their own income, to various sectors (including education), as well as within sectors. Regions and woredas also have the authority to create teacher and other staff positions, fill those positions, and take disciplinary actions relating to staff. Likewise, regions have the authority to issue directives within the framework of federal education regulations. In contrast, decentralization of the academic aspects of education remains weak in the country, largely because the ETP does not envision decentralization of the secondary curriculum.

Table 6.1 Assessment of Progress toward Decentralization to Subnational Governments

	Progress toward decentralization: General			Progress in Ethiopia	
Function	Strong	Moderate	Weak	Status	Rating
Financial management					
Financing of local schools	Block grants	Block grants for recurrent expenditures and earmarked capital expenditures; earmarked funding is larger than block grants	Earmarked or line-item transfers	Regions and woredas get block grants; block grants are much larger than earmarked funding	Strong
Personnel administration					
Creating teacher and staff positions	Full authority	Authority to create temporary or contract positions	No authority	Regions and woredas have full authority	Strong
Hiring of teachers and other staff	Full authority	Authority to hire on temporary or contract basis; authority to hire lower-level staff and teachers	No authority or authority to hire on temporary or contract basis	Regions and woredas have full authority	Strong
Disciplinary actions for nonperformance	Full authority	Authority to take moderate disciplinary action	No authority	Regions and woredas have full authority	Strong
Legal authority					
Issuing directives	Full authority within the framework of applicable national laws	Authority within narrow scope	No authority	Full authority	Strong
Academic management					
Secondary curriculum development and implementation	Full authority according to national standards or curriculum framework	Authority for region- and/or school-specific work plans of teachers	Prescribed curriculum and implementation modalities to be followed	Regions have authority for primary education only; woredas have no authority with regard to the curriculum	Weak

Progress toward School-Based Management

Although official documents presently do not refer to school-based management, the policies implemented in Ethiopia have been moving school management in this direction for over a decade. The current government policy with respect to school management is stated in the ETP, Blue Book, and ESDPs. Its overall policy objectives are listed in box 6.3. Table 6.2 assesses progress toward the decentralization of educational management to the school level, or school-based management. This assessment is based on measures defined in the table as "strong," "moderate," and "weak," depending on the depth of decentralization. It should be noted here that interpretation of the Blue Book and school practices are not uniform nationwide. Information collected during field visits were used for the assessment presented in the table, so it may not be accurate for the entire country.

According to the information in table 6.2, the transfer of financial management authority to the school level is moderate in Ethiopia. The current status of decentralization is as follows:

- In principle, schools have the authority to mobilize, retain, and use local resources, but the kebeles have overlapping authority in this area. For example, the latter play a role in fixing community contributions to local schools. Similarly, there is a perception that preparatory fees are a federal mandate, based on a previous circular. In practice, however, preparatory fees are fixed by PTAs. The Blue Book does not specifically identify the body that has the authority to establish preparatory school fees.
- Schools have full authority to use school grants as they see fit, including for related procurements. But this is an arrangement specific to GEQIP. Some schools exercise similar authority for block grants, while others do not. The Blue Book envisions schools making only small procurements using petty cash.
- Schools do not receive government budget funds for capital expenditures.

Decentralization of personnel management authority is assessed as weak because Ethiopian schools do not have the authority to hire principals, teachers, or staff; promote teachers or other staff; or reprimand principals. In practice, schools do hire teachers and other staff using local resources, but this arrangement is not based on formal policies. They also have the authority to take simple disciplinary actions with respect to delinquent teachers and other staff, such as verbal and written warnings and the deduction of one-month's salary. In practice, however, this authority is reduced to advising the kebeles.

Finally, decentralization of academic management authority is also assessed as weak, as schools have to follow a prescribed curriculum and use prescribed textbooks, reference books, and curriculum implementation strategies. Decentralization to the school level thus falls short of articulated government policy goals and the status of school-based management is accordingly weak. To address these issues, the MOE is now preparing a policy on SBM.

Table 6.2. Assessment of Progress toward School-Based Management

Function	Progress toward SBM: General			Progress in Ethiopia	
	Strong	Moderate	Weak	Status	Rating
Financial management					
Internal (local) resources	Full control over mobilization and utilization of local resources	Authority to mobilize local resources, approval required for spending OR Authority to mobilize local resources, but no authority to adopt a mobilization and utilization policy	No authority to mobilize local resources OR such resources must be returned to the treasury	Authority to mobilize, retain, and use local resources; kebeles have a role in fixing community contributions	Moderate
Procurement	Full authority to execute budget	Authority within a specific threshold	No authority OR authority for using petty cash	Full authority for school grants; full or no authority for block grants. Blue Book allows petty procurement only	Moderate to strong
Recurrent budget approval	Full authority	Authority for local resources only	No authority	Full authority for school grants and, in some schools, block grants	Moderate
Execution of capital budget	Full authority	Authority within a specific threshold	No authority	No authority	Weak
Personnel administration					
Hiring of teachers and other staff	Full authority	Authority to hire teachers on temporary or contract basis	No authority	No authority	Weak
Hiring and firing of teachers and staff financed by local resources	Full authority	Authority for selected positions	No authority	Practiced, but no authority	Weak
Hiring of principal	Full authority	Participation in selection process	No authority	No authority	Weak

(table continues on next page)

Table 6.2 Assessment of Progress toward School-Based Management *(continued)*

	Progress toward SBM: General			Progress in Ethiopia	
Function	Strong	Moderate	Weak	Status	Rating
Disciplinary action for nonperformance	Full authority	Authority to take moderate disciplinary action	No authority	Authority to take simple disciplinary actions, but in practice superseded by overlapping kebele authority	Weak to moderate
Reprimanding principal	Full authority	Authority to take moderate action	No authority	No authority	Weak
Promotion	Full authority	Authority for selected positions	No authority	No authority	Weak
Academic management					
Curriculum development	Authority to deliver instructions to achieve defined competencies	Authority to define local content and/or nonexaminable subjects	Prescribed curriculum to be followed	No authority	Weak
Curriculum implementation	Full authority to choose textbooks, reference books, and instructional strategies	Authority to choose reference books and instructional strategies, as well as offer elective subjects	Prescribed textbooks, reference books, and instructional strategies	Prescribed textbooks, reference books, instructional strategies	Weak

Source: Author's analysis, based on a review of the existing legal framework and site visits to secondary schools in Ethiopia.
Note: SMB = School-based management.

Strengthening School-Based Management

Existing policies give the government a mandate to strengthen school-based management. There are a wide range of SBM options being practiced worldwide. The choice and evolution of a particular option are mainly influenced by country context and policy choices. This section reviews the most suitable SBM option for Ethiopia and outlines how it might be implemented.

Decentralization Model

The existing Ethiopian model of school management is close to the balanced-control model defined in box 6.1, but also shares features of the community-control variant, manifested in an influential PTA formed for a three-year tenure by a parents-teachers' congress (that is, meeting) (PTC).

The strength of the balanced-control model is the perception that power is shared between parents and teachers. In this model, the key challenges are managing the competition between these two parties and the risk that decentralized authority will revert to the government (that is, to the woredas or kebeles), together with the possibility that full management authority is not transferred to the school level.

The main strength of the community-control model is that it establishes a clear line of accountability to the main stakeholders: the parents. In this model, the School Management Committee or School Board, formed by parents and operated under their leadership, has overall responsibility for school performance and the authority to make major decisions. However, a School Management Committee primarily focuses on generating resources, establishing external linkages, and monitoring school activities and performance, while the school principal focuses on school administration and academic management. The main challenge of this model is gaining the acceptance of teachers, who may not easily agree to the new role of parents.

The primary factor to be considered when choosing an SBM model is the nature of decentralization that is sought in an education system. Given the Ethiopian government's policy goal of having local communities exercise full control over schools, as articulated in the Blue Book, and the concomitant expectation of significant community contributions to schools, it would be most appropriate for Ethiopia to opt for the community-control model.

Decentralizing Functions, Staff, and Funds

The Blue Book defines the function of schools only in general terms. Based on practice on the ground, the primary responsibility for creating a learning environment that ensures students acquire the competencies described in the curriculum lies with schools. To fulfill this responsibility, they are required to complement government resources with community resources. This is a daunting task. The move toward school-based management is not just about delegating more functions to schools, it is, most importantly, about better resourcing schools so that they can shoulder this responsibility.

Staff and discretionary funds are the key resources needed to undertake any school management function. The paradox in Ethiopia is that schools are being asked to deliver quality education efficiently without being able to manage their own staffs and with little or no discretionary funds.[5] Although the overall goals of SBM are to give schools control over their staffs and the funds required to fulfill their responsibilities, many countries have implemented SBM only partially; as a result, the outcomes of the reforms have been mixed.

Key challenges associated with the transfer of authority over staff and funds to schools in Ethiopia are: (1) the possible reluctance of the woredas and kebeles to cede their authority over these inputs; (2) the usual preference of teachers and other staff to be managed by woredas and kebeles; and (3) building the capacity of schools to manage these two elements. When woredas, kebeles, and teachers are not fully on board with school-based management, they can slow down or even halt the reform process, citing the inadequate capacity of schools to manage decentralized functions.

Strong political commitment is a prerequisite for addressing the first and second challenges. The third challenge—capacity building at the school level—is more difficult, but critically important. One option for implementing SBM reforms is to simultaneously transfer responsibility for staff and funds, while concurrently building the administrative capacity of schools. But many countries have chosen to transfer staff functions and funds in phases in order to make the transition smoother. If Ethiopia chooses to adopt this path, the phases should be short and implemented according to a predetermined timetable. Otherwise the chances of the reform becoming stalled will be high. The next section presents an example of how these reforms could be phased.

Implementing SBM in Phases

A possible approach to the phased implementation of school-based management is presented in table 6.3. This table includes only the financial and personnel management aspects of SBM. From the perspective of carrying out the full reform, it is advisable to set the duration of each phase at not more than two to three years.

The first phase is designed to build the capacity of schools to make independent decisions on resource generation and the use of all school resources, including government grants and locally mobilized resources. During this phase their capacity to manage funds, assets, and procurement—together with accountability mechanisms—will be strengthened. Personnel management capacity will be built through independent decisions on staff appraisals, simple disciplinary actions, training selection, and recognition for good work. In addition, schools will be able to further strengthen their personnel management capacity if they put in place a formal transparent system for the recruitment of teachers and other staff who are paid with local resources.

During the second phase schools will develop the full capacity to manage financial, procurement, and contract matters through the administration of

Table 6.3 Possible Phased Implementation of School-Based Management in Ethiopia

Authority	Phase 1	Phase 2	Phase 3
Financial management			
Determine cost sharing in grades 11–12, household contributions to grades 9–10, and other charges	X		
Merge block and school grants	X		
Convert all in-kind supplies to cash grants[a]	X		
Finance school budget by local resources, school grants, and block grants	X		
Operate school bank account	X		
Execute school budget, including procurement	X		
Administer capital expenditures funded by government		X	
Administer salary budget		X	
Approve full school budget, including salaries and capital expenditures		X	
Personnel management			
Fix terms of employment of teachers and staff paid with local resources	X		
Hire and fire teachers and other staff paid with local resources	X		
Conduct performance appraisal of teachers and other staff	X		
Take simple disciplinary actions with respect to teachers and other staff (for example, give verbal and written notice, deduct one month's salary)	X		
Take simple disciplinary action with respect to principals (for example, verbal notice, notice in writing)	X		
Reward teachers and staff	X		
Approve leaves of principal, teachers, and other staff	X		
Select teachers and other staff for training	X		
Hire principals		X	
Take moderate disciplinary action with respect to principals, teachers, and other staff (for example, deduct up to three months' salary, bar promotion for up to two years)		X	
Hire teachers and other staff			X
Promote teachers and other staff			X
Take serious disciplinary action with respect to teachers and other staff (for example, reduce salary and job classification levels, dismiss)			X
Take serious disciplinary action with respect to principals (for example, dismiss)			X

Note:
a. With the exception of textbooks until such time as schools are allowed to purchase them.

salaries and capital budgets. Their personnel management will be further strengthened through decisions on moderate disciplinary actions and most other staff management functions except hiring, firing, and promotion. By appointing principals who are accountable to them, schools will develop the skills to take full responsibility for school management in the third phase.

The key functions transferred during the third phase are the hiring, firing, and promotion of all staff, including teachers and principals. At the end of the third phase schools will have become autonomous institutions owned and managed by the community in partnership with the local government—that is, woredas and kebeles—as envisioned by the ETP and the Blue Book. The school administration is accountable to the community, as represented by a School Management Committee or School Board, and the local government.

Upon full implementation of SBM, the relationship between schools and the government will be similar to that between a service provider (the school) and

Strengthening Governance and Management

a client (the government). Financing will be tied to the quantity and quality of services that the government contracts the school to deliver, giving the government greater leverage over the school to deliver these services according to agreed specifications.

Structure for School-Based Management

As part of the SBM approach, overall responsibility for management is usually assigned to a body that represents key stakeholders (parents, teachers, the local administration and/or government, students, and in some cases, employers), most often known as the School Management Committee or School Board. The composition of local PTAs, or Parent-Teacher-Student Association (PTSAs) in Ethiopia,[6] is close to that of a School Management Committee (SMC) or School Board. PTAs and parent-teacher-student committees (PTSCs) do not, however, include representatives of the local government or local employers. To avoid confusion with either existing PTA/PTSCs or Kebele/Woreda Education and Training Boards, it may be better to refer to this body as an SMC.

In the case of the community-control model of school-based management, SMCs are accountable to parents—as a rule, to a parents' meeting and/or congress. In the case of the balanced-control model, they are accountable to teachers and parents and, through teachers, to the local government and/or administration. An example of the composition of a School Management Committee that would be applicable to the community-control model is presented in table 6.4. This composition largely draws on that of existing PTA/PTSCs. The size of the committee presented in table 4 may, however, be

Table 6.4 Composition of School Management Committee in the Community-Control SBM Model

Position	Selection process	Number
Chairperson	Parent or community member (other than a current schoolteacher) chosen by the local parent-teacher congress (PTC)	1
Member	Female parent chosen by PTC	2
Member	Male parent chosen by PTC	2
Member	Male representative of teachers	1
Member	Female representative of teachers	1
Member	Male representative of students	1
Member	Female representative of students	1
Member	Representative of kebele administration	1
Member	Donors from the community and/or prominent social workers chosen by the PTC	2
Member	Representatives of local employers and/or enterprises	2
Member	Representative of youth association	1
Member	Representative of women's association	1
Member and secretary	Principal	1

Note: PTC = Parents-teachers' congress.

somewhat too large to be manageable. If this becomes a concern, it is possible to reduce its size. While doing so, it will be important to ensure that parents, together with parental appointees, maintain the majority of SMC membership.

To ensure the effective functioning of SMCs, it is desirable to establish a mechanism to monitor their work. In some countries this role is fulfilled by a committee comprised of parents, students, and teachers. Teachers and parent members of this committee are elected by the parent-teacher congress, and student members, by students. This committee may be entrusted with, among other tasks, monitoring the implementation of the annual school plan, auditing the school's statements of account on behalf of the community, and reviewing its annual report.

Capacity Building for School-Based Management

Sustained progress toward school-based management will require an enabling environment—first and foremost, effective arrangements for strengthening the capacity of School Management Committees, principals, and PTA/PTSCs.

Capacity Building for Principals

Robust research evidence demonstrates that quality school leadership is one of the most significant factors in improving educational quality (Verspoor 2008). In light of current conditions in Ethiopia, however, programs to strengthen school leadership face several challenges. First, turnover of principals is reportedly high, with the Addis Ababa Education Bureau reporting that, on average, a principal stays in a post for two years. Some move up the career ladder, but others move out of education into other sectors. Moreover, the MOE is now introducing a requirement that all principals of preparatory schools have a master's degree. This may make it more difficult to find qualified principals. Second, opportunities for training are limited. Few principals and vice-principals have benefited from induction or training programs. Some have taken university courses in educational leadership and management at the bachelor's, diploma, or master's level—sometimes as part of the Leadership and Management Program (LAMP) of MOE—but this accounts for only a minority of principals. Several new initiatives are in preparation, including a new master's-level program in educational leadership and planning to be delivered by public universities. Existing principals will be able to complete this program during vacations over a three- or four-year period.

The ETP specifies that "[e]ducational management will be democratic, professional, coordinated, efficient, and effective" (Ethiopia 1994, 30). This implies that secondary school principals, as the head teachers of their schools, need to be familiar with curriculum, pedagogy, and assessment issues. Just as important, they also need to be "professional" in strategic leadership; planning; and managing human resources, finances, and client relationships. In addition, principals will be required to both conduct performance appraisals of teachers and set agreed performance targets as schools move toward greater control over their staffs. Many principals will not have all the skills required for their evolving responsibilities when they are appointed. Therefore leadership and management skills need to be provided as cost effectively as possible once an appointment is made. Given the current rapid turnover of principals and the need to avoid long absences for training, courses that take principals out of schools or go beyond what is essential to carry out their duties effectively should clearly be avoided.

Box 6.4 presents a number of options for principal training that may be considered. Given the need for practical, cost-effective courses, options based on existing Teacher Education Institutions (TEIs) and the Ethiopian Management Institute (and its regional equivalents) appear to offer the best solution. An alternative would be for Regional Educational Bureaus (REBs) to define the skills required of principals as a set of specifications (not a curriculum), then call for proposals for suitable courses from public and private universities and management institutes and TEIs.

Box 6.4

Options for Capacity Development Training for Principals

Full-time university courses. Master's-level courses in education management and leadership are available. They are attractive to individuals because the higher qualification attracts a higher salary, but such courses are expensive and take principals out of active service for a long period. In addition, existing courses are theoretical and provide neither practical skills nor on-the-job learning. As the time a principal stays in a post is short (in Addis Ababa, the average is two years), the return on investment in long-term training is very limited.

Part-time university courses. MOE has been offering Leadership and Management Program (LAMP) courses through universities on a part-time basis (typically over three summers). As with full-time courses, these courses are attractive to individuals due to the promise of a higher salary. However, LAMP courses have also been criticized for being too theoretical and lacking trainers who have the techniques to transmit skills, not simply information. Impact assessments, moreover, have not shown that these courses change principals' working practices. The courses are now being redesigned, but may require four (rather than three) summers to complete. Given the rapid turnover of secondary school principals, this cannot be considered a cost-effective option.

Education Management Institute or staff college. Ethiopia does not have a dedicated education management institute or staff college (such as the Kenya Education Staff Institute or the U.K. National College for School Leadership). While the total number of secondary principals and

(box continues on next page)

Box 6.4 Options for Capacity Development Training for Principals *(continued)*

vice-principals to be trained may not justify creating such an institute, the total number of primary and secondary school heads combined possibly would. Courses offered by such an institute would need to be short and practical in nature, ideally delivered by former successful principals, and offer some sort of follow-up support. The Oromia REB has, in fact, proposed that its regional government set up such a college specifically for Oromia, although it may be difficult to justify a college for a specific region.

Teacher Education Institutions (TEIs). Establishing a department (or section) for principal training in one or more TEIs would be more cost effective than establishing a dedicated education management institute because the facilities would be shared with teacher training courses. Again, courses would need to be short and practical in nature, ideally delivered by former successful head teachers (most likely recruited for specific courses rather than hired as permanent staff), and offer follow-up support.

Ethiopian Management Institute and its regional equivalents. The Ethiopian Management Institute (EMI) is a national-level educational institution that runs short, practical courses (from three days to three weeks) on such topics as basic managerial skills, human resources management, and finance for nonfinance managers. Courses are provided either at its head office in Addis Ababa or its residential center in Debrezeit. EMI already provides these types of courses to MOE staff. Its regular training programs focus on individual sectors, although the Institute also offers tailor-made courses. The regions each have similar facilities and the EMI has a strategic relationship with them to develop their capacity.

Courses delivered by the REBs. Certain REBs have already provided training courses, but these tend to be very short in nature—for example, initial induction courses for new principals that focus on rules and regulations.

Source: Smith 2011.

These capacity-building efforts can only be successful if issues of selection and retention are addressed. Along with the development of training programs, consideration needs to be given to the retention of competent principals. Guidelines for the recruitment of principals by schools should, among other things, consider:

- Selecting principals and vice-principals based solely on merit and making appointment criteria transparent
- Determining the most appropriate (or minimum) required selection criteria for the post, avoiding unnecessarily advanced qualifications, and prioritizing management skills over academic qualifications
- Selecting principals and vice-principals from the locality whenever possible
- Incorporating a performance element into principals' remuneration package; for example, incentive payments to principals who achieve or exceed agreed performance targets

- Over time, increasing principals' salary scales proportionate to those of teachers in order to make the posts more attractive to good managers
- Introducing longer-term succession planning with the support of school communities, including the fast-tracking of outstanding vice-principals.

Strengthening the Capacity of School Management Committees

The outcomes of school-based management will to a large extent be determined by the capacity of the SMCs. Some capacity-building efforts are already underway (for PTAs) as part of GEQIP, which is supporting the development of school improvement planning, but these efforts need to be expanded. The chairperson and other members of an SMC should be encouraged to participate, alongside the principal and/or vice-principal, in short training courses. In addition, short-term induction training packages should be developed for SMC members. Given the logistical challenge of reaching adequate numbers of SMC members through face-to-face training, the development of self-learning kits—printed as well as computer-based—should be considered.

In-service Support

There is overwhelming evidence that one-shot training programs are by themselves insufficient for real capacity building; such programs need to be supplemented by follow-up support. In-service support essentially needs to: (1) provide school management teams the skills and systems that have not been and cannot be provided by other means (that is, through formal training courses); (2) support school management teams in dealing with a range of issues, the particular mixture of which will be unique to each school, including lack of discipline, poor teacher performance, and low pupil motivation; and (3) identify other means of support that might be available and facilitate access to them. Networking solutions, as suggested in box 6.5, are likely to be effective and should be tested.

Information and Transparency

Setting targets and establishing well-functioning accountability systems requires having the information needed to make a realistic analysis of the present situation of a school, monitor its progress, and know what is going on elsewhere in order to benchmark the school's performance against that of others. At present, there are significant limitations on information sharing and communication between different levels of the education system and between schools.

Lack of relevant and timely information sharing limits the potential effectiveness of reforms at the school level. Strengthening information-sharing processes will be fundamental to improving the effectiveness and efficiency of education service delivery, including improving the quality of the education delivered. In order for schools and their communities to be able to make evidence-based decisions, data from educational management information systems need to be available to schools, including data for other schools and their woreda and regional comparators.

Box 6.5

Networking Options for In-Service Support to Secondary School Management Teams

- *Strengthen links between schools and capacity-development institutions* so that the latter can provide professional follow-up support. The institutional provider may be a dedicated education management institute, a principal training department (section) of a Teacher Education Institution, or the Ethiopian Management Institute and/or its regional equivalent.
- *Make greater use of information technology,* for example, enabling the relevant Woreda Education Office (WEO) or Regional Educational Bureau to keep in touch with schools via email or by putting management materials online so that school management teams can access them as required.
- *Develop networks of schools that are moving toward school-based management,* creating a system of mutual support. Schools learn what works and what does not work from each other. Schools in a network also generate new ideas and incorporate and adapt the best practices identified by other schools, developing their own capacity in the process. This enhances the opportunity to impact learning outcomes across the network.
- *Develop a mentor system* using former principals who have demonstrated effective leadership and management of their own institutions. These individuals would not hold permanent posts, but form a pool that schools could call on as required.
- *Develop a professional network,* such as an association of secondary school principals, enabling members to learn from one another.
- *Develop a professional network of secondary School Management Committees,* so that SMC members are able to learn systematically from other SMCs and thus strengthen the support that they provide their schools.

Source: Smith 2011.

Implications of School-Based Management for the Secondary Education System

The functions of woredas, regions, and the MOE will change as school-based management is implemented. All functions and authority that may in the future be transferred to schools (table 6.3) are presently being exercised by the woredas or kebeles, with the exception of hiring principals and teachers, a process in which both Regional Education Bureaus (REBs) and woredas are involved.

The new management model will entail significant change in the scope of work of the woredas and kebeles. These two administrative units will ultimately no longer be involved in decisions related to the management of schools, except in the capacity of members of relevant School Management Committees. Their main functions with respect to schools will be to negotiate a results framework, in addition to handling financing, monitoring and evaluation, and technical support matters. In the process of implementing SBM, certain staff redundancies in woredas and kebeles could be transferred to schools to meet the additional staff requirements associated with the transfer of personnel and financial management functions.

With the introduction of competitive hiring of teachers by individual schools, the current system of teacher recruitment and deployment managed by the REBs and woredas will no longer be required. To control the quality of teachers hired by schools, the MOE and/or REBs will need to certify the quality of eligible teachers through a licensing and relicensing system (chapter 5), which is now being prepared by the MOE.

Once schools are allowed to choose their own instructional strategies to deliver the competencies defined in the national curriculum, the MOE will no longer need to develop mandatory work plans for teachers. The MOE and REBs may, however, develop and make available to schools good examples of teacher work plans.

Preparations for SBM Reform

Many countries have embarked on the implementation of school-based management in their quest to achieve more effective and efficient schools and reach national education goals. But the models of SBM that have been adopted to date differ considerably from country to country (figure 6.2). The weakest versions do not transfer authority over staff and funding to schools, but open some space for community engagement in school affairs—very often by providing feedback and funds. The strongest versions transfer full control over funds and staff to schools.

Available evidence suggests, however, that the full potential of SBM can be exploited only when schools are given full control over these two inputs (staff and funds). Transferring this authority is almost always politically difficult because of the entrenched interests of various stakeholders in perpetuating an existing system—even an inefficient one. This difficulty has led to the adoption of various SBM models, as well as frequent discrepancies between the strength of a model and its expected outcomes. As a result, the new management system does not produce anticipated results. Hence, it is critically important to conceptualize the SBM framework. There are two options for doing so: (1) defining outcomes and then determining the compatible degree of authority over staff and functions that will be transferred to schools; or (2) deciding on the degree of transfer of authority and then determining expected outcomes. Though the first option is preferred, many countries consciously or subconsciously choose the second.

Agreement on the features of a school-based management model needs to be followed by the drafting of a comprehensive but concise legal framework for the model. Given the political sensitivities of the required reforms, SBM cannot

> **Box 6.6**
>
> **Preparing for School-Based Management Reform in Ethiopia**
>
> 1. Conceptualize the SBM framework.
> 2. Draft comprehensive but concise legislation for SBM.
> 3. Conduct intensive consultations on the draft so that all concerned stakeholders, including parliamentarians, are aware of the intent and content of SBM and arrive at a consensus model for the reform.
> 4. Adopt the legal framework.
> 5. Prepare an implementation plan, including a capacity-building plan, and provide an orientation that makes the commitment of the government very clear to all concerned stakeholders, including those in the education bureaucracy.
> 6. Launch the capacity-building plan, together with a nationwide communication campaign on SBM.
> 7. Implement SBM and monitor and evaluate the program.

be implemented without being backed by law. For example, some aspects of the Blue Book have either not been fully implemented or are interpreted differently because these aspects are not fully backed by a proclamation passed by the Ethiopian parliament (and then issued by the president) or by regulations issued by the Council of Ministers. In contrast, decentralization reforms in the regions have been implemented more rigorously because they are backed by a corresponding proclamation.

Finally, it is important to allow for consultations with as broad a range of stakeholders as possible and to accompany implementation with sustained capacity building. The capacity-building effort must go beyond one-shot training and be designed to provide regular local-level support to school management teams and SMC members. Box 6.6 describes steps that may used to deepen school-based management in Ethiopia.

Conclusion

Decentralization of the public education system is a global trend. The first stage of this trend is the decentralization of management functions from national to subnational levels, and the second stage, from subnational levels to schools. This second stage constitutes school-based management. Ethiopia has had remarkable success with the first stage, transferring school management functions to the regional and woreda levels by introducing block grants and devolving full control over staffing.

The country has now set an ambitious target for the second stage of decentralization: transforming schools into autonomous institutions owned by communities. Ethiopia has managed to attain a significant level of community participation in school management by institutionalizing PTAs elected by parents. This participation takes the form of parents being involved in school financing, planning, monitoring, and to some extent, implementation of school plans. A sound foundation has thus been created for decentralization to continue to the school level.

The main responsibility for accomplishing national goals for secondary education lies with secondary schools themselves. More often than not, however, schools face this daunting responsibility without preparation and only limited authority over their own staff and funds. School-based management is an attempt to address this disconnect. As noted throughout this chapter, SBM reforms in different countries transfer control over school finances and staff to schools to different degrees, but the full potential of SBM can be exploited only upon the full transfer of this authority to schools.

SBM can make a significant contribution to achieving national goals for secondary education by substantially enhancing the effectiveness and efficiency of schools. Implementation of these reforms requires strong political commitment throughout the entire period of the reform. To produce expected results, the Ethiopian government may wish to consider an SBM reform package that, over time, transfers full authority over staff and funds to schools. For the reform to succeed, it is critical that its duration not be very long—preferably five or six years. This report provides an option for implementing the reform in three phases, one after another. Finally, a comprehensive but concise legal framework for SBM is indispensible for successful implementation. Similarly, broad-based dialogue on the reform agenda will go a long way toward both its smooth conceptualization and implementation.

Notes

1. This chapter is based on Smith (2011).
2. A charter school in the United States operates independently under a performance agreement that spells out its educational program and goals and is largely funded on a per-pupil basis.
3. Harlem Children's Zone Inc. is a community-based organization serving over 17,000 children living in a 100-city block area in Harlem in New York City. It runs elementary, middle, and high schools (including Promise Academy Charter Schools) and colleges.
4. Education and Training Management Boards are established at the woreda, kebele, and subcity levels to lead and supervise educational work within their respective administrative areas.)
5. Discretionary funds are funds controlled at the school level that can be used according to criteria and procedures established by the School Management Committee.
6. Parent Teacher Student Committees (PTSCs), rather than PTAs, exist in the City Administration of Addis Ababa.

References

Abdulkadiroglu, Atila, Josh D. Angrist, Susan M. Dynarski, Thomas J. Kane, and Parag A. Pathak. 2011. "Accountability and Flexibility in Public Schools: Evidence from Boston's Charters and Pilots." *Quarterly Journal of Economics* 126 (2): 699–748.

Angrist, Josh D., Susan M. Dynarski, Thomas J. Kane, Parag A. Pathak, and Christopher R. Walters. 2010. "Inputs and Impacts in Charter Schools: KIPP Lynn." *American Economic Review: Papers & Proceedings* 100 (2): 1–5.

Barrera-Osorio, Felilpe, Tazeen Fasih, and Harry A. Patrinos. 2009. *Decentralized Decision Making in Schools: The Theory and Evidence on School-Based Management*. With Lucrecia Santibáñez. Washington, DC: World Bank.

Bruns, Barbara, Deon Filmer, and Harry A. Patrinos. 2011. *Making Schools Work: New Evidence on Accountability Reforms*. Human Development Perspectives. Washington, DC: World Bank.

Caldwell, B. 2005. "School-Based Management." Education Policy Series. UNESCO International Institute for Educational Planning, Paris.

Clark, Damon. 2009. "The Performance and Competitive Effects of School Autonomy." *Journal of Political Economy* 117 (4): 745–83.

Dobbie, Will, and Roland G. Fryer. 2011. "Are High-Quality Schools Enough to Increase Achievement Among the Poor? Evidence from the Harlem Children's Zone." *American Economic Journal: Applied Economics* 3 (3): 158–87.

Duflo, Esther, Pascaline Dupas, and Michael Kremer. 2011. "Peer Effects, Pupil-Teacher Ratios, and Teacher Incentives: Evidence from a Randomization Evaluation in Kenya." *American Economic Review* [American Economic Association] 101 (5): 1739–74. http://www.aeaweb.org/articles.php?doi=10.1257/aer.101.5.1739.

Elmore, Richard F. 2004. *School Reform from the Inside Out: Policy, Practice, and Performance*. Cambridge, MA: Harvard University Press.

Ethiopia, Federal Democratic Republic of MOE (Ministry of Education). 2002. "Directive for Educational Management, Organization, Public Participation, and Finance." MOE, Addis Ababa.

Ethiopia, Transitional Government of. 1994. "Education and Training Policy." Transitional Government of Ethiopia, Addis Ababa. Quoted in Dufera 2011.

Gertler, Paul, Harry A. Patrinos, and Eduardo Rodríguez-Oreggia. 2010. "Parental Empowerment in Mexico: Randomized Experiment of the *Apoyo a La Gestion Escolar* (AGE) Program in Rural Primary Schools in Mexico: Preliminary Findings." World Bank, Washington, DC. Unpublished manuscript.

Gertler, Paul, Harry A. Patrinos, and Marta Rubio-Codina. 2012. "Empowering Parents to Improve Education: Evidence from Rural Mexico." *Journal of Development Economics* 99(1): 68–79.

Hanushek, Eric A., and Ludger Wößmann. 2007. "The Role of Education Quality in Economic Growth." Policy Research Paper 4122. World Bank, Washington, DC.

Hoxby, Caroline M., and Sonali Murarka. 2009. "Charter Schools in New York City: Who Enrolls and How They Affect Their Students' Achievement." NBER Working Paper 14852. National Bureau of Economic Research (NBER), Cambridge, MA.

Hoxby, Caroline M., and Jonah E. Rockoff. 2005. "Findings from the City of Big Shoulders." *Education Next* 5 (4): 52–58.

Jimenez, Emmanuel, and Yasuyuki Sawada. 1999. "Do Community-Managed Schools Work? An Evaluation of El Salvador's EDUCO Program." *World Bank Economic Review* 13 (3): 415–41.

King, E. M., B. Özler, and L. B. Rawlings. 1999. "Nicaragua's School Autonomy Reform: Fact or Fiction?" Working Paper 19. Impact Evaluation of Education Reforms Series. Development Research Group, World Bank, Washington, DC.

MOE (Ministry of Education) Office of the President. 2000. "Strengthening of the Management and Administration of Schools (Amendment) Proclamation 217/2000." MOE, Addis Ababa.

Smith, Harvey N. J. 2011. "Governance and Management of Secondary Education: From Decentralization to School Autonomy." Background paper prepared for *Secondary Education in Ethiopia*. World Bank Ethiopia Office, Addis Ababa. Unpublished manuscript. (Available upon request of Rajendra Joshi, rjoshi@worldbank.org.)

Verspoor, Adriaan. 2008. *At the Crossroads: Choices for Secondary Education in Sub Saharan Africa*. With the SEIA Team. Africa Human Development Series. Washington, DC: World Bank.

World Bank. 2003. *World Development Report 2004: Making Services Work for Poor People*. Washington, DC: World Bank and Oxford University Press.

———. 2007a. "Guiding Principles for Implementing School-Based Management Programs." Online toolkit. Education Unit, Human Development Network, World Bank, Washington, DC. http://go.worldbank.org/4169W4FI70.

———. 2007b. "What Do We Know about School-Based Management?" Education Unit, Human Development Network, World Bank, Washington, DC.

———. 2008. "What is School-Based Management?" Education Unit, Human Development Network, World Bank, Washington, DC.

CHAPTER 7

Diversifying the Provision of Secondary Education

The nongovernmental education sector currently enrolls only five percent of secondary education students in Ethiopia. Reaching the target of universal secondary education is unlikely to be realized without a substantial increase in nongovernmental school enrollments. Such an increase will require some changes in policy. A first step will be to streamline the regulatory environment to allow nongovernmental providers to respond more efficiently to market demand. But unsubsidized nongovernmental schools will be affordable only to a small percentage of the secondary school population. Public-private partnerships would enable the government to support the enrollment of eligible disadvantaged poor students in nongovernmental schools through full or partial scholarships or vouchers. These partnerships would reduce demands on public resources, accelerate progress toward universal general secondary education, and free up resources for quality-enhancing inputs in government schools.

In many countries, the ministry of education has traditionally interpreted the task of managing secondary education to mean managing government-run secondary schools.[1] This inclination is increasingly inappropriate as new channels of service delivery—including distance education courses, short vocational courses, and informal training programs—emerge. These programs are often delivered by a proliferation of alternative providers, such as private for- and not-for-profit organizations, nongovernmental organizations (NGOs), faith-based organizations, and communities. This trend has important implications for the way in which secondary education is financed and delivered.

In many countries—including lower-middle-income countries—public schooling is increasingly organized through partnerships that involve formal or informal collaboration between government agencies and faith-based organizations, communities, and parents. The financing of secondary education is progressively becoming a joint effort of governments and parents, as parents pay fees to government schools and governments subsidize private providers. In this environment, the task of the government is no longer to manage government schools, it is to manage a system characterized by a number of different providers, decentralized decision making, and multiple sources of financing.

Some of these institutions are elite schools that charge fees affordable only to relatively wealthy parents; others are low-cost, low-quality "dwelling house" schools owned by small private for-profit operators (as in Malawi, India, and Kenya).[2] In many countries community schools run by parents or community associations (for example, "people's schools" in Vietnam and community schools in Nepal) have proliferated. Some of these schools are formally recognized by the government, usually based on government standards for educational provision. Others are unrecognized and operate as part of the informal economy (Harry Anthony 2007; Verspoor 2008a).

Nongovernmental Schooling in Ethiopia

In Ethiopia these changes are still at an early stage. The government currently remains the almost exclusive provider of general education, enrolling some 95 percent of students in primary and secondary education. Nongovernmental schools played an important role in the education sector prior to the mid-1970s, accounting for some 30 percent of institutional capacity in 1975. In that year, the military government outlawed the establishment of nongovernmental schools and nationalized those then in existence. The government that came to power in 1993, after the collapse of the military government, reopened the education sector to nongovernmental providers. Its commitment to the nongovernmental sector is reflected in the Education and Training Policy (ETP), which articulates a policy of "[creating] the necessary conditions to encourage and give support to private investors to open schools and establish various educational and training institutions" (Ethiopia 1994, 32).

As a result of this policy change, enrollments in nongovernmental institutions increased rapidly: doubling between 2006 and 2009 in technical and vocational education and training (TVET) programs, and more than tripling in tertiary undergraduate programs. In secondary education, the share of enrollments in nongovernmental (that is, private) secondary schools has increased steadily since 2000 (figure 7.1). Even more impressive, the number of secondary students enrolled in these schools increased from 57,000 in 2007/08 to about 92,000 in 2010/11, an annual growth rate of almost 17 percent—faster than the growth of enrollment in government schools. Yet the nongovernmental sector enrolls a relatively small proportion of Ethiopian students. The 92,000 secondary students enrolled in the sector in 2010/11 represented only about 5.2 percent of total enrollments, a much lower share than that in countries such as Mauritius (55 percent), Indonesia (43 percent), Chile (57 percent), Vietnam (21 percent in upper secondary), Jordan (18 percent), and Ghana (16 percent) (EdStats).[3]

Rationale for Nongovernmental Provision

In many countries where a high share of secondary enrollment is in nongovernmental schools, deliberate government policy recognizes the private sector as a

Figure 7.1 Enrollments in Nongovernmental Secondary Schools, Selected Years
percentage of total

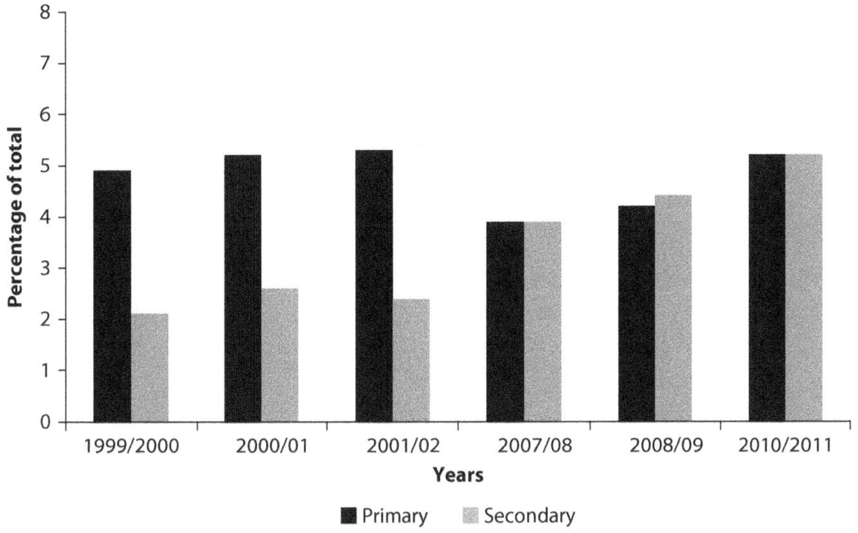

Sources: MOE 2000, 2001, 2002, 2008, 2009, 2011.

partner in the effort to reach national education development goals. The reasons differ according to national context and historical legacy, but the most important include (Latham 2011):

- Mobilizing additional financial resources
- Supplementing the limited capacity of government schools to absorb growing numbers of children, thereby expanding access and helping reduce class sizes
- Sharpening competitive pressures in the education sector, thus generating efficiency gains and spurring greater innovation in education delivery
- Tapping private sector knowledge, skills, and innovation—whether related to pedagogy, technology, or management—that may not be available in the government sector
- Allowing government education authorities to focus on core functions, such as policy, planning, curriculum development, and quality assurance, in which they have a comparative advantage over the private sector, rather than devoting resources to areas where they may not have such an advantage.

The most common rationale—certainly at the early stages of secondary education development—is the potential of the nongovernmental sector to reduce the public financial and infrastructure constraints on expanded enrollment. Increased nongovernmental provision can be supported through a regulatory framework that encourages the private sector to provide secondary education, but does not offer financial incentives. This approach can be effective in the early stages of secondary education expansion, but has limitations because unacceptable inequities in access will result—many qualified students from poor families will neither be able to find a place in a public school nor afford private school fees, leaving them unable to pursue education at this level.

In some countries inequities take the form of high-quality nongovernmental schools catering to students from higher-income families, while government schools provide relatively low-quality education to students from lower-income families. In other countries poor students—many of whom have lower scores on entrance examinations—do not qualify for limited places in high-quality government schools and are obliged to pay for their educations in nongovernmental schools. In both cases, students from poor backgrounds are at a disadvantage with regard to educational opportunities.

Several countries (for example, Mauritius and the Republic of Korea; see box 7.1) have engaged the private sector in partnerships that include public financial support for nongovernmental provision of secondary education. These partnerships are part of a strategy designed to rapidly expand access and do so equitably, but without large immediate capital investments. In Vietnam the government recently initiated a scholarship program to provide access to secondary education for disadvantaged students; the scholarships can be used in both public and private schools.

Strategies for Engaging with the Nongovernmental Sector

Partnerships with nongovernmental institutions allow governments to directly finance students (demand-side financing) or encourage private investments by improving private sector access to affordable financing, thus lowering the cost of the private provision of education. Specific arrangements are usually the result of a mixture of the historical legacy of private provision and deliberate policy choices. Several countries in Sub-Saharan Africa, for example, have a long tradition of faith-based education providers that have helped expand access, but these providers increasingly rely on public support to continue their operations, especially since many seek to enroll eligible poor students.

Common strategies for engaging with the nongovernmental sector include the public acquisition of:

- *Student places*, sometimes through voucher programs. In this strategy, a government enters into formal contractual arrangements with private schools and either pays an agreed amount for each student enrolled or provides students a voucher that can be used against tuition payments.
- *Professional and support services*. In this strategy, the government contracts private providers to deliver such services as school evaluations or reviews, teacher training, and textbook publication, as well as such noninstructional services as school construction, transportation, and school meals.

> **Box 7.1**
>
> ## Private Schools in Mauritius and Korea
>
> *Mauritius.* The introduction of free secondary education in 1977 transformed the way in which secondary education is provided in the country. Pupils enrolled in private schools do not pay tuition fees. The national government pays the staff wages and operating expenses of these schools through the Private Secondary Schools Authority (PSSA), based on a grant formula. In 2005, 66 percent of students in the general secondary stream and 58 percent of students in prevocational secondary education were enrolled in private schools.
>
> The PSSA exercises control over private secondary schools (both confessional and nonconfessional) and offers a range of incentive grants to encourage school managers to improve facilities. Denominational schools are administered by religious authorities (for example, Catholic, Anglican, Hindu, and Islamic). Private nonconfessional schools are administered by autonomous private entrepreneurs. In an attempt to establish equity in the secondary sector, the government tops up PSSA grants with other incentives, such as loans at preferential interest rates from the Development Bank of Mauritius. The loans are made available to private schools for infrastructure upgrades.
>
> *Korea.* To deal with inequities in educational access the Korean government implemented a national equalization program in 1974 that banned entrance examinations, established catchment areas, and instituted a lottery for schools in high demand. As a result enrollments soared and private providers stepped up to provide needed capacity. The equalization program guaranteed any deficit in the operating costs of private schools. Today most private schools receive direct financial assistance, subsidies, and tax exemptions from the government. In return the schools cede control over key areas—such as the curriculum, tuition, and teachers' salaries—to the government.
>
> *Source:* Verspoor 2008b.

- *Infrastructure.* In this strategy, private providers are responsible for the financing and design of new buildings, in exchange for the right to operate a school in these facilities for a specific period of time.

Box 7.2 provides examples of public-private educational partnerships established for different purposes.

Expanding Nongovernmental Provision of Secondary Education

In the context of a rapidly growing secondary education system, even the challenges of maintaining the proportion of students enrolled in nongovernmental institutions are considerable. Increasing the share of enrollment in these institutions at the secondary level will thus require special policy attention. For general

Box 7.2

Examples of Public Support for Private Provision of Secondary Education

Direct payments or vouchers

Uganda: Universal Secondary Education Program

- Government pays tuition fee for each eligible student enrolled in participating private secondary schools.
- Participating private schools are in areas where there are no places available in government schools.
- Per-student tuition fee paid by the government is well below the average per-student cost of public schools.
- In 2008, there were some 430 private secondary schools in the program serving approximately 56,000 students.

Pakistan: Foundation-Assisted Schools (FAS) Program

- FAS is a program of the Punjab Education Foundation, an independent autonomous institution established and funded by the Government of Punjab with the overall objective of promoting quality education for the poor through partnerships with the private sector.
- Participating private schools are located in poor urban and rural areas and are paid a monthly fee of 400 Pakistani rupees for each secondary student enrolled; no fees can be charged to students.
- Student learning performance is closely monitored and the continued participation of schools in the program requires that their students meet specific performance standards.
- The program was introduced in late 2005 and has expanded rapidly: from 54 schools and 20,000 students in late 2005 to 1,157 schools and 500,000 students in early 2008.

Chile: Vouchers

- The government pays a monthly fixed fee to subsidized private schools according to their enrollments. There is price discrimination among private subsidized schools depending on their location and level of education.
- Subsidized schools must meet minimum requirements, but enjoy management flexibility.

Thailand

The government provides monthly subsidies to private schools on a per-student-cost basis.

Korea

Private schools receive direct financial assistance, subsidies, and tax exemptions. In return, private schools have ceded control over the curriculum, tuition, and teachers' salaries to the government.

(box continues on next page)

Box 7.2 Examples of Public Support for Private Provision of Secondary Education *(continued)*

Professional services

Indonesia: Whole School Improvement

The Sampoerna Foundation is a philanthropical and corporate social responsibility organization that has implemented whole-school development projects in strategic locations across Indonesia. One of the projects involves 17 government schools and 5 Islamic (*madrasah*) schools, to which the Foundation provides school leadership training, professional development services for teachers, and education quality improvement programs.

Malaysia: Trust Schools-Private Management Support for Public Schools

Trust Schools are public schools that are managed jointly by private sector partners and Ministry of Education school leaders. The Ministry provides Trust Schools with more autonomy and in return requires accountability for improved student outcomes. Schools maintain their public status and funding, but their management responsibilities are transferred to a qualified private sector partner that works in collaboration with school leaders. The private partner is expected to provide operational, management, and educational expertise and, if necessary, additional funds to the schools. Successful applicants are required to establish a nonprofit foundation. This initiative is managed by the Khazanah Trust Schools Network. The network is led by the Government of Malaysia's investment holding arm, the Khazanah Nasional Berhad, which views education as a strategic industry and a critical driver of human capital development.

Infrastructure

Burkina Faso

The government has been providing no-interest loans for the construction of classrooms in private schools operated by nongovernmental organizations (NGOs) or private providers, on the condition that the education provider build one classroom for each one constructed with government funds within a maximum period of one year. The loan payback period is five years, following a grace period of two years. The government has also provided construction funding for classrooms on a matching-grant basis.

Thailand

Private schools that provide basic education can qualify for state-subsidized loans to build new school buildings or renovate old ones. The government also has a revolving fund that offers 4 percent-interest loans with a repayment period of 10–15 years to schools that can offer collateral.

Sources: Latham 2011; Verspoor 2008b (Burkina Faso).

---

secondary education (grades 9–10), even a target of only 5.2 percent of total enrollment for 2014/15 (a percentage equal to the 2009/10 share of total enrollment) would increase the number of students in nongovernmental schools from 73,000 in 2009/10 to about 135,000 in 2014/15, constituting an average annual increase of more than 13 percent.

At the preparatory level (grades 11–12) increasing enrollment in nongovernmental schools from 7.9 percent in 2009 to 10 percent of total enrollment by 2014/15 would double the number of students in these schools, from 19,139 to 38,315—representing an annual rate of growth of 15 percent. Because of the projected rapid growth in total secondary general enrollment, this pattern will continue over the longer term.

Even the comparatively modest 10 percent targets for nongovernmental secondary and preparatory school enrollments imply sustained rapid growth in absolute numbers. Over the period 2009–19 enrollments would triple in grades 9–10 and double in grades 11–12, implying annual growth rates of more than 12 percent and 7 percent, respectively. Progress toward a 20 percent target (of total secondary enrollments) by 2024/25 would require a growth rate of almost 20 percent for 15 years for grades 9–10 and 17 percent for grades 11–12. Dealing with this growth challenge is likely to require *improvements in the regulatory environment* and strategies for further engagement with nongovernmental providers through *negotiated partnerships.*

Streamlining the Regulatory Framework

The role of the private sector in education is recognized in Regulation No. 206/1995 of the Council of Ministers (Ethiopia 1995). This regulation permits the establishment of nongovernmental education institutions in the country, defines these institutions, and sets out broad rules for their governance at all levels of education. Table 7.1 describes the main elements of the regulatory framework for such schools in Ethiopia.

A key concern with the existing regulatory framework is the often lengthy process required to establish nongovernmental schools. The main reason for this situation is the difficulty of obtaining access to land and incentives, such as exemptions from import duties. In both cases, the problem is not the design of the regulatory framework, but rather, its implementation.

To ensure that the private sector can play a more significant role in the development of secondary education, as it does in the countries discussed in box 7.2, it may be necessary to strengthen the existing policy framework. New policies would focus on improving the way in which private schools are regulated, as well as the volume of information on private schools available to students, parents, and regulators.

Access to Land

Under current policy, regional governments allocate land for approved investment projects. By the mid-1990s, a number of regions in Ethiopia had adopted a policy that allows them to provide land to educational operators free of leasing charges. Only two regions then had a policy that charged fees for at least some levels of education (Amha et al. 1998).

Pursuant to Investment Proclamation No. 37/1996, regional governments are required to provide land to private investors within 60 days of receiving an

Table 7.1 Regulatory Framework for Nongovernmental Schools in Ethiopia

Aspect of regulation	Details
Recognition of private sector role in education	The role of the private sector is recognized in Regulation No. 206/1995 (Ethiopia 1995). New educational policy commits the government to creating the necessary conditions for increased private sector investment in education. The policy objective is to "provide choice for education service seekers who have the ability to pay."
Governing authority	Main elements of the regulatory framework for nongovernmental schools are contained in Regulation No. 206/1995.
Responsibility for private education	Responsibility for school education is split across different levels of government. Responsibility for private schools generally rests with the Regional Education Bureaus (REBs).
School licensing	Private schools must be licensed in order to operate legally in Ethiopia.
	The rules regarding the licensing of private schools are contained in Regulation No. 206/1995, which defines a private school as an educational institution run by a private investor and established for the purpose of conducting formal or nonformal education or training at any level (including kindergarten).
	Private schools can be for-profit or not-for-profit organizations; they can also be foreign owned.
Licensing process	Each individual school must be licensed by the relevant REB to operate legally. The approval process for licensing private schools involves the woreda, zonal, and regional education administrations.
	There is a one- or two-stage approval process, with preliminary approval from the woreda, zone, and REB. Final approval is given by the REB once buildings have been inspected and approved.
	The approval process takes approximately only one month, but the process of establishing a private school can take a long time because of delays in getting approvals for the use of land.[a]
	School licenses are renewable every two years, subject to satisfactory assessments.
	Schools can be closed if they do not meet government standards.
	REBs look at existing school provision when determining whether or not to approve applications.
Fees	Nongovernmental schools are free to set tuition fees. There are limits on fee changes, however, which can only be implemented at the end of an academic year and require several months' prior notification of parents.
Government subsidies	Private, NGO, and faith-based schools do not receive public subsidies. Public schools receive some subsidies in the form of paid teachers, materials, and free training.[b]
	There are no demand-side financing arrangements.
Human resources	A centrally established salary scale exists for government and public school teachers, who are paid by the government.[c] Nongovernmental schools negotiate their own salary contracts.
Curriculum, review, and qualifications	The curriculum for primary schools is set at the regional level and for secondary schools, at the national level. Nongovernmental schools and public schools must follow the curriculum, but can teach additional subjects.
	Regional examinations are required after grade 8 and national examinations, after grades 10 and 12, respectively. These exams determine students' progression to higher levels of education.
Operations	The school year is set by the REBs.
Provider representation	No genuine private school associations exist, although groups of schools associate.

Source: Latham 2011.
Note: REB = Regional Education Bureau, NGO = Nongovernmental organization.
a. In Ethiopia land is owned by the government, which provides land to entrepreneurs upon approval of investment projects.
b. Public schools are considered part of the nongovernmental sector; they are established and managed by local communities. They are not-for-profit, nongovernmental institutions financed by government subsidies and student fees.
c. Public schools receive partial support for teacher salaries from the government.

application for an approved investment (Ethiopia 1996). Yet delays in obtaining access remain a significant constraint, including in the education sector. It is important that a more transparent and timely land allocation process be implemented. One possibility would be to identify and "bank" land that is available to, and suitable for, the education sector, as well as establish in advance a schedule for land allocation to investors. Together, these steps would allow investors to better plan their investments, as they would know up front what land was available and when the allocation would take place.

Standards

There are a number of standards that schools must meet, including minimum requirements for classroom size, a playground area, and parking (Latham 2011). These standards mean that private investors must have a considerable amount of land in order to build a school. The objectives of these regulations—to ensure the quality and safety of private schools—are often laudable. The risk is that standards may drive up the cost of educational provision or indeed, make it unfeasible (for example, due to space limitations, as in cities such as Addis Ababa). Setting standards too high can frustrate government objectives by restricting private investment in education. It is therefore important to ensure that standards are "fit for purpose" and reflect local conditions.

Information

Access to timely information for making school, policy, and regulatory decisions can improve parental choice and regulatory decision making. Poorly performing schools are more likely to pay a price for not delivering the quality of education desired in a system in which consumers and regulators are better informed. Currently there is limited information available on school quality—such as examination scores, school review and assessment results, and other indicators—that can help parents and students make decisions on which school to attend.

Measures that could be introduced to improve available information include: (1) requiring nongovernmental schools to disclose information to regulators and the general public (regarding, for example, fees, performance indicators, or examination results) as a condition of licensing, and (2) maintaining a directory of nongovernmental schools with individual descriptions. The government may also wish to consider encouraging and facilitating the development of a private school association; such an association could carry out the information dissemination role outlined above and drive the self-regulation of quality in nongovernmental schools.

Toward Public-Private Partnerships

Despite low per capita incomes in Ethiopia, an increasing number of families are able to send their children to nongovernmental schools. Nongovernmental education and training provision, particularly of TVET and higher education, is expanding rapidly. Nevertheless the inability of much of the population to afford private school fees is likely to constrain the expansion of nongovernmental secondary education and create a system with unacceptable inequities in access.

Financing students in nongovernmental educational institutions would expand the educational opportunities of students from poorer backgrounds, reduce pressure on the limited Ethiopian government budget, and accelerate progress toward secondary education enrollment objectives. The total cost per student in government secondary schools in 2009/10 was estimated at about Br 3,000. It is quite likely that places in nongovernmental schools could become available for government-sponsored students at a considerably lower rate if policies more conducive to the expansion of nongovernmental schools are put in place. The savings the government could realize through public-private partnerships (PPPs) are thus potentially significant and would enhance its ability to increase expenditures on quality-enhancing inputs in government schools.

Experience suggests that the most efficient way to provide funding to nongovernmental providers through a PPP is to link subsidies to the enrollment of eligible students. Financing mechanisms for this purpose could be introduced in a variety of ways, for example, by allocating vouchers or scholarships to students at the woreda or kebele level, using education opportunity grants provided by the central government and supplemented by local or external funds. Such a decentralized system would allow local authorities to accurately target those families and groups most in need, such as those living in remote areas with no access to government schools and insufficient income to pay private school fees. The voucher or scholarship would allow students to enroll in a nongovernmental school with boarding facilities, if necessary.

Another approach would be to target areas without a secondary school or with a government school that lacks adequate capacity, then contract nongovernmental schools in the area to provide places for an agreed price (fee) per student, to be paid by the government. This is essentially the strategy the government of Uganda has followed in its quest to achieve universal secondary education. In other areas (Francophone Africa, for example) governments negotiate with nongovernmental providers (or their association representatives) the per-student fee and the number of places that will be made available for government-sponsored students. The ministry of education of the country then assigns students to specific schools. Some governments that have adopted this approach allow nongovernmental providers to ask parents to complement the government subsidy with a payment, which brings total tuition up to the usual level (Verspoor 2008b).

Facilitating Access to Financing

At present, education entrepreneurs have a limited range of available financing sources. Banks are often not interested in lending to the education sector, which is still seen as social in nature. Even when banks do lend to the sector, they are typically not interested in financing long-term investments. In addition, bank

> **Box 7.3**
>
> **IFC Private Sector Support Program in Africa**
>
> Through a partial risk-sharing guarantee concluded with local commercial banks, the International Finance Corporation (IFC) is helping local banks expand their lending to the private school sector in Africa. Under the Private Sector Support Program (PSSP), the IFC shares with local banks the risk on loans extended to eligible private schools. These loans are used to finance construction, the purchase of educational materials, and other capital expenditures. In parallel, the IFC supports a technical assistance program that comprises an *introductory workshop* for all targeted schools, *school development services* (in the form of workshops and one-on-one consulting), the development of a series of *school operating manuals*, and the building of sustained local capacity (that is, a *local service provider*) to deliver these services after the end of the IFC program.
>
> *Source:* World Bank; IFC PSSP.

interest rates are often at levels that make private school investments unfeasible for prospective operators, given the relatively long lag time before they reach profitability.

To help address this problem, the government could consider a number of initiatives, including:

- Improving the regulatory environment and incentive policies, such as tax holidays and exemption from import duties, for nongovernmental schools in order to encourage investors—small and large—to invest in the secondary education sector
- Providing subsidized loans for school construction (box 7.2)
- Instituting a credit facility for nongovernmental schools (box 7.3) that would provide loan guarantees to prospective nongovernmental school operators that meet certain quality standards.

Strengthening Capacity

Regulators and schools need to appreciate the objectives of a new regulatory environment if it is to have any impact. The Ethiopian MOE is committed to providing a policy environment conducive to private sector education. However, it is not clear that the potential contribution of this sector and the instruments needed to harness its contribution are fully appreciated and understood at both the central and lower levels of the system. It will be important, for example, for MOE staff and other stakeholders to familiarize themselves with possible alternative PPP modalities and develop a framework that is most appropriate for the Ethiopian context.

To have a lasting impact these efforts need to be supported by actions that build the MOE's institutional capacity to manage relationships with the nongovernmental sector. This would involve assigning specific responsibility for managing relationships with private education providers and working closely with them to design the specifics of public-private partnership arrangements, including:

- Establishing a Nongovernmental Education Working Group, comprised of members of the public and private sectors, to oversee a private education study; the study would collect data on different types of nongovernmental education provision (for-profit and not-for-profit) and consider such issues as the drivers of growth of nongovernmental schools, the quality of educational provision, and the unit delivery costs of private education
- Mandating this working group to prepare a nongovernmental education development strategy and policy investment framework, complete with proposals for:
  - A regulatory framework that identifies eligibility criteria for nongovernmental providers to participate in a PPP
  - Specific financial mechanisms that provide incentives to nongovernmental providers to expand their supply of school places
  - A school review mechanism responsible for assessing the performance of nongovernmental schools
  - Coordination arrangements between central and regional education offices responsible for liaising with nongovernmental education providers.

As important as it is to strengthen MOE's capacity to engage with the nongovernmental sector, it is equally crucial to develop the capacity of the nongovernmental sector to participate in PPPs in a responsible way. The sector needs to organize itself, possibly through the creation of one or more associations of private providers.

Currently there is a lack of communication between the government and the nongovernmental education sector, as well as among different types of nongovernmental providers. There is also no forum in which the collective nongovernmental sector can interact with the government and its advisers. The absence of such an association(s) hinders broader interaction with the government and makes it difficult for the private education sector to regulate itself. Further advantages that would accrue from such an association are that it would provide a vehicle for:

- Organized participation in the Nongovernmental Education Working Group mentioned above
- Linking a possible education financing facility to accreditation standards established by the association and verified by the MOE
- Sharing best practices among private sector operators, advisors, and teachers
- Developing and coordinating school improvement initiatives, including staff and management training.

Conclusion

Continued rapid growth of secondary enrollments in the nongovernmental sector has the potential to rapidly expand the number of places available at this level of education, reduce financial demands on the government budget, ensure progress toward universal general secondary education, and free up resources for investments in quality-enhancing inputs in government schools.

Mobilizing the nongovernmental sector to support secondary education will require two parallel efforts. First, it will be important to streamline the regulatory framework and allow the nongovernmental sector to respond more efficiently to market demand. At the same time, given Ethiopia's current stage of development, it is clear that there are limitations to effective demand for private secondary education because its cost will likely be affordable to only a small part of relevant age cohort (not much more than 20 percent). Enrolling even 10 percent of secondary students in nongovernmental schools would be a considerable achievement and require rapid growth in nongovernmental school enrollment.

More ambitious targets can be envisaged over the longer term, but would require policies that move beyond accepting the nongovernmental sector as a self-financing, parallel system and develop public-private partnerships in which government resources support the sector's development. As a result, the nongovernmental sector would become an integral part of the development strategy for secondary education. Implementation of this scenario would, however, require substantial efforts to work out a partnership framework satisfactory to all parties and develop the capacity of both MOE and nongovernmental providers to manage such partnerships and fulfill their agreed roles and responsibilities. Even under the best of circumstances the development of a PPP framework may take several years—a strong argument for beginning the exploration of different policy options without delay.

Notes

1. This chapter is based on Latham 2011.
2. "Dwelling house" schools are operated in an individual's home.
3. Figures are for 2009 or latest available year.

References

Amha, Wolday, Mulat Demeke, Djene Aredo, and Assefa Admassie. 1998. "Strategy to Encourage Private Sector Investment in Education and Training." PHRD (Policy of Human Resource Development) Project, East African Development and Training Consultants, Addis Ababa. Quoted in Latham 2011.

Ethiopia, Federal Democratic Republic of Council of Ministers. 1995. Regulation No. 206/1995. Council of Ministers, Addis Ababa.

———. 1996. Investment Proclamation No. 37/1996. Council of Ministers, Addis Ababa.

Ethiopia, Federal Democratic Republic of Ministry of Education (MOE). 2000. "Education Statistics Annual Abstract (ESSA), 1992 EC (1999/00 GC)." MOE, Addis Ababa.

———. 2001. "ESSA, 1993 EC (2000/01 GC)." MOE, Addis Ababa.

———. 2002. "ESSA, 1994 EC (2001/02 GC)." MOE, Addis Ababa.

———. 2008. "ESSA, 2000 EC (2007/08 GC)." MOE, Addis Ababa.

———. 2009. "ESSA, 2001 EC (2008/09 GC)." MOE, Addis Ababa.

———. 2011. "ESSA, 2003 EC (2010/11 GC)." MOE, Addis Ababa.

Ethiopia, Transitional Government of. 1994. "Education and Training Policy." Transitional Government of Ethiopia, Addis Ababa. Quoted in Dufera 2011.

Patrinos, Harry Anthony, and Shobhana Sosale, eds. 2007. *Mobilizing the Private Sector for Public Education: A View from the Trenches.* Washington, DC: World Bank.

Latham, Michael. 2011. "Private Participation in Secondary Education in the Federal Democratic Republic of Ethiopia." Background paper prepared for *Secondary Education in Ethiopia*. World Bank Ethiopia Office, Addis Ababa. Unpublished. (Available upon request of Rajendra Joshi, World Bank, rjoshi@worldbank.org.)

Verspoor, Adriaan M. 2008a. *At the Crossroads: Choices for Secondary Education in Sub-Saharan Africa.* With the SEIA Team. Africa Human Development Series. Washington, DC: World Bank.

———. 2008b. "The Power of Public-Private Partnership: Coming Together for Secondary Education in Africa." Working Document Draft. Association for the Development of Education in Africa, Paris.

CHAPTER 8

Financing the Development of Secondary Education

Ethiopia's current pattern of public education expenditures reflects its legacy as a slow-growth, low-income economy. Given that the country's economy is now growing rapidly, it is essential to adjust this pattern by reducing per-student public expenditures in tertiary education and the share of tertiary education in the education budget. The analysis presented in this chapter demonstrates that, assuming a continued high rate of economic growth and strong government commitment to education (that is, a high level of budget allocations for the sector), it will be possible to finance the expansion of secondary education to reach the enrollment levels typically found in lower-middle-income countries. However, this goal is possible only if the country also implements policies that enhance the efficiency of public resource use in secondary education and accelerate the mobilization of private resources in the sector.

Secondary education systems throughout the developing world face the "twin challenges" of expanding access equitably and improving the quality and relevance of education at the same time (World Bank 2005). Responding to these challenges calls for broad reforms throughout the world, but perhaps more so in Sub-Saharan Africa than in any other region. Secondary education in this region is developing at a time when education systems need to respond to multiple demands and competing priorities, yet increases in public funding for the sector are largely dependent on economic growth and the ability of governments to mobilize more public resources.

A recent World Bank publication (Verspoor 2008) argues that under these conditions, expansion of secondary education as it currently exists in the region is financially and educationally inconceivable. The absence of action in the face of rapidly expanding demand for secondary school places is likely to have highly negative consequences for educational quality. Major changes in the way in which resources are deployed and mobilized are the core of reforms that countries in Sub-Saharan Africa must consider if a purposeful, orderly development of secondary education is to occur. The challenges of financing education at this level fit the pattern that many other countries in the region are experiencing, but are perhaps more challenging in Ethiopia, given both the ambitious education targets that it has set for itself and the high cost of secondary, technical and vocational education and training (TVET), and tertiary education.

The previous chapters have emphasized the importance of changing the purpose, quality, and management of secondary education. This chapter focuses on policy options that will enhance the financial sustainability of secondary education and protect its educational quality. Specifically, it explores the financial impact of changing the way in which the system currently delivers secondary education and mobilizes and allocates resources in the subsector.

The chapter begins by examining the per-student cost of secondary education in Ethiopia from an international comparative perspective; it then discusses the expected financing envelope for education in the country. This discussion is followed by a description of the simulation model used by Education Sector Development Program (ESDP) IV for financial projections and the way in which this model has been updated by the authors. Based on the updated ESDP simulation model, a base case scenario representing a likely path of education sector development within the boundaries of existing policies and practices was formulated.

There was a significant financing gap in the base case scenario. Simulations were then conducted to find out if the financing gap could be eliminated solely by increasing public financing for education within the expected resource envelope for education. The results showed that this possibility was unlikely. An assessment was then made to determine whether the financing gap could be eliminated solely through reforms that caused available resources to be used more efficiently and mobilized additional nongovernmental resources. However, results showed that this scenario was also not possible. Further simulations established that the financing gap could be eliminated through efficiency-enhancing measures, mobilization of additional nongovernmental resources, and increased public financing for education within the expected resource envelope.

Following the analysis of various policy options for the sustainable financing of secondary education, the chapter discusses the limitations of the analysis and concludes with considerations regarding the implementation of needed reforms.

Cost Per Student: Benchmarks

When assessing the financial sustainability of secondary education growth, it is important to consider the extent to which its expansion is constrained by per-student costs in government secondary schools or, alternatively, by a combination of high unit costs and unbalanced growth in other educational levels (primary or tertiary).

Table 8.1 provides international benchmarks for unit costs at different educational levels for comparison purposes. The data in the first two rows are based

Table 8.1 Comparison of Total Public Per-Student Spending
percentage of GDP per capita

	Year	Primary	Secondary	Tertiary
1. Fast-growing economies	Late 1990s	11	18	55
2. Slow-growing economies	Late 1990s	13	24	265
3. India	2004	8	27	60
4. Vietnam	2008	20	17	61
5. Indonesia	2008	11	12	16
6. Kenya	2004	22	24	275
7. Philippines	2007	19	23	10
8. Ethiopia[a]	2009	9	26	591

Source: World Bank 2005 (rows 1 and 2); World Bank 2009 (row 3); EdStats (rows 4–7).
Note: GDP = Gross domestic product.
a. Average ESDP IV simulation model data for the years 2006–09 (see Ethiopia 2010).

on World Bank analysis; they refer to spending patterns that were typical in the late 1990s in 15 developing countries selected for either their rapid or slow economic growth. These unit cost data are complemented by more recent data for a number of middle-income countries that have expanded their secondary education systems. The table shows that fast-growing economies and countries that have succeeded in expanding secondary enrollment have had much more balanced public per-student spending. In fast-growing economies, expenditure per secondary student was 64 percent higher than that per primary student; in slow-growing economies, the figure was 86 percent. Vietnam, India, Indonesia, and the Philippines show expenditure patterns consistent with that of the sample of fast-growing countries.

Table 8.2 shows differences in public per-student spending in relation to rates of economic growth and secondary enrollment expansion. These data are not meant to present causalities, they simply reflect international experience that should be taken into consideration when planning a secondary education development strategy. As the table demonstrates, expenditure per tertiary student was only about 3 times the expenditure per secondary student in fast-growing economies, compared to 11 times per secondary student in slow-growing economies.

The absolute numbers in table 8.1 make it clear that the divergence in expenditure patterns between fast- and slow-growing economies is created by a divergence in expenditures at levels beyond primary education, especially the tertiary level, where spending is too high in slow-growing economies. The relative numbers in table 8.2 clearly show that slow-growing economies and education systems that did not succeed in expanding secondary education had much less balanced spending across levels of education than did fast-growing economies. In the former group of countries, the ratio of public spending per secondary student to public spending per primary student was higher compared to the latter group of countries. Similarly, the ratio of spending per tertiary student to spending per secondary student was much higher in slow-growing

Table 8.2 Typical Per-Student Spending Patterns in Relation to Rates of Economic and Secondary Enrollment Growth

	Ratio of per-student spending	
	Secondary to primary	Tertiary to secondary
1. Economic growth		
Fast-growing economies	1.4	3.0
Slow-growing economies	2.2	11.0
2. Countries succeeding in expanding secondary enrollment	1.4	3.2
3. Countries not succeeding in expanding secondary enrollment	2.6	9.3
4. Ethiopia	2.8	22.2

Sources: Rows 1–3: reproduced from World Bank 2005, 143, table 7.6; row 4: ESDP IV simulation model (see Ethiopia 2010).

economies than in fast-growing economies. This means that less funding was available to expand access to secondary education.

Relative per-student spending in Ethiopia for secondary education (table 8.2) is double the level seen in fast-growing economies and countries that are succeeding in expanding secondary education, possibly because of limited cost sharing and the cost of infrastructure in Ethiopia. In fact, per-student public spending in the tertiary sector in Ethiopia exceeds all comparators in table 8.2 by a large margin. These comparisons suggest that when analyzing financing options for a rapidly expanding secondary system, the cost effectiveness of service delivery at all educational levels needs to be examined closely. Ethiopia's current pattern of public education expenditures reflects its legacy as a slow-growth, low-income economy. Given that the country's economy is now growing rapidly, it is essential to adjust this pattern by reducing per-student expenditures in higher education, implementing efficiency-enhancing measures in general secondary and preparatory education, and mobilizing nongovernmental resources wherever possible.

Fiscal Envelope for the Education Sector

For the period 2010/11–2014/15, ESDP IV assumes that the national budget is 19.7 percent of gross domestic product (GDP) and the education budget, 20.8 percent of the national budget (which is equivalent to 4.1 percent of GDP).[1] Recent trends in public education expenditures in Ethiopia are presented in table 8.3. In 2010/11, the actual share of GDP represented by the education budget was 4.6 percent.

The Ethiopian Growth and Transformation Plan (GTP) for 2010/11–2014/15 projects that the national budget as a share of GDP will increase to 23.7 percent by 2014/15. This appears to be an optimistic projection, given that public expenditures in 2010/11 were equal to 18.5 percent of GDP. In recent years, the national budget reached its highest share of GDP (20.8 percent) in 2006/07

Table 8.3 Trends in Public Education Expenditures in Ethiopia
percentage

Fiscal year	Actual expenditures					Budget[a]
	2006/07	2007/08	2008/09	2009/10	2010/11	2011/12
National budget as share of GDP	20.8	18.8	17.2	18.9	18.5	23
Education budget as share of national budget	23.6	21.3	22.1	23.8	24.9	22.6
Education budget as share of GDP	4.9	4	3.8	4.5	4.6	5.2

Source: Data provided by MOFED, May 2012.
Note: GDP = Gross domestic product.
a. Budget applies only to 2011/12.

and its lowest (17.2 percent) in 2008/09. The original ESDP IV model assumes that the share of the national budget allocated to education will be 20.8 percent. However, the actual share of education in national expenditures was 24.9 percent in 2010/11—the highest in the recent years. Even its lowest recent share—21.3 percent of the national budget in 2007/08—still exceeds the original EDSP IV projection of 20.8 percent. Moreover, the allocation for education in 2011/12 is 22.6 percent of this budget.

Very often the actual share of education in the national budget ends up being higher than the planned share because of relatively large recurrent expenditures in the education budget. Therefore, the recent increase in education expenditures to 24.9 percent of the national budget cannot be taken as intentional on the part of the government. It would be more prudent to assume that education expenditures will represent 22.6 percent of the national budget. If, as projected, the national budget as a share of GDP reaches 23.7 percent and the share of education in the national budget is maintained at 22.6 percent, education as a share of GDP could reach 5.4 percent—slightly higher than the 5.2 percent planned for 2011/12 (already the highest such share in the last six years).

Figure 8.1 presents a comparison of education budgets as shares of gross national product (GNP) for a number of countries and regions. As the figure shows, the share of GDP allocated to education in Ethiopia in 2011/12 (5.2 percent) is about the same as that allocated to education in developed countries. It is also higher than the GDP share for education in developing countries (leaving aside the difference between GNP and GDP)—even in lower-middle-income countries like Indonesia, the Philippines, and India. But it is substantially lower than the GDP share for education in Kenya and Tanzania, and substantially higher than that in Uganda. Given that the education budget as a share of GDP for 2011/12 in Ethiopia is roughly the same as the average GDP share for developed countries, it would be imprudent to expect education expenditures in Ethiopia to increase much beyond this level. Given the examples of Kenya and Tanzania, however, it is not inconceivable that the education budget could increase beyond 5.2 percent of GDP if the government so chooses. Based on the above discussions, the

Figure 8.1 Education as a Share of GDP, Selected Countries, Groups, and Regions

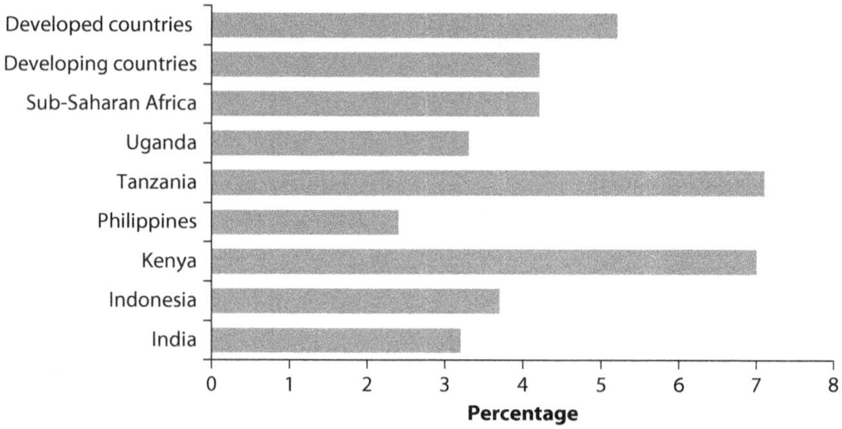

Source: UNESCO 2011.
Note: Data for 2008 or latest available year. GDP = Gross domestic product.

analysis in this chapter assumes that public education financing of 5.4 percent of GDP is the maximum fiscal envelope that Ethiopia could afford.

Updated ESDP IV Simulation Model

The cost and financing requirements of ESDP IV (see Ethiopia 2010) were projected through 2024/25 by a simulation model, which was updated for the purposes of this study. The updated model largely maintains the assumptions of the original model, with revisions based on actual 2009/10 data from the *Education Statistics Annual Abstract*, budgetary data from the Ministry of Finance and Economic Development (MOFED), and recent construction costs incurred in Ethiopia's regions. In addition, the following adjustments were made:

- Dated ESDP targets—such as the intake rate in grade 1 and dropout and repetition rates for all grades—have been maintained, but the linear trajectory has been adjusted to take account of progress realized to date, based on 2009/10 data. Enrollment numbers; intermediate gross and net enrollment rates; and efficiency, quality, and expenditure data have been adjusted accordingly.
- Teachers' salaries have been adjusted for the 2009/10 salary structure and are assumed to remain a fixed percentage of GDP per capita.
- Secondary classroom construction costs have been adjusted to reflect a cost of Br 425,000 per classroom (as compared to Br 223,000 in the original model). Other construction costs have been increased by 30 percent to reflect recent price increases.
- Community contributions to capital costs are assumed to increase from 10 percent in 2009/10 to 30 percent by 2014/15, instead of from 0 percent in 2009/10 to 50 percent in 2014/15.

A linear forward projection of the key enrollment parameters of the updated ESDP IV model results in a 2024/25 gross enrollment rate (GER) of 98 percent for grades 9–10 and 20 percent for grades 11–12. Assuming average annual real GDP growth of 11.2 percent, total education expenditures required to achieve these targets would increase from 4.3 percent of GDP in 2009/10 to 6.4 percent in 2012/13 and 6.6 percent in 2017/18, before decreasing to 5.8 percent in 2024/25. The financing gap—using the public financing parameters shown in table 8.4—would thus amount to some 38 percent of total projected education costs for the period 2009/10–2024/25. The gap for 2024/25 would be 30 percent. In absolute terms the financing gap increases from about Br 10 billion in 2011/12 to Br 17 billion in 2014/15, Br 30 billion in 2019/20, and Br 36 billion in 2024/25 (in constant 2010/11 birr).

In reality the financing gap is likely to be much smaller than that suggested by the updated ESDP IV projections for three reasons. First, the experience of lower-middle-income countries (LMICs) suggests that a GER of 98 percent—an ESDP IV assumption—for lower secondary education is not a feasible target for financial planning. As discussed in chapter 3, there is always a group of young people who, upon completion of primary education at the age of 14 years, do not have the interest or ability to continue to general secondary education and instead directly enter the labor market. Second, ESDP IV targets for reducing the dropout and repetition rates in grades 1–8 to 1 percent each by 2014/15 are unlikely to be reached; the grade 1 repetition rate in 2010/11 was 8.5 percent and the dropout rate, 13.1 percent, resulting in a grade 8 completion rate of less than 50 percent. This rate of completion constrains the growth of secondary enrollments. Third, at the end of grade 10, a number of students will directly enter the labor market and enroll neither in preparatory nor in formal vocational training programs.

In addition to overestimating costs, the updated EDSP IV model does not fully reflect the government's readiness to mobilize the resources needed to rapidly expand secondary education. For example, the model assumes that education funding comprises 20.8 percent of the national budget, whereas in fact, the actual education share of the budget was 23.2 percent in 2010/11. On the other hand, the updated model underestimates financing requirements, specifying nonsalary expenditures as 22 percent of total recurrent secondary education expenditures. This figure most likely underestimates the funding required to deliver curricula at an acceptable level of quality. A recent World Bank study of

Table 8.4 ESDP IV Education Budget Parameters, 2009/10

percentage

Variable	Recurrent (%)	Capital (%)	Total (%)
National budget/GDP	9.1	10.6	19.7
Education/ national budget	26.9	15.6	20.8

Source: ESDP IV financial simulation model, as updated by the authors in September 2011.
Note: GDP = Gross domestic product.

countries in Sub-Saharan Africa (Mingat et al. 2010), for example, considers nonsalary costs in the range of 38 percent to 45 percent of recurrent expenditures to be reasonable for lower secondary education, and in the range of 42 percent to 50 percent for upper secondary education. These parameters suggest that it is essential to gradually increase the current allocation of 22 percent to 40 percent by 2024/25 as part of the nation's effort to enhance the quality of secondary education.

Base Case Scenario

A "base case scenario" for assessing the financial implications of expanding secondary education to LMIC levels was developed for this analysis. This scenario represents a likely path of expanding secondary education, based on existing trends and guided by existing policies. It differs from the updated ESDP IV simulation model in that it incorporates the adjustments to enrollment and budget parameters discussed in the preceding section. The specific values for these and certain other important updated variables are shown in table 8.5.

Table 8.5 Key Parameter Values of Base Case Scenario

Assumptions	Target base case		Actual 2009/10	ESDP IV target[a]	
	Year	Value		Year	Value
Transition to grade 9, %	2024/25	90	78.7	2014/15	98
Transition to grade 11, %	2024/25	30	26.6	2009/10	20
Transition to higher education, %	2024/25	60	81.8	2014/15	95
Dropout rate after grade 10, %	2014/15	20	7.1	2014/15	0
Dropout rate for grades 1–8, %	2019/20	1	13.1	2014/15	1
Repetition rate, grades 1–8, %	2019/20	1	8.5	2014/15	1
Dropout rate, grades 9–10, %	2019/20	1	12[b]	2014/15	1
Repetition rate, grades 9–10, %	2019/20	1	12[b]	2014/15	1
Dropout rate, grades 11–12, %	2019/20	2	10[b]	2014/15	2
Repetition rate, grades 11–12, %	2019/20	3	11[b]	2014/15	3
National budget/GDP, %	2009/10	19.7	19.7	2009/10	19.7
Education budget/national budget, %	2009/10	23.2	23.2[c]	2009/10	20.8
Share of enrollment in nongovernmental schools, grades 9–10, %	2014/15	10	5.2	2014/15	5
Share of enrollments in nongovernmental schools, grades 11–12, %	2014/15	10	7.9	2014/15	10
Teacher-section ratio, grades 9–10	2014/15	1.60	1.6	2014/15	1.5
Teacher-section ratio, grades 11–12	2014/15	1.70	1.7	2014/15	1.8
Nonsalary recurrent cost (% of total cost)[d]	2009/10	40	22	2014/15	20
Classroom construction costs (e)	2009/10	425,000	425,000	2010/11	223,000
Classrooms with double-shift use, %	2009/10	0	0	2014/15	0

Source: ESDP IV financial simulation model, as updated by authors in September 2011.
Note: ESDP IV = Education Sector Development Program (ESDP) IV, GDP = Gross domestic product.
a. As specified in the ESDP IV model updated by MOE in August 2011.
b. Estimates based on actual data in the ESDP IV model updated by MOE in August 2011.
c. Budget allocation for 2010/11.
d. Includes nonteacher salaries, textbooks, instructional materials, and school operating costs.

These variables were selected because of their impact on the financial sustainability of an expanded secondary education system. The key challenge of a sustainable financial framework will be to mobilize the governmental and nongovernmental resources required, and then spend these resources efficiently for optimal school performance and student learning.

A large number of options likely to increase school performance have been discussed in the preceding chapters of this report. Those that are expected to lead to substantial cost reductions have been included in the financial sustainability analysis presented here. It is important to note, however, that many policy options recommended for consideration have not been included in the simulations, as they do not add significant financial costs.

Specifically, the analysis does not include the cost of reforms related to the curriculum discussed in chapter 4, teacher preparation and development (chapter 5), or school-based management (chapter 6). Estimating the cost of these reforms—the details of which remain to be worked out—is beyond the scope of this report. Nevertheless their cost is not expected to be large and hence, will not have a significant impact on the results of the analysis presented in this chapter, as discussed below:

- *Curriculum differentiation* will not significantly affect the cost of service delivery, provided that: (1) policies encouraging teachers to be certified in more than one subject are implemented; (2) teachers teach a number of periods closer to the official teaching load than is currently the case (chapter 4); and (3) electives are predominantly applied versions of existing subjects and can be taught by existing teachers. (A simulation of the potential savings associated with a decrease in the teacher-section ratio has been included in the financial analysis).
- *Improvements in teacher education* (chapter 5)—that is, establishing standards, accrediting universities, and providing regular school-based support—are largely organizational and will incur only limited costs. An estimated increase in funding for in-service training is assumed to be included in the increased allocation for nonteacher salary expenditures.
- *School-based management* will incur some capacity-building costs, but these are unlikely to significantly affect the financing gap (chapter 6).
- *An improved regulatory framework for nongovernmental education provision* is a legal and organizational issue that does not have a significant cost element.
- *Minimum enabling conditions* (chapter 9) should be possible within projected salary and nonsalary resource allocations.

The results of projections for the base case scenario are shown in figure 8.2. Total projected education expenditures over the period 2015/16–2024/25 represent an average of about 30 percent of the projected national budget for that period. The financing gap, shown on the right-hand side of the figure and expressed as a percentage of total education expenditures, averages about

Figure 8.2 Base Case Scenario

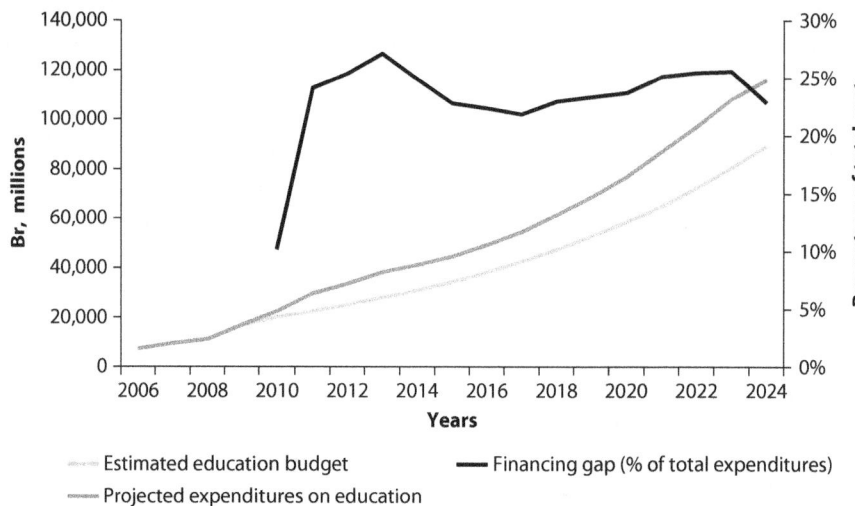

Source: Projection by authors, using the ESDP simulation model updated in September 2011.
Note: In this scenario, the total education expenditures account for 4.6 percent of GDP. ESDP = Education Sector Development Program (ESDP) IV, GDP = Gross domestic product.

Br 18 billion each year, or 24 percent of total education expenditures between 2015/16 and 2024/25.

Large investments in higher education and ambitious enrollment targets for TVET and secondary education are included in the base case scenario, which result in important shifts in how the education budget is allocated among subsectors between 2009/10 and 2024/25. As shown in figure 8.3, the share of TVET increases from 3.8 percent to 6.2 percent, and the share of secondary education, from 11.5 percent to 35.0 percent. (The category "general education secondary" in the figure actually includes allocations for both general and preparatory secondary education.)

These trends are the result of different rates of enrollment growth in the different education subsectors and the large variation in infrastructure costs between them. In the base case scenario primary enrollments are projected to increase by 40 percent over the 15-year period 2009/10–2024/25 and secondary enrollments, by 230 percent. The remarkable decline in the share of higher education in the total education budget, from 41.4 percent to 16.7 percent (figure 8.3), is mainly the result of a projected slowdown in tertiary education infrastructure investments after 2015, following an extremely rapid increase in these investments, from a low base, over the period 2009/10–2014/15. Investments in this subsector are projected to increase only moderately thereafter to accommodate projected growth in enrollments.

The base case scenario shows a significant shorter-term financing gap for the secondary sector for the period 2009/10–2014/15. This gap is caused by: (1) a slower-than-expected startup of ESDP IV, which results in larger financing requirements for the remaining years of the plan, as enrollment targets for

Financing the Development of Secondary Education 171

Figure 8.3 Base Case Scenario: Allocation of Education Budget by Subsector, 2009/10–2024/25
percentage

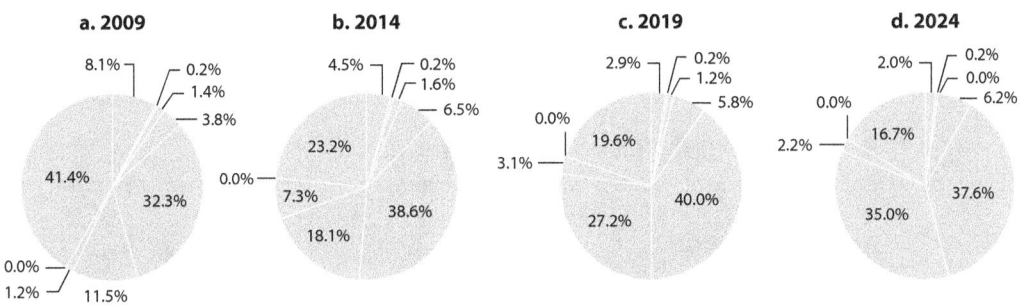

	2009	2014	2019	2024
Advisory & support services	8.1%	4.5%	2.9%	2.0%
Special education	0.2%	0.2%	0.2%	0.2%
Teachers' training centers	1.4%	1.6%	1.2%	0.0%
Vocational training	3.8%	6.5%	5.8%	6.2%
General education primary	32.3%	38.6%	40.0%	37.6%
General education secondary	11.5%	18.1%	27.2%	35.0%
General education other	1.2%	7.3%	3.1%	2.2%
Pre primary	0.0%	0.0%	0.0%	0.0%
Tertiary	41.4%	23.2%	19.6%	16.7%

Source: Projection by authors, using the ESDP IV simulation model updated in September 2011.
Note: In this scenario, total education expenditures account for 4.6 percent of GDP. ESDP = Education Sector Development Program (ESDP) IV, GDP = Gross domestic product.

2014/15 will need to be reached in a shorter period; and (2) certain large investments, especially in university construction and textbooks, envisaged for the early years of ESDP IV. The scenario assumes a national budget equal to 19.7 percent of GDP and aeducation budget equal to 23.2 percent of the national budget (the actual education allocation for 2010/11), which is equivalent to public financing for education of 4.6 percent of GDP.

Reducing the Financing Gap

Building an education system that effectively supports the economic development trajectory of Ethiopia (that is, reaching middle-income status) requires resolving the financing gap without jeopardizing educational quality. In fact, it means simultaneously ensuring sustained progress toward quality improvement and expanded access. It also means achieving these goals with additional national resources, as external support is already accounted for in the base case scenario.

What follows is an analysis of the financial implications of a number of longer-term options for secondary education policy reform. All of these options relate to the efficiency of resource deployment and the mobilization of nongovernmental resources. The government may wish to consider these choices as it attempts to reach its quantitative and qualitative objectives for secondary education in a financially sustainable way. The simulations discussed here are not intended to present a concrete recommendation on a package of policy reforms to bridge the financing gap, but to offer policy choices that can help guide the development of secondary education.

Reform Options for Reducing the Financing Gap

Policy reform options that may help bridge the financing gap in the base case scenario can be broadly grouped into two categories: those that *use available public funds more efficiently* and those that *mobilize additional nongovernmental resources*. Among the possible options for using available public funds more efficiently are decreasing the teacher-section ratio, continuing the practice of double-shift classroom use, and decreasing classroom unit costs. Increasing both the share of secondary enrollment in nongovernmental schools and community contributions to classroom construction costs are potential options for mobilizing more nongovernmental resources. Simulations of the base case scenario were conducted to see how these policy options would help reduce the financing gap in the base case scenario. The results of these simulations are presented in table 8.6.

Proportion of Financing Gap to be Borne by Secondary Education

Before analyzing these reform options further, it is important to identify how much the cost of secondary education delivery must be reduced in order to help

Table 8.6 Potential of Policy Options to Reduce Financing Gap in Base Case Scenario

Policy options		Projected reduction in financing gap, 2015/16–2024/25	
		Amount (Br, millions)	% reduction
Enhance efficiency	Decrease teacher-section ratio from 1.6 to 1.2 in general secondary education, and from 1.7 to 1.4 in preparatory secondary education, by 2024/25.	29,046	3.01
	Continue double-shift use of 20 percent of classrooms until 2024/25.	3,042	0.30
	Decrease classroom unit costs from Br 425,000 to Br 340,000 as of 2014/15.	3,650	0.37
Mobilize nongovernmental resources	*Alternative 1:* Increase nongovernmental school enrollments to 20 percent[a] by 2024/25 (compared to 10 percent by 2014/15 in base case scenario).	19,556	2.00
	Alternative 2: Increase nongovernmental school enrollments to a total of 30 percent[a] by 2024/25 (compared to 10 percent by 2014/15 in base case scenario).	40,563	4.27
	Increase community contributions to classroom construction from 30 percent to 50 percent of costs by 2014/15.	5,941	0.60

Source: Projections by authors, using the ESDP IV financial simulation model updated in September 2011.
Note: Br = Ethiopian birr, ESDP = Education Sector Development Program (ESDP) IV.
a. Starting from the 2009/10 enrollment levels of 5.2 percent in general secondary and 7.9 in preparatory secondary education.

Table 8.7 Share of Financing Gap Assigned to Various Education Subsectors
percentage

	Primary	Secondary	Tertiary	Other[a]	Total
Subsector share of total education financing in 2024/25	37.60	35.00	16.70	10.7	100.00
Subsector share of total financing for primary, secondary, and tertiary education[b]	42.10	39.20	18.70	n.a	100.00
Apportionment of financing gap for education budget of 4.6% of GDP	10.05	9.36	4.47	n.a	23.88
Apportionment of financing gap for education budget of 5.2% of GDP	5.70	5.31	2.53	n.a	13.54

Source: Projections by authors, using the ESDP simulation model updated in September 2011.
Note: GDP = Gross domestic product, n.a. = Not applicable.
a. "Other": includes all education subsectors except for primary, secondary, and tertiary education.
b. Shares have been derived by neglecting the share of other sectors in education financing.

close the financing gap. The gap identified for the base case scenario pertains to the entire education sector. Sustainable financing of secondary education will thus be possible only when all educational subsectors act in tandem to reduce this gap. The scope of this study is limited to identifying measures that can help reduce the gap within the boundaries of secondary education. Therefore it is important to determine the specific share of the financing gap that needs to be bridged by secondary education.

As shown in figure 8.3, the three major education subsectors are primary, secondary, and tertiary education. The average education budget financing gap of 23.88 percent for the period 2015/16–2024/25 is apportioned to these subsectors, based on their projected weight in the education budget over time (figure 8.3). Assuming an education budget of 4.6 percent of GDP (that is, the actual budget for 2010/11), the portions of the gap to be addressed by the primary, secondary, and tertiary subsectors would be 10.05 percent, 9.36 percent, and 4.47 percent (table 8.7).

If, however, the education budget is increased to 5.2 percent of GDP, the financing gap is reduced to 13.54 percent from 23.88 percent, and these percentages change to 5.70, 5.31, and 2.53, respectively. Given the relatively lower shares of the total education budget allocated to secondary education in the early years of the 2015/16–2024/25 time period, the portion of the financing gap assigned to it is on the high side. Nevertheless, it will be used as a yardstick for the analysis in the following sections.

Alternative Scenarios for Secondary Education Financing

The preceding analysis established the following: the financing gap in the base case scenario, the portion of this gap that secondary education must cover through policy reforms to ensure sustainable financing, the potential of various reform options to reduce the gap, and the maximum fiscal envelope that will likely be available for education sector financing. Using the values established by that analysis, this section will attempt to identify alternative scenarios for sustainable financing of secondary education.

Two packages of policy reforms—"deep reform" and "moderate reform"—are used to build the scenarios. These packages, shown in table 8.8, differ only in the value that they assign to nongovernmental enrollment and community contributions to school construction costs. Similarly, three alternative levels of public financing for the education sector—4.6 percent, 5.2 percent, and 6.0 percent of GDP—are used (table 8.9). Alternative scenarios for expanding secondary education were then generated based on the different combinations of reform packages and financing levels shown in table 8.9.

Simulations showed that the "no reform and education budget of 6.0 percent of GDP" scenario fully eliminates the financing gap for the education

Table 8.8 Policy Reform Packages for Reducing Cost of Public Service Delivery

Reform package	Policy options
Deep reforms[a]	• Decrease teacher-section ratio from 1.6 to 1.2 for general secondary education and 1.7 to 1.4 for preparatory secondary education by 2024/25
	• Continue double-shift use of 20 percent of classrooms until 2024/25
	• Decrease per classroom cost from Br 425,000 to Br 340,000 by 2014/15
	• Increase enrollment in nongovernmental schools to 30 percent by 2024/25 from 5.2 percent and 7.9 percent, respectively, for general and preparatory secondary education in 2009/10
	• Increase community contribution to classroom construction to 50 percent in 2014/15 from 10 percent in 2009/10
Moderate reforms	Same as deep reform, but with the following changes:
	• Increase enrollment in nongovernmental schools only to 20 percent
	• Increase community contributions to classroom construction costs to 30 percent 2014/15 from 10 percent in 2009/10

Note: Base case scenario projects an increase in nongovernmental enrollment to 10 percent of all secondary enrolment.
a. This reform package is referred to as "deep reform" because the reforms are very radical.

Table 8.9 Alternative Scenarios for Expanding Secondary Education

	Policy dimension		
Financing dimension	No reform	Moderate reform	Deep reform
4.6% of GDP	Base case scenario (no reform and education budget of 4.6% of GDP)	n.a.	Deep reform and education budget of 4.6% of GDP
5.2% of GDP	n.a.	Moderate reform and education budget of 5.2% of GDP	n.a.
6.0% of GDP	No reform and education budget of 6.0% of GDP	n.a.	n.a.

Note: GDP = Gross domestic product, n.a. = Not applicable.

sector. But as discussed above, an education budget of 6.0 percent of GDP is beyond the maximum resource envelope for education. It is thus unfeasible to expand the secondary sector solely by counting on additional public resources. Given that the financing gap cannot be eliminated solely by increasing public financing, initial simulations were conducted to determine whether the gap could be eliminated relying solely on policy reforms. Simulations were accordingly run for a package of deep reforms and an education budget of 4.6 percent of GDP (figure 8.4). In this scenario, the average educational sector funding gap over the period 2015/16–2024/25 is 16.0 percent, compared to 23.9 percent in the base case scenario (that is, no reforms and an education budget of 4.6 percent of GDP). To eliminate the financing gap assigned to secondary education (9.36 percent; see table 8.7), however, the gap should have been reduced to 14.5 percent. Therefore, the financing gap cannot be bridged solely by policy reforms.

Clearly it is impossible to eliminate the financing gap assigned to secondary education solely by increasing public financing or implementing deep policy reforms. Further simulations were thus conducted to find out if a combination of the moderate reform package with expanded public financing (within the limits of the maximum expected fiscal envelope) could eliminate the share of the financing gap assigned to secondary education. After multiple iterations, the scenario identified in table 8.9 was shown to do so: public financing for education equal to 5.2 percent of GDP and the package of moderate policy reforms outlined in table 8.8.

This conclusion was reached after conducting simulations for various education budget levels with moderate reforms. For each level of education budget,

Figure 8.4 Deep Reform with Education Budget of 4.6 Percent of GDP

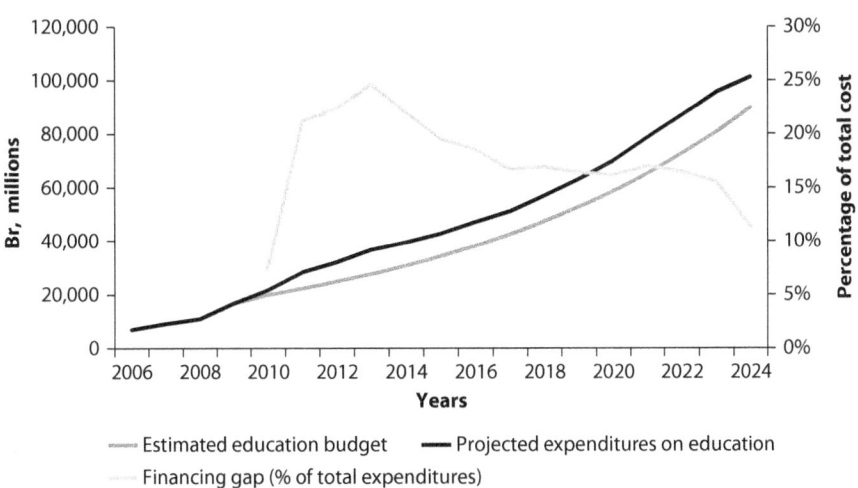

Source: Projection by authors, using the ESDP simulation model updated in September 2011.
Note: GDP = Gross domestic product, ESDP = Education Sector Development Program (ESDP) IV.

the gap to be reduced by secondary education was determined using the approach illustrated in table 8.7. Subsequently, simulations were carried out for moderate reforms and various education budget levels to find out which budget would enable moderate reforms to fill the financing gap apportioned to secondary education.

The moderate reform package and an education budget of 5.2 percent of GDP scenario (figure 8.5) reduced the financing gap for the period 2015/16 to 2024/25 to 7.1 percent; however, this gap needed to be reduced only to 8.2 percent (table 8.10). During this period the financing gap was below 8.2 percent for all years except for 2015/16 and 2016/17, when it was 9.7 percent and 8.8 percent, respectively. At the beginning of the reform period the gap was

Figure 8.5 Moderate Reform with Education Budget of 5.2 Percent of GDP

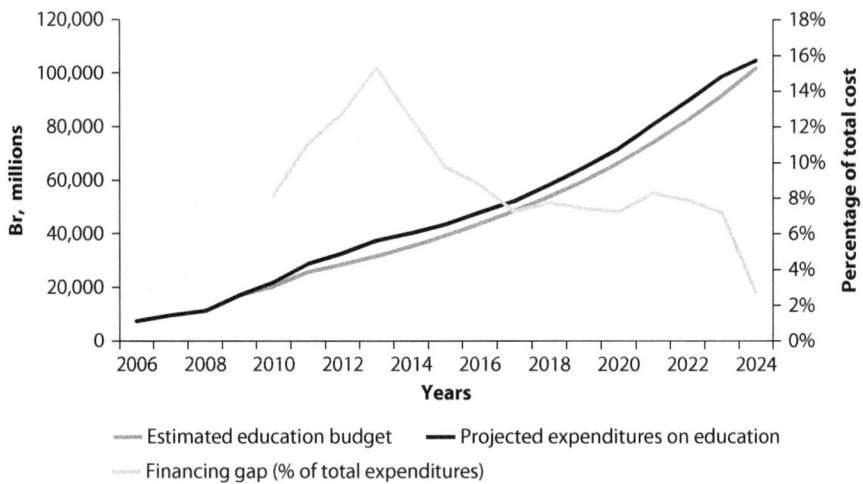

Source: Projection by authors, using the ESDP simulation model updated in September 2011.
Note: GDP = Gross domestic product, ESDP = Education Sector Development Program (ESDP) IV.

Table 8.10 Ability of Alternative Scenarios to Cover the Education Sector Financing Gap

Item	Deep reform with education budget of 4.6% of GDP	Moderate reform with education budget of 5.2% of GDP
Gap without reforms, % (1)	23.9	13.5
Gap to be reduced by secondary reforms, % points[a] (2)	9.4	5.3
Gap to be reduced to by secondary reforms, % (3 = (1) − (2))	14.5	8.2[b]
Gap after secondary reforms, %	16.0	7.1
Gap reduction adequate?	No (16.0>14.5)	Yes (7.1<8.2)

Source: Author's analysis, using the ESDP IV financial simulation model updated in September 2011.
Note: Financing gap is for the years 2015/16–2024/25. Total reductions resulting from individual policy interventions do not tally with total reductions resulting from the combination of all interventions because of the difference in public financing involved in the two scenarios. GDP = Gross domestic product, ESDP IV = Education Sector Development Program (ESDP) IV.
a. See table 8.7.
b. This number is smaller than that for the base case scenario due to a greater projected sector budget.

higher by design, as the reform intensifies gradually. In 2024/25 the gap was reduced to 2.8 percent because the maximum impact of reforms is achieved by that point. This result confirms that the financing gap can be bridged through a combination of moderate policy reforms and enhanced public financing for secondary education within the expected available resource envelope.

Table 8.10 compares how well the deep reform scenario and the moderate reform scenario with greater public financing close the financing gap for the period 2015/16–2024/25.

Limitations of the Analysis

Although the education sector needs long-term planning, it is impossible to do reliable long-term financial projections because of uncertainties related to economic growth over time. Therefore, the results presented here should be regarded as indicative rather than definitive and the analysis presented in this chapter, as a framework for the periodic updating of projections for secondary education financing.

Another limitation of the financial analysis in this chapter is that governments make a political decision when they allocate a certain share of the national budget to education. While the education budget as a share of either GDP or the national budget is widely watched and monitored, the decision on the size of the share of the education budget allocated to the secondary subsector is mostly left to education ministries—a decision that does not come under the same rigorous public scrutiny. In addition, there are no established norms for establishing this share, making it impossible to project the secondary education budget alone.

Consequently, the analysis apportions part of the total education financing gap to secondary education by distributing the total gap among the primary, secondary and tertiary education sectors proportionate to their shares in the education sector budget over time. This is another reason for treating the results of the analysis presented here as indicative rather than definitive. Finally, the reform packages used to formulate the alternate financing scenarios are simply two among many possible such packages. While updating financial simulations, it would be useful to explore other possible policy reform options, as well as other packages of reforms, in order to make the analysis richer.

Implementing Reforms

This chapter has attempted to outline an approach to closing the financial gap. The analysis is meant to provide policy makers information about the choices available for expanding secondary education, and thus support Ethiopia's transition to a middle-income economy. The actual choice of reforms and the level of public financing for education are political decisions better handled by policy makers themselves.

This section considers issues related to the implementation of policy reform options. Decreasing the teacher-section ratio, for example, can yield significant cost reductions. The proposed reform does not seek to increase the workload of teachers beyond existing norms, but to maintain this workload closer to these norms. Though at first glance this reform may not seem difficult, in reality it is. Among the enabling conditions for implementing this reform are:

- Teachers prepared to teach more than one subject with incentives offered for doing so, which would give them a workload in line with existing norms, particularly in small schools
- A standards-based career promotion system that encourages teachers to work hard
- A school-based management system that provides schools incentives to optimally use their teachers.

This list of enabling conditions makes clear that reforms related to financing cannot be implemented as stand-alone reforms. Rather, they should become part of a broader secondary education reform. Because reducing the teacher-section ratio will require serious preparation, the target date of 2024/25 was chosen for this change. The contribution of this intervention to decreasing delivery costs would be even higher if it was implemented at a faster pace.

Another policy reform that can significantly reduce the cost of public service delivery is increasing the share of secondary enrollment in nongovernmental schools. As mentioned in chapter 7, the share of nongovernment enrollment in many countries is over 20 percent—the level envisaged in the moderate reform package. For example, enrollment in nongovernmental schools in Indonesia is 43 percent; in Pakistan, 31 percent; and in Bangladesh, 96 percent. These countries have managed to expand secondary education with public education expenditures that represent a relatively low share of GNP: 3.7 percent in Indonesia and 2.9 percent in both Pakistan and Bangladesh (UNESCO 2011). While some countries have done this via public-private partnerships (PPPs), others have done so without such partnerships. For example, Bangladesh heavily subsidizes private schools by paying the salaries of teachers, as its resources permit.

Though a rapid expansion of nongovernmental enrollment is an attractive option in terms of freeing up scarce resources for quality inputs and a rapid expansion of access to secondary education, it is important not to lose sight of the possible inequities in access that such an expansion could produce. In addition, a large private sector may result in poor-quality schools. Taking this factor into consideration, it is advisable to choose an appropriate mix of unsubsidized private provision and private provision via PPPs (chapter 7). For example, the target of 30 percent for nongovernmental enrollment included in the "deep reform package" could be reached by combining 20 percent unsubsidized private enrollment and 20 percent subsidized enrollment (at the rate of 50 percent of the per-student cost established by the government). Since this policy reform also requires significant upstream work, the distant time horizon of 2024/25 was chosen as the target date for reaching the target of 30 percent. The actual cost savings produced by this reform will be larger or smaller, depending on the pace and depth of the reform.

Community contributions to classroom construction can also significantly reduce the cost of public service delivery in secondary education. Many countries have succeeded in expanding secondary education with small public investments in classroom construction. Nepal is a notable example—a country where all costs of classroom construction associated with the creation of secondary schools are borne by local communities. Nevertheless, the gross enrollment rate for general secondary education (grades 9–10) has reached 66 percent in that country (Nepal 2010). Ethiopia already has a tradition of significant community contributions to classroom construction. It thus makes sense to encourage this tradition further; it may be possible, for example, to have community contributions cover 50 percent of classroom construction costs, as envisaged in the deep reform package. However, it will remain important to channel government resources to schools in poorer communities so that such communities are not disadvantaged in terms of their children's access to secondary education.

The temptation to phase out the double-shift use of classrooms is understandable because this practice can contribute to a deterioration in educational quality, especially when it results in a reduced hours of classroom instruction. Yet there are ways to mitigate the negative impact of double-shift use; in any case, there is no hard evidence that shows that phasing out this practice would significantly improve educational quality. Even a rich country like Singapore continued double-shift use of classrooms until 2000, while maintaining superior educational quality. Therefore, it is advisable to carefully weigh the pros and cons of the planned phase-out of double classroom shifts in Ethiopia. And it makes sense to study how the negative effects of this practice can be mitigated.

Decreasing the cost of classrooms is another reform included in the reform packages. Low-cost classrooms are common in many countries. Where there is a practice of community construction, the cost of community-built classrooms is usually lower than that of classrooms built by the government. Yet the specifications of the former are almost universally inferior to the specifications of the latter. The issue is not whether better classrooms are desirable, but whether the increased cost of better specifications is justifiable.

As noted earlier, community-constructed classrooms already exist in Ethiopia. One possibility to expand this tradition might be to prepare several low-cost classroom designs that draw on this experience, recognize the availability of local construction materials and local construction practices, and apply the lessons of international experience with low-cost classroom construction. It should be noted here that the classroom unit cost used in the base case scenario was derived from the total cost of building classrooms, laboratories, libraries, and offices. Therefore there should be scope to reduce the unit cost of classrooms by economizing the cost of these facilities as well. In light of the upstream work needed to introduce such designs and reduce unit costs, the alternative scenarios do not envisage the implementation of low-cost classrooms before 2014/15.

Cost sharing at the preparatory level was also assessed (outside the simulation model) as way to reduce costs. Estimates revealed that revenues from cost sharing at the preparatory level could reach approximately 2.4 percent of annual public costs of secondary education by 2024/25, given the following assumptions: (1) the share of total secondary enrollment in government schools is 70 percent; (2) 20 percent of students in government schools receive fee waivers; and (3) the cost-sharing rate is 50 percent of recurrent costs. Considering that a policy of cost sharing already exists at the preparatory level, it makes sense to consider this reform as well.

Conclusion

To conclude, the base case scenario (figure 8.2) considered in this chapter, in which all public financing (that is, the government budget) for education represents 4.6 percent of GDP, incurs an education sector financing gap of 24 percent for the period 2015/16–2024/25. This gap indicates that if existing policies on financing, service delivery, and mobilization of nongovernmental resources in secondary education do not change, the subsector will be unable to produce adequate numbers of graduates with the skills needed in a lower-middle-income economy.

The results of the simulations discussed in this chapter show that an allocation of 6.0 percent of GDP for education would be required to secure the funding needed for secondary education if no reforms are undertaken. Yet this figure is likely beyond the capacity of the Ethiopian economy. Therefore achieving the goals of secondary education solely by increasing the level of public financing, that is, without policy reform, is not an option.

By choosing the right set of policy options, it should be possible for Ethiopia to meet the challenge of producing the required quantity and quality of secondary graduates to support a lower-middle-income economy, even within a constrained financial framework. But similar reforms need to be undertaken concurrently across the other education subsectors, particularly in primary and higher education.

The scenario of deep reform with an education budget of 4.6 percent of GDP (figure 8.4) would

- Decrease the teacher-section ratio from 1.6 to 1.2 for general secondary and from 1.7 to 1.4 for preparatory secondary education by 2024/25.
- Continue double shifts in 20 percent of classrooms until 2024/25.
- Decrease classroom unit costs from Br 425,000 to Br 340,000 as of 2014/15.
- Increase enrollment in nongovernmental secondary schools to 30 percent of all secondary enrollment by 2024/25.
- Increase community contributions to classroom construction from 10 percent of costs in 2009/10 to 50 percent in 2014/15.

However, the simulation of this scenario demonstrated that even with deep policy reforms, the financing gap could not be bridged within the existing financing framework. For financial sustainability, the financing gap must come down to 14.5 percent from the projected 24 percent, but this scenario would reduce it only to 16 percent.

Alternatively, simulation of the scenario of moderate reform with an education budget of 5.2 percent of GDP (figure 8.5) demonstrated that both enrollment and quality objectives can be met if public financing for education is increased to 5.2 percent of GDP, in tandem with the implementation of the same set of policy interventions (with the exception that enrollment in nongovernmental schools would be increased to 20 percent of all secondary enrollments by 2024/25 and community contributions to classroom construction costs increase from 10 percent of costs in 2009/10 to 30 percent in 2014/15). In this case, the financing gap would need to be reduced to 8.2 percent, but is actually reduced to 7.1 percent—indicating the robustness of the scenario. Given that the available public resource envelope for education is likely to be 5.4 percent of GDP, the latter scenario looks financially sustainable.

As noted earlier, the two sets of policy reforms used for analysis in this chapter are among many permutations possible. They do not constitute a recommended set of reforms; rather, they are offered to help guide the choice of reforms based on closer analysis of reality on the ground. Depending on the set of reforms chosen, the scale of enhanced financing required to expand secondary education to meet lower-middle-income country requirements may vary.

It is important to remember that the results of the scenarios described in this chapter are based on several key assumptions about the national economy and secondary education over the long term, specifically:

- The high annual rate of growth of GDP of 11.2 percent, as assumed in the GTP, will be maintained. This growth rate will ensure the availability of public resources and provide the opportunity for productive employment of an increasingly well-educated labor force in the modern sector of the economy.
- Changes in teacher education policies and teacher deployment practices will be implemented. These changes are critical to efficiency improvements that drive the projected decrease in the teacher-section ratio, which can only occur when teachers are qualified to teach more than one subject and curricula are sufficiently flexible to adapt to the needs of schools that have only a few secondary sections.
- The contribution of the nongovernmental sector in secondary education will expand under an improved regulatory framework; however, it will reach the projected levels only through robust public-private financing partnerships.

Note

1. The national budget is financed through revenues, domestic borrowing, foreign borrowing, and grants. Therefore, donor aid to education sector has been accounted for in the analysis.

References

EdStats (database). World Bank, Washington, DC. http://go.worldbank.org/85XM5TBQA0.

Ethiopia, Federal Democratic Republic of Ministry of Education (MOE). 2010. "Education Sector Development Program IV (ESDP IV) 2010/11–2014/15 (2003 EC–2007 EC), Program Action Plan." MOE, Addis Ababa.

Mingat, Alain, Blandine Ledoux, and Ramahatra Rakotomalala. 2010. *Developing Post-Primary Education in Sub-Saharan Africa: Assessing the Financial Sustainability of Alternative Pathways.* Washington, DC: World Bank.

Nepal, Federal Democratic Republic of Department of Education. 2010. "Flash I Report 2067 (2010/11)." Department of Education, Kathmandu.

UNESCO (United Nations Educational, Scientific, and Cultural Organization). 2011. "EFA Global Monitoring Report 2011; The Hidden Crisis: Armed Conflict and Education." UNESCO, Paris.

Verspoor, Adriaan. 2008. *At the Crossroads: Choices for Secondary Education in Sub-Saharan Africa.* With the SEIA Team. Africa Human Development Series. Washington, DC: World Bank.

World Bank. 2005. *Expanding Opportunities and Building Competences for Young People: A New Agenda for Secondary Education.* Directions in Development Series. Washington, DC: World Bank.

———. 2009. "Secondary Education in India: Universalizing Opportunity." Human Development Unit, South Asia Region, World Bank, Washington, DC.

CHAPTER 9

Conclusion: Priorities for Policy Reform and Action

Developing the human resources necessary for a middle-income economy requires policies that expand secondary education. These policies need to simultaneously ensure equitable access to this education, as well as its quality and relevance—and do so in a financially sustainable manner. Key required steps will be to: (1) increase the flexibility of the secondary system to respond to the differing needs and aspirations of young people, (2) align secondary education with the evolving demands of the economy through curriculum change, while promoting the transferability of acquired knowledge and skills; (3) ensure financial sustainability by enhancing the efficiency of public expenditures and mobilizing nongovernmental resources at the postprimary level; and (4) institute a balanced allocation of resources across all levels of the education system. These steps call for a profound transformation of both the secondary curriculum and the governance and management of the secondary education system. Successful implementation should be based on careful sequencing of priority interventions and ongoing monitoring and evaluation.

A large number of policy options for the development of the secondary system have been discussed in preceding chapters. This chapter focuses on those policy changes that are especially critical to building a secondary system consistent with the requirements of a middle-income economy. The most important actions for policy attention and reform, discussed in the following sections, are to:

- *Implement curriculum reform* so that a choice of secondary programs is available, enabling all students to learn and succeed in school in accordance with their aspirations and abilities.
- *Ensure sustainable financing* so that the expansion of secondary education does not lead to a deterioration in graduates' learning achievement, but conversely, draws on sufficient resources to improve this achievement.
- *Strengthen governance and management* of the secondary sector so that accountability for public service delivery is in enhanced, scarce public resources are used more efficiently, and inherent incentives are put in place to improve performance.

- *Expand access* by ensuring that all young people who are capable and interested can complete at least 10 years of schooling, which prepares them for further education and training according to their abilities and aspirations.
- *Promote equity* by providing access to secondary education to girls across the country and students from emerging regions, pastoralist areas, and sparsely populated rural areas, as well as from poor and disadvantaged families.
- *Improve quality* to enhance students' learning achievement, readiness for further education and training, and employability.

Implement Curriculum Reform

As noted earlier in this book, a "one-size-fits-all" curriculum will not allow all students to learn to the maximum of their abilities. To provide all students the opportunity to successfully complete 10 years of education and prepare them either for a job or further education and training prior to employment, the secondary curriculum needs to become more flexible and offer differentiated opportunities for learning (chapter 4). The next round of curriculum revisions therefore needs to consider changes that would:

- Allow students in general secondary education (grades 9–10) to pursue subjects at different levels of depth beyond a common core study program suitable to the abilities of all students. Toward this end students would be offered a choice of elective subjects to help prepare them for preparatory education, the world of work, or technical and vocational education and training (TVET). This approach would be taken further at the preparatory level (grades 11–12) by introducing curriculum options with more applied tracks.
- Develop a strategy for curriculum delivery at an acceptable level of quality in small schools, including, possibly, the integration of the natural sciences into a single subject, with the same option considered for the social sciences.

The single most important policy choice to be made at this juncture is whether to measure the success of general secondary education in terms of students' competence for higher education, or alternatively, their chance to learn according to their abilities and aspirations and, ultimately, be of use to society. Though this is a choice specific to secondary education, it will have a significant impact on the development of human resources in Ethiopia and, as a consequence, its ability to become a middle-income country. As such, this issue deserves to be discussed in a broad forum that includes politicians, development practitioners, teachers, academics, and civil society representatives, among others. Moreover, this discussion needs to be informed by the experience of middle-income and developed countries.

Full implementation of this kind of curriculum reform may take a decade; it may also require a few years of preparation. In the meantime, it may be possible to make some adjustments to the existing curriculum to make it more flexible.

These adjustments would impact all other education subsectors and thus need to be discussed across the system. Given the long gestation period required for a reform that will offer differentiated curricula for secondary students, there may not be a need to bring forward the schedule for the next round of curriculum revisions. Rather, the proposed reform may be planned for this round.

Ensure Sustainable Financing

The share of gross domestic product (GDP) spent on education in Ethiopia—approximately 4.5 percent over the period 2003/04–2007/08—and the share of education in the national budget (23.2 percent in 2009/10) are both high by international standards, relative to per capita income. In addition, the composition of the education sector is relatively top heavy, with higher education taking almost half of the total education budget and absorbing more public resources than primary schools.[1] Secondary education has been squeezed between these two subsectors. In 2009/10, for example, it was allocated less than 10 percent of all public resources available for education, compared to 30 percent or more in countries such as India and Indonesia (EdStats average for 2007–09). To meet expanded access targets, a substantial increase in expenditures on secondary education will be required. This challenge is particularly daunting given the important unfinished agenda in primary education and the high cost of secondary and tertiary education in the country.

Two financial approaches to expanding secondary education are to develop a plan and hope that the needed resources will be available, or develop a plan that can be financed sustainably. A plan based on the first approach is likely to undergo serious adjustments due to financial constraints; in the end, the implemented plan may not come even close to achieving the objectives of the original plan. By contrast, a plan based on the second approach is more likely to achieve its original objectives, as sustainable financing is a part of the plan. The framework for financial analysis provided in chapter 8 can help guide the development of a plan that follows the second approach.

Based on an updated Education Sector Development Program (ESDP) IV simulation model that reflects recent data and ties growth in teacher salaries to growth in GDP, a "base case scenario" was formulated in chapter 8. This scenario represents one of the most likely options for developing secondary education in Ethiopia, given existing policies and practices. Simulations using the "base case scenario" showed that the country is unlikely to be able to fully fund the development of secondary education solely by increasing public financing because it would require an education budget of about 6 percent of GDP (the likely public financing envelope for education in Ethiopia is about 5.4 percent). However, an education budget of around 5.2 percent of GDP, complemented by policies that enhance the efficiency of resource use and mobilize additional nongovernmental resources, may be adequate to achieve the goals of the subsector.

The policy options considered in successive simulations in chapter 8 were related to the teacher-section ratio, the extent of double-shift classroom use, low-cost classrooms, the share of total secondary enrollment in nongovernmental schools, and the share of community contributions to classroom costs. Among these, the policy options with the highest potential for contributing to sustainable financing are decreasing the teacher-section ratio and increasing enrollment in nongovernmental schools. It is possible to achieve sustainable financing of secondary education through numerous sets of policy reform packages comprised of different mixes of policy measures. One of the critical next steps in preparing a plan to expand secondary education is to choose the most suitable reform package for sustainable financing.

Financing reforms are not, however, implemented in isolation. Rather they should be a part of a broader secondary education reform package, given that an enabling environment is critical for successful implementation of a financial reform package. For example, reducing the teacher-section ratio without increasing the workload of teachers beyond official norms may not seem difficult, but in reality it is. Among the enabling conditions for implementing this reform are preparing teachers and providing them incentives to teach more than one subject (so that their workload adheres closer to existing norms), particularly in small schools; establishing and/or strengthening a standards-based career promotion system so that teachers are encouraged to work hard; and implementing school-based management so that schools have incentives to make optimal use of their teachers.

The chances for successful implementation of the policy package that is ultimately chosen by the government will be higher if it is selected through a participatory process. Among the stakeholders who need to engage in this discussion are teachers, parents, principals, government officials responsible for managing the education system (including from the Ministry of Education, or MOE), representatives of nongovernmental schools, civil society representatives, public finance experts, and officials of the Ministry of Finance and Economic Development (MOFED). Policy options need to be discussed, moreover, in the context of the education system as a whole, given that the sustainability of secondary education will be possible only if concurrent measures are taken to achieve the financial sustainability of the other subsectors of the system.

Strengthen Governance and Management

Ethiopia has gone a long way toward defining a management policy framework, the design of which reflects many lessons of international experience, as documented in recent research (see Wößmann 2000). Important responsibilities have been transferred to the regional and woreda levels and parent-teacher associations (PTAs) elected by parents have been institutionalized, which have notably increased community engagement in the management and financing of school education (that is, primary and secondary education).

Moving forward, the priority must be to build on these achievements and deepen existing decentralization. Specifically, the scope of school-based management (SBM) should be expanded. This process involves transferring authority for academic administration, financial and human resources management, and procurement to the school level (chapter 6) in a phased process. School-based management would provide the foundation for improving the quality and effectiveness of secondary schooling (grades 9–12). Sustained progress toward this goal will require:

- *Regulatory changes*, preferably through a parliamentary proclamation or a Council of Ministers' regulation that clearly defines the authorities devolved to schools, with appropriate changes made to other legal instruments governing the management of schools by MOE, the regions, and the woredas
- *Strong political commitment* and continuous monitoring and support at the highest level, given that school-based management radically changes the power structure of the education system
- *Investments in capacity building*, as SBM changes the respective roles of the MOE, regions, zones, woredas, and schools. These new roles need to be understood and internalized by all staff of the agencies concerned. In addition substantial efforts will be needed to build the capacity of School Management Committees and PTAs, as well as implement a transparent, accountable management system with appropriate checks and balances.

Having already completed a radical decentralization of the education system that handed significant authority over secondary education to the woredas and regions, Ethiopia is in the process of articulating a framework for school-based management. International experience indicates that initiatives associated with SBM may stall due to the perceived contradiction between school-based management and the devolution of authority to local governments. International experience also indicates that this devolution of authority is not a substitute for SBM; in fact, the two are complementary. Although in principle local governments should be engaged to a greater degree in aspects of governance, and schools in aspects of management of secondary education, different countries have opted for different arrangements. The critical political choice in preparing a framework for school-based management is deciding which functions will be given to local governments, and which to schools.

Accountability for Performance

A deepening process of decentralization that gradually shifts responsibilities for planning, implementation, quality assurance, and financial management further toward the school level will require clear horizontal accountability mechanisms, including the regular provision of comparative data on school performance. Some countries have developed school report cards that are made available to stakeholders at the school level, as well as to administrators at different levels of the education system. These report cards include information that compares input availability (that is, teachers, textbooks, specialized facilities, etc.) at the school level, as well as student performance data (for example, examination results or assessment data) among schools. These data can also help managers at Woreda and Regional Educational Bureaus identify schools that are performing poorly and need assistance. Further, item analysis can help identify subjects with which students have difficulty and that may require improved instructional approaches.

Expand Access

Ethiopia is making great strides toward universal primary education; the net enrollment rate for grades 1–8 now exceeds 85 percent. Current policies aim to rapidly increase the number of students admitted to general secondary schools, culminating in universal education at this level by 2025.

The transformation of the education pyramid from one typical of a low-income country to one typical of a middle-income country (chapter 3) will require, first and foremost, successful implementation of quality improvement programs at the primary level. A grade 8 completion rate of 49 percent is a weak basis for developing a labor force in which one-half of workers have completed 10 years of education, as is common in lower-middle-income countries. But without a supply of basic education graduates who master the knowledge and the skills specified in the primary curriculum, the proportion of the age group that completes primary education and is ready for the demands of secondary education will remain too low to bring about the necessary inversion of the education pyramid.

At the same time education at the postprimary level needs to evolve if it is to provide educational opportunities to students who successfully complete the primary cycle. The challenge is to develop a system that is supportive not only of the general, technical, and vocational education and training of young people before they enter the labor market, but also of their lifelong education and training needs after they become employed. This shift implies that in addition to expanding access to formal education at the secondary and preparatory levels, policies need to recognize multiple routes to skills acquisition, among them, institution-based training by public and nongovernmental providers, as well as enterprise-based training in the formal and informal economies (including traditional apprenticeships). Policies will thus need to recognize that public education is only one route to skills acquisition.

The expansion of access needs to be managed in such a way that it does not erode the quality of secondary education, but on the contrary, improves this quality as part of a strategy to ensure that graduates acquire the knowledge and skills necessary to function in a middle-income economy. Evidence that the level of learning achievement—especially in mathematics and the sciences—is more important for economic growth than the number of years spent in school is robust and cannot be ignored (see, for example, Hanushek 2007).

To summarize, developing a solid human resource base for a middle-income economy means designing a policy framework (chapter 3) that ensures:

- All primary education graduates who are academically able and interested have access to further formal general education at the general secondary level (grades 9 and 10).
- Preparatory education evolves into a program that has a broader purpose than simply preparing students for university entrance.
- The proportion of students admitted into grade 11 gradually increases to reach middle-income levels.
- Learning achievement, especially in mathematics and the sciences, is an integral part of the development strategy for secondary education.
- A diverse range of TVET and "second-chance" general education programs (see World Bank 2006b) are available to graduates of primary, general secondary, and preparatory education who do not wish to continue formal general education programs, but seek further education or training either after leaving academic programs or later in life.

As noted throughout this report, expanding access to secondary education is a policy priority in all countries that aim to reach middle-income status. Countries have chosen different pathways to address these challenges, taking into account their respective institutional legacies in education, past policy choices, and the context of national social and economic development. Box 9.1 summarizes the experience of Thailand in this regard, where access to secondary education remained limited until the late 1980s. At that point, shortages of educated workers jeopardized economic growth, making a rapid expansion of secondary education imperative.

Promote Equity

Chapter 3 suggested options for possible policy and enrollment targets for the education development strategy for 2014/15–2024/25, including options for ensuring equitable access to secondary education.

Gender

Notwithstanding the progress that has been made in recent years (chapter 2), gender inequities in access persist. At the primary level, there is rapid progress toward gender balance: the gender parity index (GPI) for grades 1–4 is 0.90, and for grades 5–8, 0.86. Progress is also being made in secondary education, especially in the first cycle (grades 9–10), for which the GPI in 2009/10 was 0.80. But significant challenges remain for the second cycle (grades 11–12), for which the GPI is only 0.57.

The first step in reducing the gender gap in secondary education is to continue and, where necessary, intensify efforts to establish gender equity at the

Box 9.1

Expanding Secondary Education in Thailand

Until 1970, secondary schools in Thailand prepared students mainly for employment as civil servants, professionals, and teachers. Enrollment in secondary education represented only 14 percent of young people aged 13–18 years, although primary education then reached more than 83 percent of children aged 7–12 years. Lack of investment in secondary education eventually led to an undereducated workforce.

By 1990, the great majority of workers had completed only primary education. With a rapidly growing economy, the need to modernize the workforce made it urgent to rapidly expand secondary education. This expansion was brought about chiefly through a revised conceptualization of this educational level as basic education for the general public and the workforce, as well as for the preparation of professionals. Compulsory education was expanded from six to nine years and a multipronged strategy for secondary education was adopted that included:

- Expansion of more than 4,000 primary schools to include the lower secondary level, as well as the conversion of primary facilities that were underused due to a declining birthrate
- Establishment of more than 500 new secondary schools in rural areas where no secondary or extended primary schools existed
- Revision of the highly competitive admission policies of exclusive secondary schools to provide enrollment opportunities for students from varied backgrounds
- Gradual abolition of tuition fees, starting with extended primary schools and rural secondary schools
- Recognition of alternative forms of education, including nonformal education programs, and the establishment of special schools for disabled children and welfare schools for marginalized children, especially HIV/AIDS orphans and street children

By 2005, the secondary enrollment rate exceeded 70 percent and junior secondary education had become almost universal, enrolling 90 percent of the relevant age group.

Sources: Varavarn 2006, World Bank 2006a.

primary level. The rapid increase in the GPI at the general secondary level between 2004/05 and 2009/10 (from 0.57 to 0.80) suggests the likelihood that this rate will increase further at both this and the preparatory level. However, experience indicates that these increases are not automatic and that providing access to schools close to home, building awareness among parents, gender-appropriate role models, gender-sensitive instructional strategies, and sanitary facilities are all part of the package of measures needed at the local level to ensure consistent progress in girls' enrollment and learning achievement.

Rural Populations

Disadvantaged groups, especially those living in sparsely populated rural and pastoralist areas, continue to have limited access to secondary education. Currently most postprimary schools are located in urban areas in Ethiopia (chapter 2). The pace of progress in expanding secondary education will therefore be determined by the strategy that is adopted to expand access in rural and pastoralist areas. It is unlikely, for example, that the standard model of an urban school with a large number of sections will be appropriate for rural areas with much smaller populations in school catchment areas (chapter 5).

At the primary level, the Alternative Basic Education program recognizes that a single model of schooling cannot meet the needs of students in a country as large and diverse as Ethiopia. Providing opportunities to these populations to enroll in secondary schools is also likely to require an alternative service delivery model. This model must be appropriate for sparsely populated areas, but still provide education of equivalent quality to that offered by urban schools. This will inevitably have to be a "small-school" strategy based on cost-effective delivery of quality education in secondary schools that have, at most, two or three sections. These schools will often be extensions of existing primary schools (see box 9.1) and may:

- Integrate grades 9 and 10 into an existing primary school to create one school for grades 1–10 under a single head teacher, with shared infrastructure such as laboratories and offices.
- Share qualified teachers in specific subjects among grades 7–10.
- Qualify teachers to teach either more than one subject or integrated subjects, or both.
- Use innovative approaches, such as traveling teachers who teach a year-long course in one semester and then move on to another school.
- Provide financial incentives to teachers willing to work in the remote areas where many small schools will be located.
- Combine natural science and social science subjects into respective integrated natural sciences and social sciences curricula.
- Use multigrade classes in very low-population-density areas.
- Use information and communication technology to support teachers and students, as well as provide enrichment learning activities not usually available in rural areas.

No one school will adopt all of these options; it is important to allow different combinations to be tested and share the lessons of experience in responding to the constraints of different contexts. Finally there will be areas where the number of students in the catchment area is so small that students may have to be served by government schools with boarding facilities. Because such schools are costly, it will often be more cost effective for the government to provide such students scholarships to existing nongovernmental schools, where such schools exist (as in Uganda, see chapter 6), or even to private boarding schools.

Poor Families

Poverty remains the dominant factor explaining low educational achievement in the country (see chapter 2). There are two reasons for this. First, poor people often cannot afford the direct or indirect costs associated with schooling. Although general secondary education is free in Ethiopia, there are, in fact, "residual" school fees in many parts of the country and communities are encouraged to contribute labor, materials, or cash to establish, expand, and maintain schools, as well as cover the cost of teaching materials. Schools, woredas, and regions are expected to ensure that no child is excluded from school because of an inability to pay, but this commitment may not always overcome the financial constraints of poor people.

The second reason for low educational achievement is that poor people rarely have access to schools that offer education of acceptable quality. Their children frequently drop out and do not complete even four years of education, leaving them unable to access high-paying jobs and thus continue a cycle of economic poverty and educational underachievement.

Breaking this vicious pattern has to start at the primary level and continue at the secondary level by removing obstacles for lower-income students who—often against the odds—complete the primary cycle. Policy measures may involve instituting:

- Fee waivers for the poorest students when formal or informal fees are imposed by government schools
- Scholarships for poor students in nongovernmental preparatory schools
- Scholarships to governmental and nongovernmental boarding schools for students from areas that lack an accessible public school.

To be financially sustainable, this kind of financial support needs to be carefully targeted. Over time, its scope will diminish as the network of secondary schools expands geographically. The challenge is to ensure that limited public resources actually reach the neediest students.

Improve Quality

Effective schools are the backbone of a high-quality education system; students in these schools have the opportunity to learn to the best of their ability and acquire the knowledge and skills specified in the national curriculum. Research on effective schools has identified their key characteristics, which include enabling conditions that give students the opportunity to learn and, perhaps most important, school leadership capable of delivering instructional effectiveness and providing a well-structured environment for learning. But identifying the characteristics of effective schools is not enough. The challenge of quality improvement is how to transform poorly performing schools into effective ones. Successful strategies for doing so are school focused and typically involve several mutually reinforcing components, including *enabling conditions for effective instruction, teachers, and strong leadership by head teachers.*

The school focus underscores the need to adapt reforms to local conditions and build local commitment and capacity which, in turn, highlight the importance of institutional arrangements for improved governance and management—especially school-based management. It is these arrangements that provide a decentralized framework for the implementation of school improvement plans.

Enabling Conditions

Enabling conditions define the physical, learning, governance, and management environment of a school that create the conditions for effective teaching and learning. The physical environment includes school buildings in good condition, adequate classrooms, separate toilets for girls and boys, and drinking-water facilities. The learning environment includes the availability of qualified and trained teachers; a suitable curriculum, textbooks, and other instructional materials; effective teacher time-on-task practices; and extracurricular activities. A good governance and management environment includes a school management accountable to its primary stakeholders—parents—and fair evaluation processes and career paths for teachers that encourage them to perform.

Ethiopia has made considerable progress in several of these areas: 77.4 percent of secondary school teachers are qualified (2009/10), the textbook supply has greatly improved with the support of the General Education Quality Improvement Program (GEQIP), 70 percent of secondary schools have water (2009/10), 86 percent have library facilities, and 91 percent have at least one laboratory. PTAs contribute in important ways to managing individual schools.

Yet challenges remain, especially in the most disadvantaged areas, with 35 percent of secondary schools not having a sufficient number of classrooms and only 20 percent having Internet access. Perhaps more crucial is the question of how effectively these facilities are being used. Many laboratories lack basic equipment and supplies; it is not clear how well libraries are stocked; class sizes in general secondary education have recently grown to reach an average of 64 students in 2009; and PTAs are often constrained in their ability to contribute to a school's educational performance (Smith 2011).

It will be important to agree on the minimum enabling conditions for effective education service delivery as part of guidelines for school improvement plans. On the basis of these minimum conditions, investments can be targeted to schools where remaining resource gaps are so large that they, in effect, preclude effective instruction.

Teachers

The capability of teachers is central to educational quality. The critical policy tasks in this arena include quality assurance of initial teacher training and the creation of incentives and opportunities for continuous professional development. International experience suggests that bringing about changes in teaching practices is a process that is only successful when sustained over a long period of time through a succession of small changes that the average teacher can handle (Beeby 1966), but which add up over time to meaningful changes in instructional effectiveness.

A long-term strategy for teacher development in Ethiopia thus needs to be designed with a focus on three priority areas (chapter 5):

- *Ensuring an adequate supply of teachers* for a system that will have a large number of schools with only a few general secondary sections; staffing these schools efficiently will require teachers who are capable of teaching more than one subject area. Toward this end it will be important to provide new and currently serving secondary teachers incentives and opportunities to qualify in more than one subject area.
- *Improving teachers' instructional competence* by providing quality university training for a Post-Graduate Diploma in Teaching (PGDT), continued induction support to beginning teachers, and continuous professional development (CPD) opportunities. The latter need to be linked to standards-based career development tracks for teachers and supported by CPD structures at the regional and woreda levels. These structures should also help principals and key resource teachers provide school-based teacher supervision and support.
- *Strengthening teacher management* by implementing a merit-based teacher career structure and establishing an independent institution to develop and implement performance standards, manage teacher registration, license and relicense teachers, and accredit teacher training institutions and courses.

School Leader Effectiveness

School improvement is critically dependent on the management skills of stakeholders. The starting point here must be a sustained effort to enhance *school leader effectiveness*. The literature is clear: the quality of school leadership is the most important factor influencing school performance. Skills of effective school leaders include instructional leadership (chapter 5), financial and human resources management, effective working relationships with the staff of line educational agencies, and winning the confidence of parents and School Management Committees. The pay-off in terms of improved student learning performance is likely to be substantial. Reaching this goal will require:

- Competency-based selection criteria for school leaders
- Well-designed pre-appointment training programs
- Decentralized arrangements for the continuous professional support and supervision of school leaders
- Effective professional networks for peer support and learning.

Implementation and Phasing of Reforms

The challenges of secondary education development in Ethiopia are multiple and daunting. Many education reforms in developed and developing countries have faltered on the rocks of implementation. The literature on school reform emphasizes that, ultimately, the quality of implementation at the school level will determine the success of a reform—that is, it will determine the extent to which schools adopt the reform. The readiness of schools and local administrators to change will decide the pace of implementation, but their mental models will be determined by the way in which reform strategies are designed, communicated, and practiced by central authorities. Four elements are important:

- *Evidence-based strategies* are the root of successful reform. If rigorous quantitative and qualitative evaluations are absent, reform lessons become based on anecdote, opinion, and prejudice.
- *Broad communication of challenges and achievements*, public discussion of policy options, and transparency in decision making are key ingredients of effective implementation.
- The *sequencing* of reform measures is critical. It is never possible to implement all desirable measures at the same time. Setting priorities and combining them into politically and technically feasible packages that mix consensus policies with those that are more difficult to accept is central to successful implementation.
- *Building local support and adapting reform packages to local conditions* is also important. Initial conditions and the local capacity for change will vary; reform packages and technical support need to reflect these realities.

These elements all underscore the importance of closely monitoring the impact of reforms, making adjustments that reflect the lessons of implementation experience, and involving all stakeholders in the process, from design through implementation. Decisions on phasing are particularly critical; a possible scenario of a phased implementation for expanding secondary education is presented in table 9.1.

It is important for the Ethiopian government to begin further analysis of the issues raised in this report as soon as possible, complete with stakeholder consultations on recommended options for the long-term development of secondary education. What is clear is that inaction is unlikely to result in a secondary education system that can effectively support the country's progress toward a middle-income economy. The policy framework for the ESDP IV period has been clearly established. The time has come to assess progress to date, consider needed adjustments, and set the stage for the design and implementation of reforms required in the medium (2015/16–2019/20) and long term (2020/21–2024/25).

Table 9.1 Possible Phasing of Secondary Education Reforms

Phase I: 2012/13–2014/15	Phase II: 2015/16–2019/20	Phase III: 2019/20–2024/25
Equitable access. Intensify GEQIP efforts to improve quality and student retention rates in primary education. Update specification for minimum enabling conditions (MECs) for quality instruction at the primary and secondary levels.	Pilot approaches for increasing access to secondary education for girls and students from sparsely populated rural and pastoralist areas, as well as students from poor families.	Scale up nationwide program for equitable access to secondary education. Continue funding schools to meet MECs.
Prepare strategy and programs for equitable access to secondary education for girls and students from pastoralist and sparsely populated rural areas, as well as students from poor families.	Fund schools to meet MECs.	
Curriculum reform. Review international experience with curriculum differentiation, including examination systems. Initiate consultations and decide on options appropriate for the Ethiopian context. Revise curriculum framework with a view to developing curriculum differentiation and an examination framework.	Revise curriculum for differentiated content; prepare new learning materials. Implement revised curriculum and examination system.	Continue implementation of revised curriculum and examination system.
Teacher preparation and development. Review the PGDT curriculum with a view to preparing teachers to teach more than one subject; prepare curricula for certification of grade 9 and 10 teachers who want to qualify to teach additional subjects. Adapt policies related to accreditation of teacher education faculties of universities.	Revise PGDT to enable teachers to teach more than one subject. Establish an accreditation system for PGDT.	Monitor, evaluate, and adjust accreditation, CPD, and licensing system.
Prepare a plan to strengthen the teacher induction and CPD system. Adopt a career progression system for teachers that is linked to a licensing (and relicensing) system and a robust performance evaluation system.	Put in place a strengthened system of teacher induction and CPD. Implement licensing and relicensing system, together with a revised system for career progression of teachers.	
School-based management. Adopt a regulatory framework for SBM and launch a communication campaign. Build the capacity of schools to implement SBM, and of the woredas, regions, and MOE to support SBM.	Implement the first phase (that is, resource generation and utilization, strengthening accountability, simple disciplinary actions, selection of teachers and staff for further training, and recognition of good staff work) and initiate the second phase (that is, management of salary and capital budget; hiring principals; moderate disciplinary actions with respect to staff).	Complete implementation of the second phase and implement the third phase (that is, hiring and promotion of all staff; serious disciplinary actions with respect to staff, teachers, and principals).

(table continues on next page)

Table 9.1 Possible Phasing of Secondary Education Reforms *(continued)*

Phase I: 2012/13–2014/15	Phase II: 2015/16–2019/20	Phase III: 2019/20–2024/25
Nongovernmental provision. Streamline regulatory framework for nongovernmental provision of education. Prepare a plan to develop public-private partnerships (PPPs).	Implement revised regulatory framework for nongovernmental provision. Pilot PPPs.	Take PPPs to national scale, making them an integral part of the financing strategy for secondary education.
Financing. Update the ESDP IV financial projection model. Chose a set a policy reforms that will ensure sustainable financing of secondary education by enhancing the efficiency of public resource use and mobilizing additional nongovernmental resources and public financing. Draw up a plan to implement these reforms.	Implement reforms.	Implement reforms.

Note: CPD = Continuous professional development, ESDP = Education Sector Development Program, GEQIP = General Education Quality Improvement Program, MECs = Minimum enabling conditions, MOE = Ministry of Education, PGDT = Post-Graduate Diploma in Teaching, PPP = Public-private partnership, SBM = School-based management.

Note

1. A typical allocation for higher education Sub-Saharan African countries is approximately 20 percent (Lewin 2006; Verspoor 2008).

References

Beeby, Clarence E. 1966. *The Quality of Education in Developing Countries*. Cambridge, MA: Harvard University Press.

Hanushek, Eric, and Ludger W. Wößmann. 2007. "The Role of Education Quality in Economic Growth." Policy Research Working Paper 4122. World Bank, Washington, DC.

Lewin, Keith M. 2006. "Seeking Secondary Schooling in Sub-Saharan Africa: Strategies for Sustainable Financing." SEIA Thematic Study #1. Human Development Working Paper Series. Africa Region, World Bank, Washington, DC.

Smith, Harvey N. J. 2011. "Governance and Management of Secondary Education: From Decentralization to School Autonomy." Background paper prepared for *Secondary Education in Ethiopia*. World Bank Ethiopia Office, Addis Ababa. Unpublished. (Available upon request of Rajendra Joshi, rjoshi@worldbank.org.)

Varavarn, Khunying Kasama. 2006. Presentation to World Bank East Asia Study Tour. Ministry of Education, Bankgok, Thailand. June.

Verspoor, Adriaan. 2008. *At the Crossroads: Choices for Secondary Education in Sub-Saharan Africa*. With the SEIA Team. Africa Human Development Series. Washington, DC: World Bank.

Wößmann, Ludger W. 2000. "Schooling Resources, Educational Institutions, and Student Performance: The International Evidence." Rev. ed. Kiel Working Paper 983. Kiel Institute of World Economics, Kiel, Germany. http://www.ifw-members.ifw-kiel.de/publications/schooling-resources-educational-institutions-and-student-performance-the-international-evidence/kap983.pdf.

World Bank. 2006a. "Thailand Social Monitor: Improving Secondary Education." World Bank Thailand Office, Bangkok.

———. 2006b. "World Development Report 2007: Development and the Next Generation." World Bank, Washington, DC.

APPENDIX A

Curriculum Documentation

The current Ethiopian secondary curriculum has served the education system well in the past, when it provided a single work plan for a homogeneous group of learners who took only one examination. This may not be the case in the future, when separating the functions of the curriculum, work plans, and examinations will become increasingly necessary. A new kind of curriculum will require improvements in several areas:

- *Clarity.* The curriculum should evolve into a leaner document, addressing the fundamental concepts that should be part of each learning area, rather than the teaching details. It should also lose the clutter of secondary materials that are a major contributory factor to the current teaching and learning overload.
- *Prioritization of topics.* The curriculum should prioritize topics to ensure that all students meet its basic requirements. It must serve as a basis for not one, but multiple work plans, according to the differing needs of secondary learners. Different ways of structuring the document can be found in curricula worldwide.
- *Differentiated purposes.* Different learners, particularly at the upper secondary level, will have different educational needs. Some learners will require a deep understanding of advanced mathematics, while others may only require mathematics of the kind useful in daily life. Some students will require in-depth knowledge of science, while others may only need an understanding of how certain important scientific concepts affect us all. The curriculum should accordingly be written in such a way that different syllabi can emerge from it.
- *Learning areas.* Many countries develop curricula for learning areas rather than subjects. The more traditional subject curricula then appear as strands of the learning area curriculum. This allows the essential unity of a learning area to emerge and ensures that gaps that have developed over time are addressed.
- The science learning area in the Qatar curriculum (see box 4.2), for example, is divided into five strands, only three of which are broadly similar to the conventional categories of biology, chemistry, and physics. Writing the curriculum for a learning area also promotes flexibility in school teaching programs. A science curriculum, for example, could be taught as a single subject by one teacher or covered by three teachers who take the physics, chemistry, and biology strands, respectively.

- *Pedagogy.* It is desirable to make a clean distinction between the curriculum and the work plans based on it. The curriculum is a policy document encapsulating what should be taught in schools, how, and how it should be assessed. Work plans are developed to suit the needs of particular schools and particular students. The Ministry of Education may wish to provide guidance to schools by preparing indicative work plans as separate documents.
- *Assessment.* The curriculum should indicate what should be assessed and how, as well as the weighting of various assessment objectives. This information should serve as the basis for a greatly expanded assessment system. It is likely that the same learning area curriculum will be assessed in more than one way as the system expands.
- *Expectations of learner achievement.* Expectations are a very useful element in curricula. Teachers need to know whether a topic is likely to be difficult or easy to teach and how well their students are likely to master it. They also find it useful to know which topics are considered basic and to be mastered by all students, and which are likely to be mastered only by the more able.
- *Language of curriculum documents.* Decisions will be needed on the language used in curriculum documents. Worldwide, some curricula are written in terms of what should be studied, others in terms of what students are expected to learn (now often referred to as "competencies"). Still others are written in terms of what students are expected to be able to do as a result of their learning (often referred to as "outcomes"). What is important is consistency, but in all cases, some indication of expectations should be included, such as the range of material that learners are expected to master.
- *Scope and sequencing.* There is much overlap and repetition in the current Ethiopian curriculum. While it is desirable that the curriculum have a spiral structure, returning to specific topics a number of times over the years, unnecessary repetition, or in-depth coverage of topics too early in the learning cycle, should be avoided. A scope and sequencing plan of the entire learning cycle from kindergarten to grade 12 is an essential tool for avoiding these pitfalls.
- *Special case of mathematics.* Mathematics, more than any other subject area, is sequential in nature. Progress depends directly on the degree of mastery of the material that has been covered before. Wide differences in achievement between learners develop at an early age, so much so that mixed-ability teaching in mathematics soon becomes very difficult.

The curriculum, and the teaching strategies based on it, must be sensitive to this challenge. This may mean, for example, developing an advanced mathematics strand at an early age (grade 9 or perhaps earlier). It also implies that mechanisms should be in place to ensure that students always gain an understanding of basic mathematical concepts at a given level before they move on to higher levels.

APPENDIX B

Facilities and Equipment for Science Teaching

This appendix contains four sections:

- Section A lists minimum recommended specifications for an upper secondary school science laboratory.
- Section B lists minimum recommended specifications for a lower secondary school science room.
- Section C provides suggestions for a suite of rooms for science, library, and information technology (IT) resources in small secondary schools.
- Section D makes recommendations on science equipment for secondary schools.[1]

A. Minimum Recommended Specifications for an Upper Secondary School Science Laboratory

The Needs of Upper Secondary Science Teaching

In the past, the main purpose of practical work in science has been to ensure mastery of concepts, with instruction characterized by formal, lengthy, "set-piece" practical sessions and demonstrations. This approach led to the traditional expensive science laboratory with fixed service benches. In recent years, there has been a considerable shift toward shorter active learning sessions in science teaching, which usually involve different kinds of class and group work and relatively simple equipment. Some group work may not involve formal science facilities at all, making a fixed-bench laboratory unnecessary.

A second change in modern science teaching is an effort to make science more part of everyday life, rather something done in special rooms with special facilities. This has meant that equipment has become more simple and "everyday" as well. It also means that much good practical science can be done in rooms without complex special facilities and fittings.

A third change in science teaching is the movement toward learner-centered pedagogy. The traditional structure of a science laboratory with benches across the room facing a teacher demonstration bench was suitable for a teacher-led approach to teaching, in which the key classroom relationship was that between learners and the teacher. Such an arrangement, however, makes learner-centered activities, in which the key relationship is among learners, very difficult.

These changes in pedagogy have considerable implications for the design of science rooms. This type of room should not have fixed benches, and services should either be located around the sides of the room or in service pillars. The latter, however, involve underfloor services and are both expensive and difficult to maintain; they are thus not recommended. Storage space is important in the preparation room for stock and in the science room itself for materials in use. Display space is also important.

Science Suites

The integration of theory and practice at all levels of science teaching means that single laboratories for each science subject, used by all groups in turn, are no longer sufficient. It is desirable that laboratories be augmented with a suite of dedicated science rooms located close to the laboratory that can be used for practical work that does not require services. Storage space is desirable in these rooms for the temporary storage of equipment removed from the laboratory. Desks or tables in this room should be the same as those specified for the laboratory. The effectiveness of such rooms will be greatly enhanced if they are serviced with electricity and water, at least at one workstation.

Science Laboratory Design

Size. The laboratory floor space (excluding the area taken up by side benches) should have the area of a normal classroom.

Services. Ideally, a minimum of six stations with electricity and water are required. Gas can be included, but it invariably leads to problems with leaks that few people have the capacity to rectify; there are, moreover, alternatives to installed gas service. The service stations should be at the edge of the laboratory to avoid taking up the main working space. This location also makes installation and servicing (particularly of waste pipes) relatively cheap and simple. Specifications for individual services are listed below.

- *Water*: a swan-neck tap into a small sink with no overflow. A hollow tubular plug should be available for use. All drainage pipes should be easily accessible and the trap easily removable by hand.
- *Electricity*: double-socket outlets (240 volts) at each station. The electrical outlets should be midway between the sinks.
- *Gas*: optional; if installed, there should be double taps at each station.
- *Isolating taps and switches*: a main gas-isolating tap, together with a main electricity-isolating switch, should be available at the teacher bench.
- *Waste pipes*: normal domestic traps, of the kind that can be removed by one screw joint, should be accessible. Waste pipes can be connected to the main sewage pipe, as harmful chemicals are no longer used.

- *Demonstration bench services:* it is desirable that the bench allow the teacher to stand on one side, facing the class on the other. The bench should have all three services, but gas can be a butane cylinder fixed below the bench. A second double electrical outlet is desirable, as some demonstrations can involve a number of pieces of electrically operated equipment. A mobile serviced demonstration bench is a possible alternative in schools where space is at a premium.

Other facilities. Other recommended facilities include:

- *Display boards* should be placed along at least two walls. The normal chalkboard should be placed at the front of the class. The demonstration bench should normally be in front of it. One section of the chalkboard should be a graph board.
- *Cupboards and shelves* could be part of the demonstration bench and a certain number of the fixed side benches. Cupboards and sets of drawers are very useful in a laboratory. They should not be placed where they would impede access to water and waste pipes. A display shelf in a place that is easily seen is also useful. It should have a minimum length of two meters.

Science Laboratory Furniture

Fixed units. Workstations should be on fixed benches along the sides of the room that measure 900 millimeters high and 600–800 millimeters deep. Experience has shown that if these benches are constructed of plastic-covered fiberboard, they will have a limited life span unless good-quality board is used and the plastic coating is continuous around the edges to avoid water penetration.

Special synthetic materials are now available for laboratory surfaces, but these tend to be expensive. Solid wood is still the best material. Concrete can be used, but is susceptible to attack by acids, which can lead to a crumbling of the surface. This problem can be reduced by sealing the concrete.

Learner benches. Ideally learners should work at tables that are 900 millimeters high by 1,600 millimeters long by 800 millimeters wide. The top area can be smaller if space is short, but two dimensions are crucial: the height of the tables must be the same as the height of the side benches and the length of the tables should be exactly twice their width in order that tables can be grouped easily. A class of 36 would ideally require 18 tables. Stools should be around 660 millimeters in height. The cost of this kind of furniture should not differ significantly from the cost of 36 individual desks and chairs.

If tables and stools are unavailable, desks and chairs can be used, but it is important that they are designed to be grouped together without gaps and the tops should be horizontal. School desks available in Africa frequently do not meet one or more of these requirements.

Preparation rooms. Two walk-in storage rooms are required, the smaller of which would be used for chemicals and the larger, for other equipment, since using one room for both leads to the corrosion of metal equipment. These rooms can be shared between the two laboratories, in which case they should be correspondingly larger. Minimum appropriate dimensions are 2 meters by 4 meters, but a larger unit is desirable. If only one preparation room is constructed, some kind of alternative, secure, floor-level storage will be required for corrosive volatile chemicals. Each preparation room should have a bench with electricity and water on a short side and strong shelving on the other sides, up to a height of 1.8 meters.

Cupboards. The preparation room bench should have cupboards below it. Additional cupboards are desirable to protect expensive equipment from dust.

Security and safety. All windows should be fully burglarproof. The main door to the laboratory should have an additional security door. The door from the laboratory to the preparation room should be lockable and preferably of solid construction.

Access to laboratories and the preparation room can frequently be gained through the roof. For this reason, ceilings should be of a robust structure that does not easily provide access. If this cannot be arranged, it is desirable that all the rooms sharing the same roof space be similarly secured.

Main gas cylinders. If gas is supplied, the main cylinder should be outside the laboratory in an appropriately ventilated room behind a closed security door. A two-cylinder unit is required, which can service more than one laboratory.

Fire precautions. A compressed gas-operated dry powder extinguisher should be installed near the chalkboard and the master switches, or near the laboratory door. The services should be installed along the walls that are remote from the door. A fire bucket filled with dry sand should be provided as part of laboratory equipment.

Exits. A second exit is desirable in all laboratories for safety reasons. It is recognized, however, that in situations where security is a problem, this door will probably be kept locked, defeating its purpose. If installed, it must be in the opposite corner from the main door.

Additional Desirable Features

Overhead projector screen. An overhead projector screen, if installed, should not obstruct the view of the chalkboard.

Information and communication technology (ICT) network and equipment. This equipment may be installed according to a school's prevailing ICT policy. A wireless router is preferable to network cables. If a large monitor is installed permanently, it should be burglarproof.

Features that have commonly been installed in school laboratories in the past but are *no longer required* include:

- Fixed learner benches
- Fume cupboard
- Lecture theater.

B. Minimum Recommended Specifications for a Lower Secondary School Science Room

The Needs of Lower Secondary Science Teaching

Lower secondary science classes increasingly require little specialized equipment or can be taught using simple equipment kits in normal rooms. Running water is, however, required. All practical work of any kind is best done standing up, as this gives students greater freedom of movement. This practice has implications for science room furniture. The use of equipment means that secure storage facilities are needed.

As with upper secondary science teaching, the concept of "set-piece" practical experiments has disappeared in favor of fully integrating practical work as a natural part of all science teaching. As with upper secondary science rooms, it is desirable that all rooms used for lower secondary science classes be close together in order to facilitate the efficient storage of materials and work.

Science room design. Lower secondary science rooms should be similar to normal classrooms, but with the following additional elements:

- At least one sink with a swan-necked tap is needed. Several sinks could be built into a service bench on one side of the laboratory.
- Movable tables should be of the same description and dimensions as specified above for senior secondary science rooms.
- A walk-in storage room with a bench is needed. One long storage room can be shared between two adjacent science rooms. The storage room should have floor-to-ceiling shelving. The bench should ideally have a sink and alternate current (AC) electricity.
- Display boards, chalkboards, safety features, security features, cupboards, and shelves should be installed as in upper secondary science laboratories.
- Gas is not needed and AC electricity is only needed at the front of the classroom.

C. Rooms for Science, Library, and IT Resources in Small Secondary Schools

A relatively inexpensive way to expand basic education to include grades 9 and 10 is to add additional classrooms to existing primary schools. This option assumes that there will be a consolidation of existing subjects into fewer, broader learning areas. In particular, the three sciences will be combined into one subject. In this scenario, all rooms are multipurpose. It is also assumed an existing school is expanded by around 300 learners, 150 each in grade 9 and grade 10.

This expansion will require two blocks of three classrooms, one of which should consist of rooms for specialized activities (see figure B.1 below). These facilities require preparation and storage space; a key component of the block is secure preparation and/or storage rooms.

Figure B.1 Diagram of Multipurpose, Science, and General Teaching Rooms

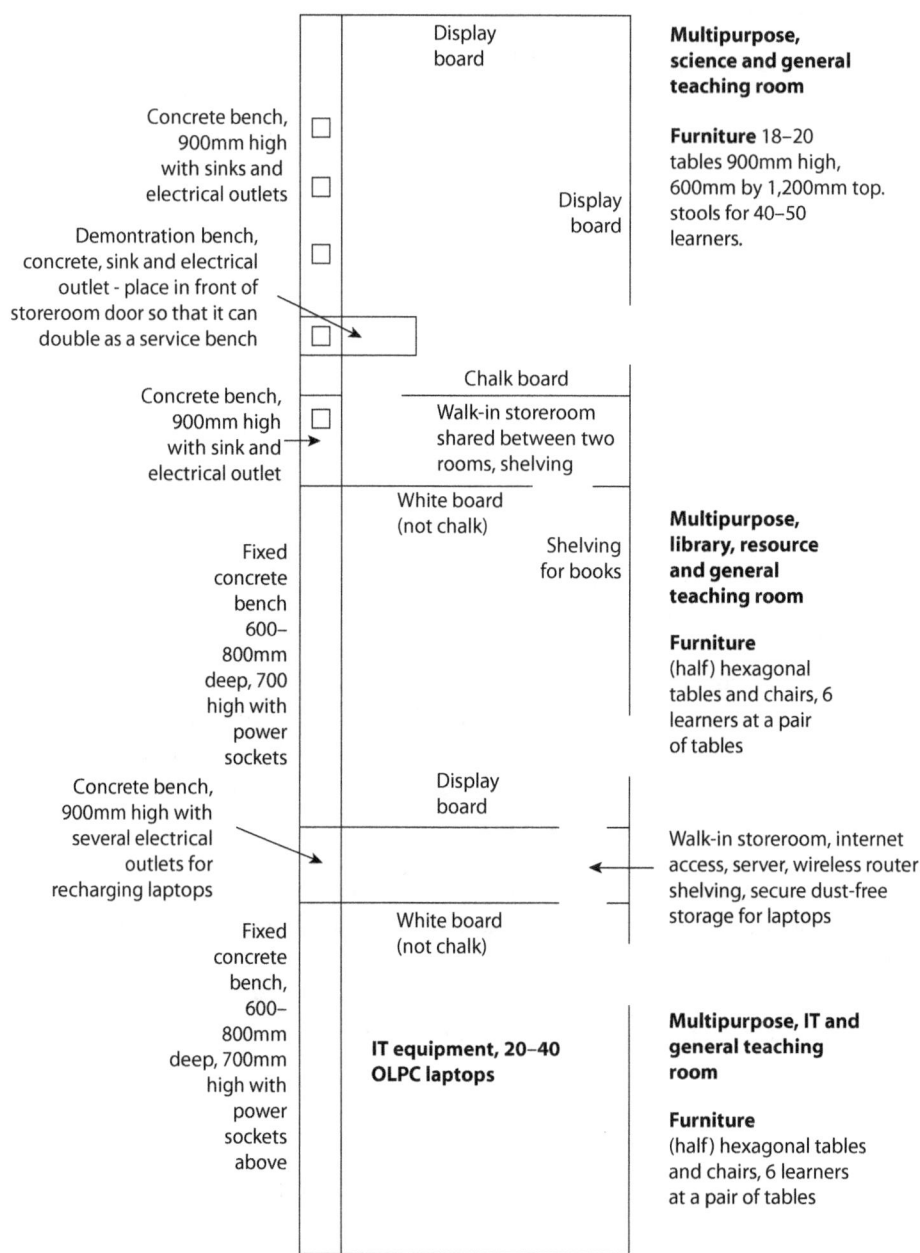

Source: Clegg 2007.
Note: IT = Information technology, OLPC = One laptop per child, mm = Millimetre, .

Information technology (IT) room. IT equipment should be based on the "one laptop per child" (OLPC) concept. These type of laptops are currently being produced at around $200 each and have built-in wireless networking. One workstation can be shared between two learners, as the screen is clearly visible at a wide angle. The machines are diskless and thus require a server for many applications. No computer network wiring will be required, as workstations should have a wireless connection. The server should be located in the storeroom; it is expected that the wireless range will allow computers in all three rooms in the block to be linked to the server. The operating system of an OLPC laptop is Open Source; its running costs and durability are not yet known.

The IT room should be a multipurpose space where laptops can be readily put away. It is not desirable for an IT room to have a chalkboard because of the problem of dust in the keyboards. Hexagonal tables (two trapezoid-shaped tables put together) are suggested. This is a space-saving arrangement for computer use that has been tried elsewhere and encourages group work. Because the room is a multipurpose space, access to a storeroom is important. It is anticipated that a certain number of computers with Internet access will eventually supplement books, therefore a side bench (of normal table height) with electrical sockets is suggested.

Science room. This room is also a general-purpose room with certain specialized facilities and services. Gas is not required, but a side bench with water and electricity is desirable. Although not necessary, it is also desirable that the bench extend the whole length of the room. The side bench should be 900 millimeters high, so that learners can work standing up. Furniture for the room should consist of tables that are also 900 millimeters high and large enough to allow two learners to sit at one table. Placing two tables together can allow 6 or 8 learners to sit around the working space. The length of the table top must be twice its width so that tables can be put together simply. Learners will sit on stools.

Tables should ideally be made of solid wood, but this is expensive. If laminated fiberboard is used, care is needed to ensure that the legs, often a metal frame, are well secured to it. Poorly made fiberboard tables are often secured to the legs with wooden screws, but these screws will not withstand normal school wear and tear.

Display boards. A big display board of good quality should be in every room on the vacant walls.

D. Recommendations Concerning Science Equipment

The nature of science equipment required for secondary education depends on its intended purpose. This section describes two kinds of science equipment used for different purposes. The first section lists everyday equipment mainly used to challenge learners to explain phenomena and address such other enquiry skills as predicting and planning investigations. The second section lists equipment suitable for illustrating specific science concepts.

Everyday Equipment

Science teachers should be encouraged to collect useful everyday equipment, such as metal objects, cotton, string, plastic objects and bags, plastic bottles and cartons, magnets from loudspeakers, and soda cans. The list is endless. The objects should then be sorted and stored in some retrievable manner.

Equipment Kits

The use of microscience materials is increasingly a worldwide phenomenon and should not be equated with "cheap" science, implying that microkits are somehow of lesser quality than "normal" equipment. Microscience has become popular partly because it more realistically mimics "real" science and partly because it is more environmentally friendly.

Equipment kits are widely used in South Africa and their use has spread to neighboring countries. Two manufacturers in South Africa have developed self-contained generic science equipment kits that address the South African curriculum: RADMASTE and Edutrade/Scientific Teaching Aids (STA). The cost of these kits is shown in table B.1 below. RADMASTE sells equipment that involves experimentation on a very small scale, while Edutrade markets more conventional equipment that is easier to handle, but more costly to buy and maintain. Both companies are usually willing to put together kits of equipment that exactly match specifications provided by ministries of education. Experience in Namibia suggests, however, that unless important items are missing from "off-the-shelf" kits, it is more cost effective to purchase them.

Both manufacturers also supply resource kits for teachers, which contain additional chemicals and spare parts. These kits are necessary; but their prices

Table B.1 Comparison of Science Kit Equipment Costs

$, 2007 prices

Secondary level/science area	RADMASTE Microscience		Edutrade/Scientific Teaching Aids	
	No. of workstations per kit	Cost per kit ($)	No. of workstations per kit	Cost per kit ($)
1st cycle/chemistry and biology	1	24	5	590
1st cycle/electricity (batteries not included)	1	20	1	60
1st and/or 2nd cycle/electromagnetics	—	—	For an entire class	320
1st cycle/dynamics (trolleys)	1	302	1	122
1st cycle/optics	1	110	1	110
2nd cycle/general	—	—	For an entire class	1,200
2nd cycle/chemistry	1	17		
2nd cycle/biology	—	—	For an entire class	940
2nd cycle/waves—light and sound	1	240	1 ripple tank only	108
Microscope kit, including some prepared slides	1	24	1	190

Source: Clegg 2007.
Note: Costs in this table are indicative only. — = not available

vary according to what they contain, making comparisons meaningless. Batteries are not included in any kit. Instructions in English are available for use with RADMASTE kits from UNESCO; they may also be purchased from RADMASTE and Edutrade/STA.

The items shown in table B.1 do not include larger, more expensive items of equipment that are useful for upper secondary science demonstrations. These items are not usually made in the region, but can be obtained through local agents. Experience elsewhere suggests, however, that such items probably will not be used even if they are supplied. It is an issue that can, and should, be addressed if a request for them is made by any school.

Note

1. This appendix is taken from Clegg 2007.

References

Clegg, Andrew. 2007. "Science Teaching and Learning in Mozambique: A Report to the Secondary Education Working Group." Report commissioned by the World Bank for Ministry of Education of Mozambique, Maputo.

APPENDIX C

Adding Value to Achievement Tests

Learning achievement tests in Ethiopia, which incorporate certain background survey questions, yield much useful information. However, these assessments could be improved by:

- Incorporating some questions that have been standardized internationally for the age group tested
- Developing a specific list of subject standards on which the test is based and hence defining subject-related attainment targets (the results would show the extent to which the targets are met)
- Analyzing the results in such a manner as to identify particular problems within specific subjects.

Using Internationally Standardized Items

Online question banks exist for certain subjects and grades and include internationally standardized items.[1] Incorporating a selection of these items into national achievement tests would give educators an idea of the performance of Ethiopian students against international benchmarks. Ultimately, Ethiopia could consider taking part in the Southern and Eastern Africa Consortium for Monitoring Education Quality (SACMEQ) or, possibly, the Trends in International Mathematics and Science Study (TIMSS).

Developing Subject Standards and Attainment Targets

Ethiopian achievement tests currently use minimum learning competencies (MLCs) for the relevant grade as the basis for an examination. The competencies provide a range of performance levels, but the norm-referenced process does not give any absolute indication of these levels. Assigning attainment levels to the MLCs for each test would provide additional information, such as the proportion of learners, nationally and regionally, who meet each target. Examples of attainment levels in the curricula of other countries are available online, which Ethiopia could use to define MLC attainment levels in different subjects.[2] To expand the expected attainment range in a given subject, a number of competencies from higher and lower grades could be added to the existing ones. This practice will be especially important as the education system expands and admits students with a wider range of abilities.

Identifying Particular Problems within Subjects

An analysis of the distribution of answers for each question on an achievement test can provide useful information about specific learner difficulties, both at the school and national level. This information is particularly useful for pinpointing specific literacy and numeracy issues. Most important, sharing item analysis (in addition to advice on effective instructional strategies) with pedagogical counselors, resource persons, and teachers can be an effective element of an educational quality improvement strategy. Box C.1 provides an example of this practice from Kenya.

School Attainment Levels

Current national learning assessments in Ethiopia do not provide information at the school level because only a sample of schools participates in achievement tests. Thus, while these assessments provide interesting information at the national level, they are of little interest to parents concerned about the standard of education in their local schools. While the testing of grades 4 and 8 in all schools would be a considerable undertaking, in the longer term consideration should be given to testing all secondary schools, particularly all preparatory schools (grades 11 and 12). More immediately, it may be feasible to provide feedback to schools based on examination results.

There is serious concern within the National Educational Assessment and Examinations Agency (NEAEA) about the high failure rates in the Ethiopian education system. The agency recognizes the need to move away from the current norm-referenced system, which is appropriate for a cadre of students with largely similar abilities, toward a criterion-referenced structure more appropriate for a student cadre that varies in ability, both within and between grades. Other problem issues include:

- *Lack of clear assessment objectives in the curriculum.* The expansion of secondary education should lead to a much more complex assessment and examination environment, with multiple tests per subject that examine different aspects of the subject at different depths. It is important that in the future, these details be made explicit in curriculum documents.
- *Questions predominantly test only recall,* as well as the ability to use algorithms learned by rote. Very few questions on current Ethiopian achievement tests evaluate higher-order skills. Short-answer papers and continuous assessment techniques may be required to address this gap, both of which would take the NEAEA into areas where it has little or no current capacity and experience. Skills, too, are neither assessed nor explicitly defined in the current curriculum.

Box C.1

Examination Reform in Kenya

In Kenya in the 1970s, steps were taken to reform examinations at the end of primary school. The content of the examinations was changed to:

- Include fewer items that measured memorization of factual information and more items that measured higher-order skills, such as comprehension and application of information
- Focus on the measurement of skills that could be applied in a wide range of contexts, in and out of school

The changes were designed to affect how teachers prepared students for these examinations. In particular, they sought to encourage the teaching and acquisition of competencies that would be useful to the majority of pupils who would leave school after the examinations. Two types of information were provided to support these changes:

- Incentive information, including the publication of a district and school merit list based on examination performance (known as "league tables")
- Guidance information based on an analysis of national student performance on individual questions, which was published in a newsletter and sent to all schools.

The newsletter explained changes in the content and skills covered by examinations, identified topics and skills with which students had problems, and suggested ways of teaching these topics and skills. League tables are no longer published because schools and districts were manipulating the system by presenting only the best students for the examinations. The Kenya National Examinations Council continues to produce a newsletter, but lack of financial resources precludes the Council from sending it to all schools. It can, however, be purchased from the Council.

Source: Kellaghan and Greaney 2004.

- *Shortage of skills at all levels to implement assessments and examinations.* Because the NEAEA is an arm of government, it has difficulty attracting people with the requisite technical expertise due to its salary levels. Further, the agency frequently loses staff who it has trained at great expense. While it can overcome this problem to some extent by outsourcing, it recognizes the need to pay market rates for its technicians, as many other countries have also recognized.
- *Rising cost of examinations.* The cost of national examinations of grade 10 and 12 curricula, already high, will rise still further as additional subjects are added to the secondary curriculum and student numbers increase rapidly. This is an issue that can be addressed in part by devolving the responsibility for administering examinations to the regions, as well as designing a cost-sensitive curriculum.

Monitoring student learning achievement is a critical part of any quality improvement strategy. In addition to moving from norm- to criterion-referenced

> **Box C.2**
>
> **Criterion- and Norm-Referenced Tests**
>
> *Criterion-referenced tests* (CRTs) are intended to determine whether a student has learned the material taught in a specific grade or course. A variation of a criterion-referenced test is a "standards-based assessment" built on *content standards* (or "curriculum frameworks"), which describe what students should know and be able to do in different subjects, and *performance standards,* which define how much of the content standards students should know to reach a "basic," "proficient," or "advanced" level in a subject area.
>
> *Norm-referenced tests (NRTs)* compare test takers to each other; they are designed to sort and rank students on a curve, not to see if they meet a standard or criterion. NRTs can, however, also be used to measure student learning in relation to standards. In this case, specific cutoff scores on the NRT are chosen to separate levels of standards achievement.

(or standards-based) testing (box C.2), students will need effective guidance on further education, training, and career choices. As noted at the outset of this appendix, secondary students may also participate in international assessments of student learning, perhaps in the first instance, SACMEQ, and in the longer term, TIMSS or the Programme for International Student Assessment (PISA.)

Notes

1. Items from the Trends in International Mathematics and Science Study (TIMSS), for example, are available online for grades 4, 8, and 12 in science and mathematics. See the joint website for TIMSS and the Progress in International Reading Literacy Survey (PIRLS), Lynch School of Education, Boston College, Chestnut Hill, MA, at http://timssandpirls.bc.edu/PDF/T03_RELEASED_S8.pdf. See also the website of EDinformatics (Education for the Information Age) at http://www.edinformatics.com/timss/pop3/pop3.htm (accessed June 2012).

2. For example, curriculum attainment targets for England can be found at website of the U.K Department of Education, http://curriculum.qcda.gov.uk/index.aspx. The Victorian Essential Learning Standards can be found at the website of the Victorian Curriculum and Assessment Authority of the State Government of Victoria, Australia, http://vels.vcaa.vic.edu.au/overview/index.html. The Western Australia learning area framework can be found at the website of the School Curriculum and Standards Authority of the Government of Western Australia, http://www.curriculum.wa.edu.au/internet/Years_K10/Curriculum_Framework. (All URLs accessed June 2012.)

References

Kellaghan, Thomas, and Vincent Greaney. 2004. *Assessing Student Learning in Africa.* Directions in Development Series. Washington, DC: World Bank.

APPENDIX D

Teacher Recruitment and Screening

Basic Skills and Content Tests

Basic skills and content examinations are not used for teachers in many countries of the world, as can be seen in table D.1.[1]

Given the significant student achievement problems identified by National Learning Assessments in Ethiopia, it would appear that a range of tougher selection policies for teacher training programs would be appropriate.

Marks/Grades

Applicants' marks (or grades) in secondary school are used by Australia, the Republic of Korea, and the United States as an admission criterion for teacher education programs. Despite this screening device, some researchers have shown than a significant proportion—perhaps as high as 50 percent of future teachers—enter such programs from the bottom-achieving half of the secondary

Table D.1 Checklist Comparison of Entrance Requirements for Teacher Education Programs

	Undergraduate				Graduate		
	Basic skills test	Interview	National subject area examination	Senior secondary marks/grades	Bachelor's degree (4 years)	Bachelor's degree in subject area	Examination
Australia	—	—	—	X	X	—	—
England	—	—	X	—	X	—	X
Hong Kong	—	—	X	—	—	X	—
Japan	—	—	X	—	—	—	—
Korea, Rep.	X	—	—	X	—	—	—
Netherlands	—	—	—	—	—	X	—
Singapore	—	—	—	—	—	X	X
United States	X	X	—	X	X	—	—
Indonesia	—	—	X	—	—	X	—
Ethiopia	—	X	—	X	X	X	—

Source: ETS 2003.
Note: X = included, — = not included.

school graduating class. A serious question should be raised as to whether candidates with a mediocre record in school should be preparing to teach students, up to half of whom will likely have superior academic ability. Given the exceptional quality of candidates in countries such as Finland, Singapore, and Korea, a strong case can be made that in the case of adequate supply, only the better students graduating from secondary school should be permitted to enter teacher training programs.

High-Needs Subjects and Areas

Nations with a great need for teachers, particularly in rural or poor urban settings, often recruit teacher candidates with academic qualifications that are less than desirable. While Hong Kong, The Netherlands, and Singapore require that all candidates who enter a postgraduate teaching program have a degree or major in their subject area; this requirement is, however, ignored in many countries, often through the use of general area majors (for example, two courses in physics for a general science teacher). Ethiopia, on the other hand, appears to require more credit hours in a teacher's major field than almost any other country in the world. England and Singapore both require an entrance examination for postgraduate teacher education programs.

It is hard to draw a firm conclusion from these comparisons, except to note that the greater the evidence of poor teacher performance and/or low student achievement in a nation's schools, the greater the need for teacher training programs to put sufficient screening mechanisms in place. Of course, it is important that any screens or tests be reliable and valid indicators, not just meaningless hurdles over which a candidate must jump.

Filters or Screens in the Teacher Education Pipeline

The following table lists "screens" or "filters" used to channel students into the teaching profession. "High-stakes" filters are highly competitive and admit only a limited number of students. As noted in chapter 5, entry into teacher education programs is a high-stakes matter in Japan, Korea, The Netherlands, and Singapore. In contrast, the United States is considered a "medium-stakes" country for teacher education. Since the Post-Graduate Diploma in Teaching Program is new in Ethiopia, it is impossible to say whether the various filters or screens that have been put in place to enter the teaching profession are of the low-, medium-, or high-stakes variety. However, if the country is to continue to upgrade the quality of teachers entering its secondary school classrooms, multiple screens must be put in place and enforced to ensure quality.

As can be seen in table D.2, countries use different combinations of mechanisms to screen teacher candidates and attempt to ensure that the best candidates are actually employed in the profession. Whether any screening device is low-, medium-, or high-stakes generally depends on the demand for, rather

Table D.2 Country Comparisons of Teacher Education Programs

Country	At entry	Practicum evaluation	At exit	Certification	Hiring/ employment	Evaluation of induction period	Evaluation of professional development	Evaluation of probation period
Australia	M	M	H	M	L	L	L	M
England	L	H	L	H	L	L	L	M
Hong Kong	M	M	L	L	L	L	M	H
Japan	H	H	L	L	M	M	H	H
Korea	H	M	H	L	H	L	H	L
Netherlands	H	H	M	L	L	L	L	M
Singapore	H	M	H	L	M	M	L	L
United States	M	L	M	H	L	L	L	L
Indonesia	L	M	L	M	H	L	L	L

Source: ETS 2003.
Note: Data in cells refer to the degree of difficulty of program filters, screens, and graduation requirements. L = Low stakes, M = Medium stakes, H = High stakes.

than the quality of, teachers. If Ethiopia achieves near universal enrollment in grades 9 and 10, and significantly expands grades 11 and 12, it will likely need to keep the "filters and screens" low stakes in order to fill all of its classrooms. If the rate of growth slows, however, it should move to establish a series of high-stakes filters.

Note

1. Kraft 2011 is an important source of this appendix.

References

ETS (Educational Testing Service). 2003. "Preparing Teachers around the World." Policy Information Report, ETS, Princeton, NJ.

Kraft, Richard J. 2011. "Teacher Preparation." Background Paper Prepared for *Secondary Education in Ethiopia*. World Bank Ethiopia Office, Addis Ababa. Unpublished. (Available upon request of Rajendra Joshi, rjoshi@worldbank.org.)

APPENDIX E

Pedagogical Content Knowledge

For the past two decades, the distinction between teachers' subject-matter knowledge and their knowledge of pedagogy has begun to fade throughout much of the world.[1] This change primarily reflects growing awareness of what is now termed pedagogical content knowledge (PCK). PCK builds upon, but is different from, subject-matter knowledge and knowledge of the general principles of pedagogy. It is a form of *practical* knowledge used by teachers to guide their actions in highly contextualized classroom settings.

It is now widely accepted in the research community that PCK builds on other forms of professional knowledge and is therefore a critical element of teaching. To teach all students the competencies in demand today, teachers need to understand subject matter deeply and flexibly so that they can help students create useful cognitive maps, relate one idea to another, and address misconceptions. Teachers also need to see how ideas connect, both across fields and to everyday life. This kind of understanding provides a foundation for pedagogical content knowledge that enables teachers to make ideas accessible to others.

In sum, PCK represents the blending of content and pedagogy into an understanding of how particular topics, problems, or issues should be organized, represented, and adapted to the diverse interests and abilities of learners, then presented for instruction. Figure E.1 presents in visual form the critically important area of PCK, which falls between content knowledge and general pedagogical knowledge.

Figure E.1 Pedagogical Content Knowledge

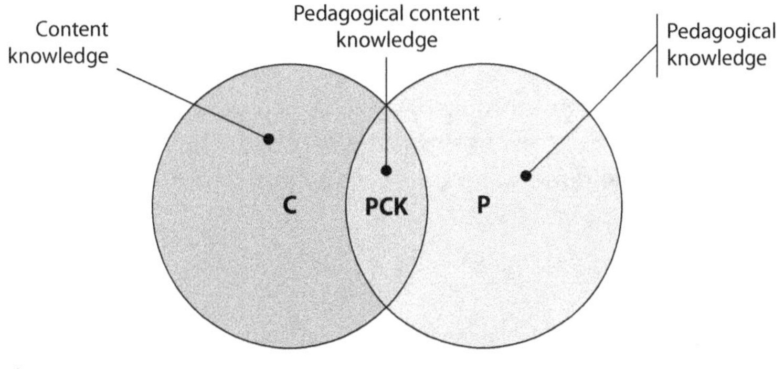

Source: Kraft 2011

> **Box E.1**
>
> **Lesson-Study Practice**
>
> A group of teachers who either teach the same grade or the same subject plan a "research" or "study" lesson together. The lesson specifically addresses a problem that they have identified and uses a technique about which they are informed, but is either untried or underdeveloped by them.
>
> Having jointly planned the research lesson in detail, one person teaches the lesson and the others observe, focusing on the behavior and learning of the "case study" pupils. The observers seek to compare what the students were predicted to do and learn with what actually happens.
>
> At a postlesson meeting, the group discusses the learning of the case pupils in detail, using their observation notes.
>
> *Source:* Kraft 2011.

One of the most successful approaches to embedding pedagogical content knowledge in a curriculum is the lesson-study approach, which has been used in Japan for many years and is now being practiced in thousands of clusters and individual schools throughout the world. Ethiopian educators have visited Japan to observe the methodology and there are plans to introduce it in both preservice training and continuous professional development (CPD) programs in Ethiopia. The lesson-study approach came to the attention of Western educators during the third Trends in International Mathematics and Science Study (TIMSS) in the 1990s. It is a process in which groups of teachers identify an area of pupil learning in their classes that is in need of improvement. They then enquire into developments in teaching that are likely to have an impact on this aspect of pupil learning (box E.1).

Lesson-study groups may involve practitioners of different ages and experience, as well as from different levels of a school's hierarchy. A group focuses on improving teaching and pedagogic knowledge (that is, PCK) regarding a particular aspect of a subject. They do so through group analysis of the specific need (that is, pupil learning), identification of the pedagogic knowledge gaps in their practice (based on evaluations of pupil performance), and finally, investigation of recent research in the area.

The lesson study model could be adapted for school-level meetings and cluster CPD settings in Ethiopia to enable all teachers in one school to participate in a study group on a problematic area of pupil learning. However, the approach is more likely to be of value if teachers at the same level and/or grade, or responsible for the same subject areas in a cluster, meet and collaboratively design and observe lessons.

References

Kraft, Richard, J. 2011. "Teacher Preparation." Background Paper Prepared for *Secondary Education in Ethiopia*. World Bank Ethiopia office, Addis Ababa. Unpublished. (Available upon request of Rajendra Joshi, rjoshi@worldbank.org.)

APPENDIX F

Quality Assurance in Teacher Education

There are basically two models of quality assurance in teacher education. The first operates through quality review within universities and the second, through accreditation by an independent body.[1] The latter is the model that many countries have adopted or are moving toward.

The model of university quality review also comes in two forms. Some countries have specialized secondary teacher training colleges, which are often affiliated with a parent university and offer a qualification accredited by that university. Other countries, including Ethiopia, offer secondary teacher training in university education departments, which often have considerable freedom to define course content, methods of instruction, and standards—subject to established university processes for quality review.

The advantage of a university review model is that it places secondary teacher training in a university environment, complete with recognized academic qualifications and standards. In addition, it places great trust in the university to set learning criteria and standards and award qualifications. The disadvantage of this model is that it does not establish common national, provincial, or regional standards and often leads to considerable variation in the knowledge and skills of teaching program graduates.

Quality assurance and teacher education qualifications are increasingly managed by independent state agencies and bodies that both license teachers and accredit teacher education institutions. The process of accreditation generally involves three steps:

- A self-evaluation is carried out by the staff of the educational institution or program, according to criteria established by the accrediting body, and a written report is submitted to the body.
- A team of peers selected by the accrediting body conducts a peer review study at the institution or program; the team then submits an assessment report to the accrediting body based on site visits, interviews, and document reviews.
- The accrediting body examines both the self-evaluation and peer review, leading to a formal decision on licensing for a certain time period. In some countries, such as the United States, the United Kingdom, and India, the accrediting agency grades and/or ranks institutions so that the public knows which are best.

The internal and external evaluation processes outlined above are equally important and, in fact, inseparable, as they feed into one another. In this framework, a university has no special status to accredit either its own courses or those of affiliated institutions; rather, primary responsibility for this task shifts to external agencies that work according to the mandates of national legislation, regulations, indicators, and qualification standards. In many cases the process emphasizes internally driven institutional development and self-regulation, which together comprise the core of external accreditation.

A teaching license is usually issued to teachers who graduate from accredited institutions. It is increasingly common for countries to require teachers to re-apply periodically for this license and in so doing, prove that they still have the requisite skills.

Current models of quality assurance and accreditation around the world differ in response to specific national conditions, but they share several common features (see Ingvarson et al. 2006):

- Institutional accreditation is closely linked to teacher registration and teacher licensing.
- Independent agencies are responsible for setting standards for the learning outcomes of teacher education programs and the awarding of teacher licenses.
- These bodies have strong representation of teachers and teacher educators, meaning that they are, in fact, self-regulating professional bodies.
- Quality assurance and accreditation bodies are funded by registration and accreditation fees.

The following sections describe examples of the role and responsibilities of teacher registration and accreditation organizations in Australia (the state of Victoria), Canada (the province of Ontario), the United States, and Thailand.

Australia

The Australian state of Victoria has a clearly defined process for the review and approval of teacher preparation courses, which is administered alongside teacher registration processes by the Victorian Institute of Teaching (VIT). The Institute:

- Registers all teachers working in all schools in Victoria.
- Works with teachers to develop standards of professional practice.
- Supports teachers in their first year of teaching with a structured induction program.
- Approves and accredits pre-service teacher education courses using national accreditation standards.
- Investigates and makes findings on instances of serious misconduct, incompetence, or lack of fitness to teach.

The VIT is governed by a 12-member council, the majority of which consists of practicing teachers from government, Catholic, and independent schools. Six members are elected by registered teachers; five are nominated by the minister of education, including the chairperson and representatives of key stakeholder groups, such as parents, teacher employers, and teacher educators. The Secretary of the Department of Education and Early Childhood Development (or a nominee of the Secretary) also sits on the Council. The institute was established in 2001 as an independent statutory authority and its funding base is provided by registration fees. The annual registration fee is determined by the Ministry of Education upon recommendation of the council.

The approval process for pre-service teacher education programs is guided by VIT's Accreditation Committee. Members of this 25-person committee include representatives from the eight universities of Victoria that offer initial teacher education courses, practicing teachers, parents, and representatives of employing authorities. The approval process for teacher education courses uses a smaller panel drawn from the Accreditation Committee and established for each course submitted for approval or review. Typically, representatives of the university that are developing a course liaise with the VIT Manager for advice. Once prepared, course documentation is reviewed by a panel and submitted with a recommendation to the Accreditation Committee (VIT 2010).

Canada

The Ontario College of Teachers (OCT) was established in 1997 to allow teachers to regulate and govern their own profession in the public interest. Teachers who want to work in publicly funded schools in the province of Ontario must be certified to teach and be members of the College. The regulatory body:

- Establishes standards of teaching practice and conduct.
- Issues teaching certificates, with the power to suspend or revoke them.
- Accredits teacher education programs and courses.
- Provides ongoing professional learning opportunities to its members.

The College is accountable to the public for how it carries out its responsibilities. The qualifications, credentials, and current status of every one of its members can be found on its public registry. The College also investigates complaints of misconduct or incompetence made against members. Disciplinary hearings are open to the public and a summary of each hearing and its outcome is published in the College's magazine. The body also investigates complaints that members are unfit to practice due to medical or other reasons. This process is not public due to the nature of the complaints (OCT n.d.).

The college is governed by a 37-member council consisting of 23 members elected by their peers and 14 members of the public appointed by the provincial government. It is funded largely by membership and accreditation fees.

The United States

The National Council for Accreditation of Teacher Education (NCATE) is a nonprofit, nongovernmental alliance of 33 national professional education and public organizations. It was founded in 1954 to accredit teacher training programs of U.S colleges and universities. NCATE currently accredits 632 colleges of education, with 78 more seeking accreditation. This accreditation recognizes that a college of education has met national professional standards for the preparation of teachers and other educators.

In NCATE's performance-based accreditation system, institutions must provide evidence of competent teacher candidate performance. Teacher candidates must know the subject matter they plan to teach and how to teach effectively so that all students learn. The U.S. Department of Education and the Council for Higher Education Accreditation recognize NCATE as an accrediting body for schools, colleges, and departments of education. The standards it uses for accreditation are not generic, but field specific. Generic standards are useful in setting out the main areas and important aspects of teachers' work, but their capacity to describe the complexity, depth, and breadth of this work is limited. Expertise in teaching, as in other professions, is domain specific (NCATE 2001).

NCATE is governed by an executive board that oversees all NCATE standards, policies, fiscal matters, and the selection and evaluation of the body's president and constitution. The board comprises 30 members, including:

- Chairs of the three governance boards (the Specialty Areas Board, State Partnership Board, and Unit Accreditation Board), plus the vice chair of the Unit Accreditation Board
- One public representative
- Six representatives of teacher organizations
- Six representatives of teacher education organizations
- Six state and local policy makers
- Six representatives of specialized professional organizations (NCATE n.d.).

NCATE is funded by dues paid by its 35 member organizations, fees charged to NCATE-accredited institutions, and foundation grants.

Thailand

KHURUSAPHA, the Teachers' Council of Thailand, was founded according to the Teachers and Educational Personnel Council Act of 2003 (KHURUSUPHA n.d.). It establishes professional standards, issues and revokes licenses for professional practice, and monitors and supervises teacher practices according to "Standards and Ethics of the Profession." Its tasks include developing the education profession and raising it to an honorable level. It has wide-ranging responsibilities, including:

- Determining professional teaching standards and a code of ethics
- Supervising the conduct and performance of professional educators to ensure their compliance with the Council's professional standards and code of ethics
- Issuing licenses to applicants to practice the teaching profession
- Suspending or revoking teaching licenses
- Supporting the professional development and promotion of teachers in line with the Council's professional standards and code of ethics
- Promoting, supporting, commending, and upholding the honor of professional educators
- Certifying degrees, diplomas, or certificates of various institutions in accordance with its professional standards
- Certifying professional knowledge and experience, including expertise in the practice of the teaching profession
- Promoting education and research relating to the practice of the teaching profession
- Representing professional educators in Thailand
- Issuing regulations of KHURUSAPHA according to its mission, as stipulated in law
- Providing consultations or recommendations to the Council of Ministers of Thailand regarding policies or problems relating to the professional development of teachers
- Providing recommendations or opinions to the Minister of Education of Thailand regarding the practice of the teaching profession or the issuance of ministerial regulations, rules, and notifications.

KHURUSAPHA is governed by a 39-member board; its secretary general serves as secretary of the board. Its members consist of:

- The chairperson, who is appointed by the Council of Ministers of Thailand from among highly qualified, knowledgeable, skillful, and experienced candidates in the fields of education, the humanities, the social science, or law
- Eight ex-officio members comprising the Permanent Secretary for Education, the Secretary General of the Education Council, the Secretary General of the Basic Education Commission, the Secretary General of the Higher Education Commission, the Secretary General of the Vocational Education Commission, the Secretary General of the Teachers' and Educational Personnel Civil Service Commission, the Director of the Administrative Office of the Private Education Promotion Commission, and the Head of the Office of the Local Administrative Personnel Standards Commission
- Seven qualified members appointed by the Council of Ministers from highly knowledgeable, skillful, and experienced candidates in the respective fields of

education administration, vocational education, special education, the humanities, the social sciences, science and technology, and law (these members must include at least three persons who previously or presently are teachers, educational institution administrators, or education administrators)
- Self-appointed members from a group comprised of the deans of faculties of teaching or educational science or education, three of which must be from public higher educational institutions and one from a private higher educational institution
- Nineteen members elected from professional educators, representing teachers, educational institution administrators, education administrators, and other educational personnel, and selected proportionately from educational districts, vocational educational institutions, private educational institutions, and local administrative organizations.

The Teachers' Council of Thailand derives its operating funds from fees, national budgetary allocations, profits generated from property management and its own operations, and funds and properties (and the interest accrued thereon) that are donated to it (KHURUSUPHA n.d.).

Note

1. This appendix is taken from Kraft 2011.

References

Ingvarson, Lawrence, Alison Elliott, Elizabeth Kleinhenz, and Philip McKenzie. 2006. "Teacher Education Accreditation: A Review of National and International Trends and Practices." ACEReSEARCH Teacher Education Report. Australian Council for Educational Research (ACER), Camberwell, Victoria, Australia.

KHURUSUPHA (Teachers' Council of Thailand). n.d. Webpage. "About Us." Khurusupha, Bangkok, Thailand. http://www.ksp.or.th/Khurusapha/en/khurusapha_AboutUs_new.php.

Kraft, Richard J. 2011. "Teacher Preparation." Background paper prepared for *Secondary Education in Ethiopia*. World Bank Ethiopia Office, Addis Ababa. Unpublished. (Available upon request of Rajendra Joshi, rjoshi@worldbank.org.)

NCATE (National Council for Accreditation of Teacher Education). 2001. "Standards for Professional Development Schools." NCATE, Washington, DC. http://www.ncate.org/Standards/tabid/107/Default.aspx.

———. n.d. "Governance." Webpage. NCATE, Washington, DC. http://www.ncate.org/Governance/tabid/103/Default.aspx.

OCT (Ontario College of Teachers). n.d. "What the College Does." Webpage. OCT, Toronto, Ontario, Canada. http://www.oct.ca/about/default.aspx?lang=en-CA.

VIT (Victoria Institute for Teaching). 2010. "Teacher Education Programs." VIT, Melbourne, Australia. http://www.vit.vic.edu.au/FINDITFAST/TEACHER-EDUCATION-PROGRAMS/Pages/default.aspx. Accessed October 28.

ECO-AUDIT
Environmental Benefits Statement

The World Bank is committed to preserving endangered forests and natural resources. The Office of the Publisher has chosen to print World Bank Studies and Working Papers on recycled paper with 30 percent postconsumer fiber in accordance with the recommended standards for paper usage set by the Green Press Initiative, a non-profit program supporting publishers in using fiber that is not sourced from endangered forests. For more information, visit www.greenpressinitiative.org.

In 2010, the printing of this book on recycled paper saved the following:
- 11 trees*
- 3 million Btu of total energy
- 1,045 lb. of net greenhouse gases
- 5,035 gal. of waste water
- 306 lb. of solid waste

* 40 feet in height and 6–8 inches in diameter

www.ingramcontent.com/pod-product-compliance
Lightning Source LLC
Chambersburg PA
CBHW081214230426
43666CB00015B/2721